UNIVERSITY OF NEBRASKA PRESS   LINCOLN AND LONDON

William Kloefkorn

New and Selected Poems | Edited and

with an introduction by Ted Genoways

Publication of this volume was
assisted by The Virginia Faulkner
Fund, established in memory of
Virginia Faulkner, editor in chief
of the University of Nebraska Press.

Library of Congress
Cataloging-in-Publication Data
Kloefkorn, William.
Swallowing the soap: new and
selected poems / William
Kloefkorn; edited and with an
introduction by Ted Genoways.
p. cm.
ISBN 978-0-8032-3405-5 (pbk.: alk.
paper)
I. Genoways, Ted. II. Title.
PS3561.L626S93 2010
811'.54—dc22
2010003405

Set in Adobe Garamond
by Kim Essman.
Designed by Ray Boeche.

Land of Heart's Desire,
Where beauty has no ebb, decay no flood,
But joy is wisdom, time an endless song.

William Butler Yeats,
"The Land of Heart's Desire"

Contents

Source Acknowledgments

A Life Like Mine. Lincoln NE: Platte Valley Press, 1984.

Alvin Turner As Farmer. Wayne NE: Logan House Press, 1973.

Burning the Hymnal. Lincoln NE: A Slow Tempo Press, 1994.

Collecting for the Wichita Beacon. Lincoln NE: Platte Valley Press, 1984.

Covenants. Granite Falls MN: Spoon River Poetry Press, 1996.

Dragging Sand Creek for Minnows. Granite Falls MN: Spoon River Poetry Press, 1992.

Drinking the Tin Cup Dry. Buffalo NY: White Pine Press, 1989.

Fielding Imaginary Grounders. Granite Falls MN: Spoon River Poetry Press, 2004.

Going Out, Coming Back. Buffalo NY: White Pine Press, 1993.

Honeymoon. University of Missouri–Kansas City: BkMk Press, 1982.

Houses and Beyond. Lincoln NE: Platte Valley Press, 1982.

In a House Made of Time. Wayne NE: Logan House Press, 2010.

Leaving Town. Menomonie WI: Uzzano Press, 1979.

Let the Dance Begin. Brockport NY: State Street Press, 1981.

Loony. Springfield IL: Apple, 1975.

Loup River Psalter. Granite Falls MN: Spoon River Poetry Press, 2001.

ludi jr. Markesan WI: Pentagram Press, 1976.

"Not Such a Bad Place to Be," "Teenage Halloween," "For My Wife's Father," "Braces," "Returning to Caves," "Thanksgiving," "Final Scenario #6," and "Epitaph for a Grandfather" from *Not Such a Bad Place to Be*. Copyright © 1980 by William Kloefkorn. Used with the permission of Copper Canyon Press, www.coppercanyonpress.org.

Out of Attica. Omaha NE: Backwaters Press, 2008.

Platte Valley Homestead. Lincoln NE: Platte Valley Press, 1981.

Sergeant Patrick Gass, Chief Carpenter: On the Trail with Lewis & Clark. Granite Falls MN: Spoon River Poetry Press, 2002.

Still Life Moving. Wayne NE: Wayne State College Press, 2006.

Stocker. Sturtevant WI: Wolfsong Publications, 1978.

Sunrise, Dayglow, Sunset, Moon. Lewiston ID: Talking River Publications, 2004.

Treehouse: New and Selected Poems. Buffalo NY: White Pine Press, 1996.

Uncertain the Final Run to Winter. Laguna Niguel CA: Windflower Press, 1974.

Walking the Campus. Omaha NE: Lone Willow Press, 2004.

Welcome to Carlos. Granite Falls MN: Spoon River Poetry Press, 2001.

Where the Visible Sun Is. Granite Falls MN: Spoon River Poetry Press, 1989.

Thanks to the following publications in which many of the new poems in this collection first appeared:

Marlboro Review: "Surgery," "Dread"

Chrysalis: "October," "Name," "Tea"

Midwest Quarterly: "Purple Iris," "What He Said," "Eating Mulberries for Breakfast," "Red Cedar," "Accessories," "Now the Juniper," "Singing Just for the Music of It," "Fairbanks, Late July," "Driving Through the Winnebago Reservation on my Way to Sioux Falls," "Moving," "Bringing up the Rear"

L Magazine: "At the Pantry"

Paddlefish: "Low Tide at Oregon's Waikki Beach," "Weeding," "Schooling," "Waiting for the End," "Arrival"

South Dakota Review: "Haywire," "Ponderosa"

Talking River: "Vista," "On the Trail Long after Lewis and Clark"

New Letters: "Confrontation" (University of Missouri–Kansas City, vol. 73 no. 4, 2007)

Virginia Quarterly Review: "Late Morning, Almost Noon," "Babble," "Memory," "Living Without It"

Nebraska Life: "Learning to Soar," "Newborn"

Introduction

A Life Like Yours

TED GENOWAYS

Bill Kloefkorn is too goddamned nice. Not his poems, mind you—they are filled with the tough-talking, clear-eyed, lovely, bloody, holy, backslid thoughts of the poet on his epic journey from a hard-scrabble boyhood in Attica, Kansas, to the book-minded life of a professor in Lincoln, Nebraska. His poems know the hard ways of the world, the kind of lessons that leave scars and wisdom and sometimes achieve love but lead us, no matter what, to the grave. There's a generosity to the poems that imbues them with a sweetness and humor uncommon in contemporary American verse, but they're not trying to bullshit anyone. They're haunted by losses great and small—from the dead of Hiroshima burned alive by the atomic bomb to Bill's aged father crushed by a drunk driver. The poems are daring and honest and accessible and lasting, and more people would know it if Bill weren't so goddamned nice.

He has spent a career, now spanning forty years, willingly—even contentedly—publishing in the relative shadows. For a decade he gave his poems to anyone trying to make a go of publishing poetry from the Midwest—Roadrunner Press, Windflower Press, Apple Press, Pentagram Press, Wolfsong Press, Uzzano Press. A virtual roll call of boosters and true believers who lacked the business acumen to get their books noticed, much less make their authors any income. Frustrated by those trials, Bill tried his hand at publishing, founding Platte Valley Press with Charles Stubblefield and bringing out four books of his own under the imprint. Along the way, he was named the State Poet of Nebraska. The not-quite-laureateship was created to avoid ruffling the feathers of lovers of John G. Neihardt (who remains the Poet Laureate of Nebraska in perpetuity), and the selection process was something of a circus to boot. Despite the chaos, the legislature emerged with the right man for the job—better, I would argue, than any other official ambassador for poetry our country has produced.

For more than a quarter century, Bill has accepted any and all invitations to speak about poetry, read poetry, teach poetry to the people of Nebraska.

I have seen him speak to packed houses at the Nebraska Literature Festival, and I have heard him speak to my mother's reading club in the living room of my parents' house. He's always the last to leave, to make sure anyone who wants to talk to him has the chance. Maybe most important, he has traveled tirelessly to elementary schools and high schools across the state, getting young people interested in the power of language. That's how I met Bill. My high school English teacher sent him poems of mine—and he responded to them with comments (which, I assure you, they did not warrant). He encouraged me to apply to the Nebraska Scholars' Institute, a summer program for high school students where he taught. After that workshop, he suggested I apply to Nebraska Wesleyan, where I was lucky enough to be a student of his for four years. Except, of course, I'm still a student of Bill's. He still teaches me, by example not dogma, that the real work of poetry happens on the page, and it gets passed on in the classroom.

I saw Bill once adrift in the grand ballroom of some cavernous conference center in Kansas City for the annual gathering of the Associated Writing Programs. He looked like Odysseus returned from his travels—a stranger in his own land. In a field that has become bizarrely commodified, Kloefkorn is a throwback. He's never lobbied for prizes, angled for high-profile jobs, or managed his career in the way so many poets do now. He taught his whole career at Nebraska Wesleyan (including Freshman Composition, right up to the end) and let his poems, and later his memoirs, be his advocates. There's a humility to it and a distinctly Great Plains sense of not calling attention to yourself. It's fed the work, but it's also left Bill in the almost singular position of being widely beloved among readers and underappreciated among poets.

I sincerely hope that this book will grab the poetry community by the lapels and show it the error of its ways. Keats wrote of reading Homer for the first time: "Then I felt like some watcher of the skies when a new planet swims into his ken." I imagine more than a few young poets will experience such awe and exhilaration on looking into this book. But, more than that, I hope that it will serve as a single-volume overview of Bill's remarkable poetic output that will appeal to his legion of fans who have only glimpsed a shadow of his magnitude by finding a few poems in slim volumes and out-of-print editions in used bookstores. There is a long overdue piecing together here, the first true retrospective of Bill's body of work, and it is a wonder to behold. Maybe now he'll finally get the literary recognition he deserves to go along with his popular appeal.

Something tells me Bill doesn't care. His work has always been more about connecting with his readers than dazzling his doubters. That's why his poems focus on clarity in their craft, the world around him (rather than the minutia of his private life) in their subject matter. The result is something far greater and rarer than the usual ego trip that a volume of new and selected poems represents; this is not the culmination of a career, it is the measure of a life. A life well lived and well written about. A life of enduring loss and soul-saving joy. A life spent striving for truth, not laurels. And yet, a life like any other. A life like yours. A life like mine.

Walt Whitman wrote of *Leaves of Grass*: "Who touches this book touches a man." Bill Kloefkorn would never say such a thing about this stunning collection of poems—he's too goddamned nice—so let me say it for him. These poems aim for nothing less than the impossible: to understand what it means to be alive and human on this moveable earth, and they succeed. They *succeed*. That's more than mere artistry. Whoever you are, this is not just a book you hold in your hands; by God, you're touching a man.

Swallowing the Soap

Eating Mulberries for Breakfast

Mostly purple, purple becoming snowdrift
as sugar falls from the small mouth
of the dispenser,

purple you gathered from the tree just
yesterday, your little brother
above you lost almost

in branches of purple, purple rising
in the bowl as the thick milk
rises, and with a silver spoon

you begin to eat what you know
your buddy Gene will laugh at
when you tell him, if you

tell him, snowdrift sugar and purple
berries and white Jersey milk
succulent in the mouth,

across the table your little brother
dribbling rivulets of juice,
slurping and dribbling

and chewing and purple teeth delighted
beyond delight, and you think
to hell with your buddy Gene,

your better-off buddy who doesn't know
what's good and what isn't, who
doesn't have the brains

he might have been born with, who doesn't
have a little brother like mine who,
when the moment is ripest,

goes out on the very highest limb.

World War Two

We did it because that's what we did when
There seemed nothing left to do.

Stephen Dunn, "Moonrakers"

When there was nothing left to do
we left whatever it was we weren't doing

to kill each other with fence-post bazookas
and to blow each other to smithereens

with grenades disguised as stones
we harvested from the dry bed of Sand Creek

where when an occasional cloudburst
gave the creek bed something to do

we rolled up the legs of our overalls and
cupped our hands to catch the minnows we

couldn't find and when the skies cleared and we
figured our worried mothers had suffered

enough we went home where in spite
of what you might have read in the papers

we remained for the rest of our endless days.

Waiting for the End

I'm the boy in the white flannel gown sprawled
on this coarse gravel bed searching the starry sky,
waiting for the world to end.

Stanley Kunitz, "Halley's Comet"

Lying in bed with its white starched sheets
and a hand-tied crazy-quilt,

a one-pound box of soda crackers open between us,
my brother and I read comic books
until the will no less than the crackers

gives out, and because I am older and my arms longer
I reach to pull the string
that will douse the light, my brother asleep
before I can settle in beside him. In darkness then
I wait not so much for the world to end

as for it to begin, so desperate am I
for the slate that was recent daylight to be wiped
clean. The truth is that the world ends
every night. The truth is that with each daybreak
the world begins again, taking you—sometimes

more, sometimes less—with it. When
I lay awake this morning listening
to the voices that awoke me,
I absorbed the purest meaning of vindictive,
the cruel hushed words of my parents

teaching me a lesson they'll never know
I learned. Batman and Robin meanwhile lie
on the floor below and beside me,
Gotham City—in the aftermath of victory—calm
and serene. What I fear most is that,

before sleep finds me, this morning's voices
will begin their whisperings at night, and those
crumbs that must have fallen from the crackers
will become the bed of ashes
the rest of my sorry life I'll toss and turn on.

Living Without It

> Let me know if you need something. If I don't have it,
> I'll teach you how to live without it.
>
> *Kansas lore*

When my father sent me to fetch a box-end wrench, and
I couldn't find it, he rolled from beneath the Model-T,
hissing goddammits between his teeth,

and, after scattering tools from one end of the yard to the other,
settled on a pair of pliers that, as he said later,
did the trick, though the knuckles

on his right hand were as red, as he put it, as a baboon's ass.
At that time in my life I had never seen a baboon,
much less its behind, but I had seen

my buddy Tub Schmidt naked in the shower at the local pool
scratching his jumbo rump until it turned
first a delicate pink, then a fire-truck

red, the rest of his flab the color of the underside of the channel
I caught out of old man Simpson's pond,
nightcrawlers gone but

plenty of doughballs left, doughballs for the carp, some of them
big enough, so my companion Larry said,
to swallow old Jonah, which I

told myself to remember to tell my Sunday school teacher,
but of course I forgot, or maybe remembered
but thought better of telling,

Mrs. Heath an elderly woman whose husband had died many
years ago, and who taught only boys because she
wanted to be frank, she said,

too frank for the sensitive ears of the girls, and though I
listened week into week to hear something
frank, I never heard it, so I just

4

went on living without it, my father meanwhile at regular
intervals lying beneath the Model-T, asking
always, or so it seemed,

for the tool we didn't have, his knuckles, like the patience
old Job must have learned as he sat
alone and bereft on a dunghill,

full of blood and just waiting to bleed.

FOR AND AFTER WENDELL BERRY

||||||||||||||||||||||||||||||||||||||||||||||||||||||||||||||||||||||||||||||||||||||||||||||||||

Rainbow

> My heart leaps up when I behold
> A rainbow in the sky.
> *William Wordsworth*

Mine doesn't. When I see a rainbow, behold! I think
of all those miserable creatures
Noah left behind,

think of them drowning in the relentless surge
of forty days and forty nights
of water falling,

the fortunate few meanwhile, in twos, high and dry
on the ark, sitting smugly
in their staterooms

drinking non-alcoholic grog and eating manna
sandwiches while observing
that—cheese and crackers!—they

haven't seen a toad strangler like this in a month
of Sundays, must already
have rained at least

a dozen cubits, until one early evening the clouds
disperse and a rainbow
appears in the west

and a youngster who has said it already seventy
times seven says it again,
Are we there yet?

llllllllllllllllllllllllllllllllllllllllllllllllllllllllllllllllllllllllllllllll

Fairbanks, Late July

FOR PEGGY AND JOE

The Chena River, there for the one
who is there to claim it,
supports also the beaver

and the mother duck
with its brood of nine, all
impervious to the speedboat, all

riding the sudden waves
with an ease that somehow eases
me, and now I can see

that the white clouds to the south
are there for the one
who is there with eyes to see them,

their soft configurations
changing ever so surely as a west wind
moves them, moments ago

the suggestion of something animal
becoming slowly the possibility
of something vaguely human,

though I am happy enough
to be here by myself, sun going
down, somewhere a moon

I am told is waning
rising, nothing now but time
with its untold list of vacancies

to lure me in.

iiiiiiiiiiiiiiiiiiiiiiiiiiiiiiiiiiiiiiiiiiiiiiiiiiiiiiiiiiiiiiiiiiiiiiiiiiiiiiiiiiiiiiiiiiiiii

What He Said

He said that at first it was the gravedigger himself
who so arrested his attention,
movements of the shovel so cleanly efficient

as the man, himself chin-deep in emptiness, so
skillfully created and smoothed
the sides to a slick reddish sheen. He said it

would be the home to his maternal grandmother.
He said the gravedigger's fore-
head was alive with sweat, his denim shirt

two shades of blue. He said most of the hole,
so the gravedigger said, had
been dug by others, said the man he was watching,

the one who at first had so arrested his attention,
was more the trimmer than
the digger, that it was up to him to make certain

that the coffin-into-hole would be a perfect fit.
And suddenly, he said, he
heard it—a meadowlark singing its five notes

(he counted them, he said) over and over again,
an accompaniment to the
rhythms of the man in the grave, the ear now

arrested no less than the eye. And later, the mind
compelled by what it could not
deny: the repetition, he said, O God the repetition!

Babble

If I can learn to think of everything as music
maybe what once upon a time was babble
I'll hear as song,

what once upon a time was screech
I'll recognize as a virtuoso singing—my
father, say, whose throat

an instant before the sot at the wheel
of a one-eyed Chevy delivered
him into silence

must surely have released what I'll hear
as music, wham and bam as
counterpoints, squeal

and thud as the sounds the woman in the
church choir made before we
ventured into song,

she the only soul in the township with
perfect pitch, and we'd sing
Amazing Grace or

I Surrender All as the congregation,
apparently having learned to hear most
babble as music,

listened intently, knowing that before
our tower to heaven could be
finished they'd be invited

to remove the hymnals from the backs
of the pews in front of them
and join in.

Confrontation

Believing myself to be moving away
from confrontation

I discover too late that I'm moving
directly into it—

so directly, in fact, that I split it
precisely down the center,

making of it the perfect dichotomy,
the unparalleled example

of divide but not conquer. It was John
Steinbeck, I believe,

who said that when you slice any-
thing precisely in half,

you don't know which half to reach
for. So you reach for

this half today, the other tomorrow.
Which is perhaps

what my parents did as, if not before,
they did it. I like

to believe that there must have been
moments when they

wanted something more than the moment,
their lives a low-

frequency radio delivering, at times,
something more

than static. I like to believe this. I like
to face confrontation,

if I must face it, wearing my best face—
Hello, whatever, who-

ever, you are, you sweet son of a bitch.
Haven't I met you, or

your other half, somewhere else before?

llllllllllllllllllllllllllllllllllllllllllllllllllllllllllllllllllllllllllllllllllll

Surgery

In the room where the heart is repaired
only the whistling of tunes
with familiar lilts is permitted.

At such a moment who wants to hear
what has yet to be tested
by time?

Above each mask are eyes you'd swap
your reservation in paradise
to look forever into.

There is a whiteness in the air, a blue-
ness in the movements you try
to follow if not understand.

Breathe evenly. You are the child of
someone dear who if not gone
would surely be here.

Is that a black fly on the ceiling defying
gravity? And are you not also,
in your own way, defying it,

rising as you seem to be from what you
were into a rare, albeit conjugal,
atmosphere?

October

This leaf from that legacy maple is the color
of the fine expensive wine
nine years ago
I gave up drinking,

and hanging from the limbs of another tree
are the amber hues of so many
many drafts and gills
so many nights ago
I said goodbye to.

Water over ice in a delicate glass
I rescued from my dead mother's kitchen.
Take it, she would have said, and
put it to good use.

I did. I lift it now to know its clarity.
Nine years or ninety-one:
At the end of any stretch there
lies another. Here's to the stretch. Here's
to the end. Here's to whatever time
it takes to have the heart it takes
once more to get there.

Dread

> Dread is our inheritance. But what sprouts out of the
> earth is our consolation, the good yellow grain, heavy
> in our arms.
>
> *Connie Wanek, "A Field of Barley"*

As much as I dread the occurrence itself
I dread the waiting, the knowing
that all things inevitable
must surely happen.

Is this why tonight your hand, waving
neither hello nor goodbye,
feels smooth as a bean?

If I had world enough and time, which maybe
I do, I'd enroll in any course
taught bass-ackward:
Middle Ages

of the Poets, for example, or The Philosophy
of Consolation. I am grateful
for anything small

enough not to be widely known. That the
door to our oven does not close
tightly, permitting the aroma
of meatloaf to escape

to find me, that nothing could be more ever-
lasting than one more
evening in.

‖‖‖

Haywire

> I cancel out the curse of God,
> defeat his greatest effort.
> I grow posies of flowers
> on the hobstone of hell.
>
> *Biddy Jenkinson*

When things go haywire
I tell myself that haywire is part
of the plan, that the dark side of the moon
isn't dark for everyone,

that the freezing rain
doesn't fall forever
on the same dog's ass, that
whatever potentate is finally in charge

draws straight with crooked lines.
None of this, of course,
prevents the burnt toast
from tasting like burnt toast,

or the clock with its withered hand
from lying about its age.
Even when things go right
their rightness is chiefly premonition:

looking quickly backward
you see that something is steadily
gaining. But the lilacs
are about to bloom,

and the one I'll choose
to decorate the sweater of the one
I gave the sweater to
will surely be the brightest, her face

above it recalling,
without saying
it, the senior prom. Just see how
perfectly full the moon is! And

before the evening ends
I'll rope it and give it to her. Jesus,
I'll say. You look like a million bucks.
What could possibly go wrong?

Horseshoes and Hand Grenades

> What I love is near at hand,
> Always, in earth and air.
>
> *Theodore Roethke, "The Far Field"*

It's what happens, or can,
when we stop just short of touching—close,

the man at the carnival says, but
no cigar. But we know better, don't we,

know that closeness can provide
its own ignition, its own plume of smoke,

know that close counts not only
in horseshoes and hand grenades, but

likewise in that distance so
deliberately sustained, hands on the table

but not quite holding, memory
recalling the sound the shoe nearly made

when it missed the stake, the silence
that follows detonation, one's flesh

intact, one's fingers most immeasurably
in love when almost they feel it.

Let There Be Music

In the beginning was the music, music
in the rippling of moving water,
music in a west wind

soughing through the grasses, waltzing
through the limbs and the leaves
of oak and maple

and sycamore and pine, music in the seed
from the cottonwood
falling,

music in words and in the absence of words,
music in the river of love, music
in the full moon rising,

music in the protest, in the harp-string,
in the fine and raucous melodies
of birdsong,

and music in the seasons that in their quaint
cantankerous schemes cannot
stop circling. Because

in the beginning was the music, let there be
music—music, and the world it
so enlightens,

without end. Amen. Amen.

Driving through the Winnebago Reservation on My Way to Sioux Falls

Because I am pressed for time
I do not stop to enroll in a course or two
at the Little Priest Tribal College,

so on my own I must learn to believe
that the earth is more than itself,
that it is our mother. And

I imagine Mary cradling not an infant
but a sack of virgin topsoil that
having reached a full maturity

is now the good earth I am traveling over,
Mary's eyes above a shirt of buckskin
cast downward, her lips

in a smile so slight I must look twice
to see its overwhelming sense of mother-
hood. How many seasons ago

might she have breathed the breath of life
into the matter she so divinely
cradles? I look at the dash

to note again that I am speeding,
but in the rear-view mirror I see nothing
but a strip of blacktop—so

I go on speeding, at my right and left
expanses giving way to more
and more expanses, good earth

doing what we little priests with our little
glories and jests and riddles cannot
seem to do—forgive, forgive.

Schooling

> Never let schooling interfere with your education.
> *Mark Twain*

On the other hand, let schooling teach you that
what you believe you have learned is
only the beginning of belief,

that what you believe you know is mostly what
others before you believed they knew,
that, regardless of whatever

form of knighthood you choose to pursue, always
there are ways—as Don Quixote put it—
of adjusting everything. Mean-

while, the bells of the future can be rung only
by those with sufficient wherewithal to
pull the ropes of the past. Mean-

while, go forth to begin the quest for where-
withal, believing as you go that one
day you will find it. Mean-

while, believe that what matters is not the matter
we believe we are made of, but the
mystery that eludes us,

mystery that sings its siren song too sweetly not
to be heard, song too distant, however near,
ever to be understood.

South Padre Island, Early Evening

FOR BERNADINE

All day the water in the gulf has been faithful
to its catechism,

wave after wave soaking the shoreline
with the ceaseless

gifts of obedience. One of them, a small shell
striated orange and aqua,

calls out to be delivered, but I walk on—because
who in this world

of flim and of flam deserves it? And, too,
maybe I misheard

its voice. Maybe instead of deliverance
it wants, very simply,

to be left alone. Who knows? And who knows
what, beyond the irregular

pulse of medical attention, might serve to keep
my lung-weary sister

breathing. Hang on, hang on, say the breakers,
as if setting an example,

as if the choice to do so is theirs. And the evening
becomes the night

with its half moon rising, moon smug in its
routine deception, one

half remarkably visible, the other too perfectly
itself to be seen.

At the Pantry

FOR JAY GERBER

Because I am sitting
in the midst of wordsong and baconsmell
how can my cup not runneth over?

To keep it brimful the woman
whose face is mostly widesmile
tips a vessel, its contents hot and black
and everflowing.

I order what my colleague orders,
biscuits and gravy enough
to please if not overawe
the village mortician.

Through a window I can see that
in a farflung world
treelimbs are bending. Each time I inhale
I inhale deeply.

Thanks to Brother Parkinson
my colleague's right hand cannot stop
waving. Hello, whoever you are. Hello,
whoever.

His voice is soft and steady
and reassuring. No, life is not
yet a treadmill to oblivion. It is instead
biscuits and gravy and wordsong

and baconsmell, goodness and mercy
between us in the guise
of time neverending counting down.

Memory

> Memory's law: what we choose to say
> about our past becomes our past.
>
> *Stephen Dunn, "Memory"*

I choose therefore to say that I lost the fight
because I was afraid I'd win, afraid
I'd not be able to endure the sight of blood

on my opponent's face. I choose to say this,
perhaps believe it, though over and
over again, when I'm not believing, I'm

cowering for another reason. Put simply, I
did not believe myself equal to my
classmate's aggressive fists. Look: the little

menace was a dynamo. Had I not covered
up, he'd have broken every bone
on my moon-shaped countenance, which

induces me to say that I lost the fight
because I didn't want to know
the pain I had seen in so many comic books

and on the screen. I wanted to choose
not to fight another day. And
what I choose now to remember is the grin

on my conqueror's face when he raised his arms
in victory, lowering them finally
to embrace me because he knew what we both

knew, that I was a little menace also and in the
heat of battle might have found
reserves I didn't know I had, might then have

rendered my buddy senseless, which possibility,
though remote, was nonetheless a
possibility, and, as I said earlier, I'm not sure

I could have seen him in such a bloody state
without breaking down, which is
maybe why I folded, after all, or maybe not,

which is why my friend was grinning, let's say,
not in triumph but in relief, his
achievement akin to all achievements, both

a curse and—in time, a memory—a blessing.

|||||||||||||||||||||||||||||||||||||||||||||||||||||||||||||||||||||||||||||||||||||||||||||||

Moving

> She taught him
> what it means to love a moving body.
> *Camille T. Dungy, "At the Alpha Phi Alpha Ball"*

And what he came to learn also was that
moving can mean likewise *changing*,
he no longer as young as he used to be,
she no longer that brilliant apple
aloft on the highest branch of a distant tree.

Now they dance mostly in the kitchen.
Because the automatic washer is on the blink
she stands in her blue robe at the sink,
her hands moving and invisible
in a lathering of suds, he beside her
holding a white cotton towel in the hand
that isn't soothing the nape
of her girl-white neck.

Beyond the window something is bringing forth
the yellow on a patch of iris—call that something
sun. She lifts a glass from the suds,

gives it for its rinsing and drying
into the hand that only moments ago had
touched her neck, had touched the body
whose hands, though invisible, were moving,
that body, so surely and so beautifully,
changing.

||||||||||||||||||||||||||||||||||||||||||||||||||||||||||||||||||||||||||||||||||||||||||||

Over the Years

Over the years
affection accumulates

until almost too much exists
for us to bear—yet

somehow we bear it,
grateful on the one hand

for the blood-sweet burden,
fearful on the other hand

that, should it be taken
from our time-worn shoulders,

the lightness derived from loss
might bring us down.

||||||||||||||||||||||||||||||||||||||||||||||||||||||||||||||||||||||||||||||||||||||||||||

Along Highway 14 in Southern Washington

> All the rivers run to the sea,
> yet the sea is not full.
>
> *Ecclesiastes*

Dry land and lava: a metaphor for life, says the man
with the good heart and the bad back,
and having had the latter before the former joined in
I do not disagree. We are in a cool bus

following the Columbia River in the direction
of the Pacific. In the seats in front of us
two ladies giggle like school girls
over a recent issue of *Glamour*. Graciously, they

share their newly-found information: jeans to fit
every description of derriere, from the flat
to the moderate to what an illustration labels
bubble. Yes, I say, but I'll give you odds

that the one with the bubble butt has a very pleasing
personality. Meanwhile, dry land and lava. And
meanwhile also the Columbia River, water enough
to slake the thirst of almost everything

but lava. And I think of the bar of soap my mother
insisted I use in an effort to make my sin-
stained body clean. After which, she said,
she'd take what was left of the bar

to cleanse my dirty mouth. And she did, and I
swallowed deliberately what was left of the bar,
pretending then to be choking. Dry land and
lava. And my mother slapped my back

and prayed to her god to spare me as I choked and
gagged, gagged and choked—until, having
decided that she had suffered long enough,
I gulped deeply and exhaled a long, low, throat-

clearing *Ahhhhhh*, and my mother closed her
eyes and bit her lower lip, then held me
so tightly I almost couldn't breathe, and
the skin at her neck smelled like the damp leaves

on the cottonwood I'd climb high onto that very
evening, my little brother with me, Johnny, the one
I'd called a son of a bitch that morning, dry
land and lava, and we sat in our treehouse

for the longest time, and that evening was the birth
of love, and the Columbia River flows
like the ongoing savior it sometimes is
all the way to the sea.

‖‖‖

What the Churchbells Say

They say *Up and Adam!* That's what
my mother, rousing me,
says they say.

What they actually say, though, isn't
really that funny. They
say *With all heads*

bowed, all eyes closed, which means
that we are about to be
asked to raise our

hands if we haven't found Jesus. Later,
I'll tell my mother I didn't
know Jesus was lost.

Will my mother know what I mean?
She never goes with me
to church. And

inside our heart of hearts, do we feel
the spirit moving? And
aren't we almost

persuaded? I have my head only slightly
bowed, my eyes only
half open. Later,

I'll remember the wad of gum on the
grass-green cover of the
hymnal. The yellow

bird that at the moment is the most
brilliant pane in the stained-
glass window. The

tremor on Carl Tredensky's potato-
fingered hand as he moves
like a man once more

dispossessed down the lonely aisle.

||||||||||||||||||||||||||||||||||||||||||||||||||||||||||||||||||||||||||||||||||||||

An Old Story

> . . . at rest there is the promise
> of flight, in flight the promise of rest.
> *Donna J. Long, "First Winter Grace"*

It's such an old, old story: landlocked and wing-
less we speak of flight

until anticipation turns to action, and off we go,
into the wild blue yonder,

air and most everything else too rare to be taken
sufficiently in, rings

on the fingers of each Bohemian, bells on the toes,
music we can't very well dance to

wherever we go,

until what was once-upon-a-time so pedestrian
becomes that faraway place

with its strange-sounding name, and having first
thought, then whispered it,

we say it aloud first to each other, then in mixed
company, then to the stars

as we hopscotch our way across the heavens like
the children we were born to be

home.

Learning to Soar

AFTER "LEARNING TO SOAR,"
A BRONZE SCULPTURE BY
DAVID R. YOUNG, AND
FOR MY WIFE, ELOISE ANN

How fortunate is the child
to have the mother who sees herself
as fortunate to have the child.

Joined at the hands, they dance
the ancient dance of the umbilicals,
each learning to soar, each

one day learning that the soaring
means something
only if there is something, however

bittersweet, to soar up and away from.
If your wings are your
own, they say, you can never

soar too high. And if the wings derive
from wings that were a mother's
own, they will find

their independence in the vast
and receptive skies
of another home.

Low Tide at Oregon's Waikki Beach

Can it be that the same sun that shone
on all those others so many, many sleeps ago
shines now on me?

I look across the water to where a fish
had its thoughts interrupted
by a gull.

Enough driftwood along the shore
to pacify, in one way or another, whatever
multitude or scavenger.

A black-tailed deer ignores me
to investigate the bleached-out trunk
of a grandfather spruce.

When the tide rises, the shore I am standing
on, on schedule, will
disappear. William, you are too old and

much too inert to build or to resurrect
anything. Go home, and take what
little is left of your senses with you.

||||||||||||||||||||||||||||||||||||||||||||||||||||||||||||||||||||||||||||||||||||||||||||||||

Late Morning, Almost Noon

> And I have felt
> A presence that disturbs me with the joy
> Of elevated thoughts; a sense sublime
> Of something far more deeply interfused . . .
>
> *William Wordsworth, "Lines Composed a*
> *Few Miles Above Tintern Abbey"*

Not the best time to be trimming the junipers,
my wife reminds me,
it being one week past the middle of August,

but I fear that if I give the bushes another hour
they'll overcome us
all, and though I love the lovely scent of cedar

I prefer not to be smothered by it—and, too,
there is something
to be said for doing something by the sweat

of one's brow, grandmother on my father's side
awash in sweat as she
walked the clothesline decapitating chickens,

my father wringing sweat from a square of blue
cotton as inch by inch
he dug a tunnel under our lopsided house

to accommodate a floor furnace no less than
to defuse a peckish wife.
Not far to the north, at a fountain in Eden

Park, a man with an orange bicycle stands
coughing
in a baritone that surely must carry all the way

to wherever mercy, or vengeance, resides. It is
difficult for me
to reach the top of this one, but on tiptoes

I manage, and with my shears I snip the branch that
with its removal
creates a symmetry that my wife, standing

in the shade of the open garage, applauds. A tall
glass of water, with ice,
sits on the trunk of the Toyota. I drop the shears

on the grass and, before joining her, turn to see
that the man with the
resonant baritone is gone. Here, she says,

handing me the glass. And I drink deeply. Is
this what the sublime
amounts to? Not the work, or the sweat, or even

the symmetry, but something that happens when
something you love
not to do but to finish, like dying, goes down?

Weeding

But the air, the air in late July!
Thank God I am alive to breathe it,
to take the scent of lilies

directly into my blood.

Connie Wanek, "Summer Yard"

Bum that I am I sit inside
watching my wife at service among the
yellows and purples of daylilies and phlox
in the flower bed.

She kneels with her gloves on, her hands
describing a ritual I trust her
parishioners understand.

When I step outside I'll learn what
all along she must have known,
the scent of an early-summer season.

But for the moment I enjoy the thrill
of postponing one joy
to enjoy another: measuring that

little distance between the found and the
lost, my earthbound wife at service among the
yellows and purples of daylilies and phlox
in the flower bed.

Upon Planning to Break My Fast a Day Early

It wasn't going very well anyway, hunger
so much stronger than promises,
so I'm planning

to break my fast a day early so that by late
afternoon I'll have made the
decision final,

and just in time, I'm guessing, for the spare-
rib special at Famous Dave's,
corn on the cob

and baked beans and hot steaming biscuits
on the side, nothing divine,
Lord, only the

fulfillment of a desire I hope doesn't hurry
me too soon into becoming
strictly the bones

soon enough, with or without the ribs, I'll
become. And, too, there is
joy of sorts

in the breaking of vows, especially those you
never honestly subscribed to,
and a certain elation

in the eating of some other animal's sweet
flesh, a fine though temporary
rush of superiority.

Later, after dessert, I'll probably repent my
decision, because there is joy
in repentance

no less than in the indulgence that induced
it, I meanwhile wandering
the acreage

like a lost boy who knows that before it's
all said and done he will
find his way.

Now the Juniper

FOR DALE CLARK

Now the juniper, leafless in the midst
of so many leaves,
reaches its twisted branches not only

to touch the morning's blueness, but
also to touch the
observer who, with his own limbs

draining, stands admiring the juniper
for its unwillingness
to yield, its voice made possible by a

breeze moving through and around its
configurations. *I am*
old, says the juniper by way of the wind,

but here or there, it says, *I am with you.*
When I move on
down the trail, I touch one arm with the

fingers at the end of the other. Now the
sky is nothing but blue, and
too distant not to be lost in.

Arrival

FOR CLAYTON ALLEN HOWREN,
BORN FEBRUARY 7, 2008

Our anticipation ends, to begin again, with
your arrival,
each day a newness moving into the newness

of another day. What I want to say is this:
Welcome! As you
might have noticed, this world beyond the

confines of your own snug world of breath
and breast, pillow and
quilt and the undiminished milk of others'

kindness, lies blanketed in snow. So here's
today's vocabulary:
brrrrrr and *brrrrrr* again. And *frostbite* and

sleet, numb and *shiver* and *chill* until another
gift shall more or less
arrive on time, *bud* and *blossom, leaf* and

grassblade and *stem,* green as far as the blue
in your eye can see.
And what I want to say is this: Let's hang

around to see it. You do whatever the new-
born does to keep
himself from becoming someone else; we'll

do the rest. And isn't that a sunrise over
yonder about to
happen? Wake up! Let's stand at the window,

just you and I, while the rest of the family
wastes its life on the
foolishness of sleep, and take it in.

|||||||||||||||||||||||||||||||||||||||||||||||||||||||||||||||||||||||||||||||||||||||||||

Tea

> It's good to have poems that begin with tea
> and end with God.
>
> *Robert Bly*

God knows it's good also to have poems
that begin with God and end with tea,

especially if the tea is hot and your fever
waning, you a day or so earlier so sick

you wanted to write an ode in praise
of death, sweet sweet death, wanted to be

not yourself but Walt Whitman, say,
that chef expansive enough to include

death as an entrée, or more likely a
dessert, but before you managed

to put pencil to paper the fever eased,
and now you find yourself sitting alive

and upright in a padded chair, easy the
chair, easy the way the one who serves you

brings relief, her hand steady as she
places the cup on the small table beside

you, aroma of something cinnamon
and divine rising to find you, and verily

it does, and you snap your pencil like a twig
while saying to hell with that ode

to death, to hell with dying, to hell with
Walt Whitman and his foolish expansiveness,

to hell with all things not blooming, and
you bring the cup to your lips

and sip, liquid hot as the center of Hades
against the tongue, liquid delivered

by someone you truly care for who
truly cares for thee—call is whatever name

you choose to believe in, you little
apostolic jerkoff, so long as you call it tea.

Birdsong

> Even the smallest wren strains
> as though it believes its voice
> is the one that sings the world into being.
>
> *Samuel Green, "Daily Practice"*

And when the last trill from the final bird
loses itself in the shelter of trees it came from,

will the world shrug its collective shoulders
and become nothing more, nothing less, than

total silence? Or will it dissolve to become
what it was before it was so ostensibly something?

I'd rather not be around to find out, would instead
rather the wren keep its self-importance intact—and

not only the wren, but also those many other voices
whose songs sustain if not invent our sometimes

glorious, sometimes pitiful, lives. Even that old crone
in the back-row pew back home in church,

her voice more gravel than the tiny pebbles them-
selves—not only the words and the tune

but also the effort, the enormous straining
to give birth to the self without which there is

no world. And the day before, a Saturday
filled with the heat and the din of commerce,

I'd watched a long line of overburdened trucks
crawl south toward an elevator where grain,

spilling from beds upraised, would sing the anthem
of high expectations, birds too many to count

nibbling and carrying away the spillage. The world:
It's what we must create each moment, each day,

to keep ourselves created. And that evening
sitting in a house of screen and light and the muttering

of a lofty projector, I watched a movie with a plot
I cannot remember, only that at its end a young boy

sat alone in a deserted farmhouse, calling out
to someone, and I heard that voice again and again

as I drifted into sleep, its straining giving birth
to what must surely lie beyond the boy's horizon, his

stance our own, his relentless calling out—our song.

―――――――――――――――――――――――――――――――――――

Newborn

> He had a heartbeat for forty-five minutes. Just think of it!
> All of his earthly life he was held by those who love him.
>
> *Sandy Fruehling*

They passed his tiny body
from the hands of one
to the hands of another

until not even the deepest
concern could sustain
his breathing, and

he was gone—quietly
as the joining of a falling
leaf to water, and

you find yourself knee-
deep in the stream
watching

the leaf—so small, so
delicate, so
beautifully intact—drift

to wherever the force you
cannot control
might take it.

II

Silence

At the memorial service the eldest son,
not much for words,
chooses to fill his time with silence,

asks all of us to join him. *When I strike
the gong*, he says,
let the silence begin. When I strike

the gong again, let the silence end. He
approaches a disc-shaped
circle of bronze, strikes it smartly

with a small padded hammer, filling the
sanctuary with a resonance that
gave the instrument its name: *gonggggg*.

Is it possible, in silence, not to think
silently in words?
In the beginning was the sound, and

*the sound was without words. Is that
the voice of the turtle
I'm hearing, or is it the coo of something*

*as yet unnamed wanting to console this
deeply furrowed land?*
When he strikes the gong a second time,

time with its relentlessness begins, and
with words we struggle
mightily to give meaning to silence

by breaking it—again and again, O my
brothers and sisters,
again and again and again!

IN MEMORY OF ALAN HANSEN

Red Cedar

When I embrace the red cedar
at DeVoto grove in eastern Idaho

I think of my maternal grandmother,
Anna, ancient German woman

who, with her inexhaustible supply
of vinegar and spite,

weathered the countless storms
of doubt and dispute

and alienation. Is it such a bad thing
to continue to love the dead,

to bring them up again and again
to embrace them, our hands

so humanly against the bark that
only one swift millennium ago was skin?

Writer in Residence at Sheridan Elementary

Does the child walking alone
toward the south entrance
of the old brick building

think of anything beyond
the next short step,
anything beyond

the enormous heft of his olive-
drab backpack? His pace
tells me his life is

filled with what he does not
understand, but because
he has forever

to sort things out he might some-
how, sooner or later,
sort them out. And

watching him I feel a sweet,
sweet sickness coming
on, my pace

becoming for a moment his own,
how one mid-afternoon
in August I sat

on the curb in front of the drug-
store knowing only the
weight of the heat

and the sense that time, because
it so barely passes, gives
even the hapless

the chance to do, and undo, every-
thing, concern for the
chance of error

therefore of no concern. Behind
me, in the drugstore, Doc
the pharmacist

would be honing his other skills
at the pinball machine.
Should the moment

pass, and then another, eventually
he will win again the long
night's competition,

leaving Bateman, again, shaking
the red hair on his head
at another incredulous

loss. I open the door for the boy,
who thanks me as he walks
into the warm

aromatic bustle of another day.
And there is no option
but to look alive,

no choice but to be moving, not
unlike those steel balls
under the care

of Doc the pharmacist, now swiftly,
now slowly, now—in spite
of whatever thrust

or drag—not really moving at all.

||||||||||||||||||||||||||||||||||||||||||||||||||||||||||||||||||||||||||||||||||||

With My Wife at the Super Saver

This morning, shopping for groceries
in a store half the size of creation,
I watched a young woman

push a silver cart slowly down an aisle
between shelves well-stocked with
canned goods and staples.

She was beautiful. Her cart was loaded
to overflowing, its contents topped
with a large white bundle

of toilet tissue. I watched her until
I heard a small voice calling. It
was a sound I have known

since the very beginning. I turned my
own silver cart to find it. And
suddenly I was older than

I have ever been, bewildered and amazed,
and saddened to know again
our fixed condition.

Ponderosa

FOR ROBERT AND BETH

He was correct, my guide, my companion: The
reddish bark of the giant ponderosa
smells like vanilla.

O how small I am, how remarkably inconsequential!
And though this country is not as high
as so many other countries

it is high enough—wrote Loren Eiseley—to deplete
the soft stuff first, and the soft
stuff begins with man.

But this early afternoon in early September is no good
time to die. To be soft, as in human,
is to look up and lose oneself

in the joy of knowing, if only for a moment, one's
immeasurable limitations. Vanilla. The
reddish bark of the ponderosa

smells like vanilla. The mouth waters. The mind
boggles. The eye blurs. The rock
I am holding in my right hand

(metamorphic, according to my guide, my companion)
begins to breathe. Can it be the ancestor
of someone soft who one day stood

where I am standing, honing a thin wedge of flint,
or inhaling the scent of a shoot
he had no name for?

I hold the rock like the marvel it is, its breathing
as if the sound of a gathering zephyr
among the far-flung branches

of the pines.

Singing Just for the Music of It

I'm in the shower,
singing just for the music of it,
amazed but not angry that nothing

in the shape of an audience
has materialized—not to join me,
but to stand in a cluster

outside the sky-blue curtain,
silent, slack-jawed, appreciative,
each ear hearing

what my own ears hear, sounds
so purely on key their intonation
makes the teeth ache,

and with all heads tilted back,
all eyes closed, you can
better appreciate

not the words but the music, tenor
to satisfy the lofty, baritone
to appease the feral,

an occasional falsetto
to illustrate that heaven is not
beyond the realm of possibility.

And when the laving is finished and
the rain reduced to a slow
metronomic drip,

you hum a final note so basso profundo
it shivers the rafters
in the attic,

whereupon you
open the curtain to take the bow
the congregation, such as it is, so

ardently demands, its arms
in the form of a thick yellow towel
opening to take you in.

||||||||||||||||||||||||||||||||||||||||||||||||||||||||||||||||||||||||||||||||||||||

Accessories

> As a woman casts off accessories one-by-one,
> why does she become so lovely?
>
> *Takamura Kotaro, "You Grow More Lovely,"*
> *translated from the Japanese by John Peters*

After we had discussed, at length,
what a *complete outfit* consists of,
she withdrew the bulk of our savings

from a jelly jar in the pantry
and with a flourish impossible not to admire
left me for a long afternoon of shopping.

I'll admit this much: She looks ravishing. No,
it isn't the slant of early-evening light
through the living-room window, igniting

her hair, that causes me to whistle.
It's the way her complete outfit
discloses its completeness—blouse

the color of chardonnay complementing
an earth-tone skirt, shoes, hose, sash
in absolute agreement. And the accessories—ah,

the accessories!—bracelet and purse, earrings
and necklace, one and one and so on
adding up to one, until

one minus one and so on become the one
I wear to complete myself
when the night wears its stars like spangles

in its far-reaching effort to be lovely.

||||||||||||||||||||||||||||||||||||||||||||||||||||||||||||||||||||||||||||||||||||||||||

Name

> It's the name that goes with me
> back to earth
> no one else can touch.
> *Linda Hogan, "Song for My Name"*

I look beyond the window
to see a bed of flowers and grasses

resisting autumn, one crimson, another
purple, another an imitation of the color

on the straw that fell in torrents
from the combine that

back home in Kansas
leveled the wheat I'd drive into town

to trade for assurance that
later we'd have something to fall

back on, and I want to name what it is
I'm looking at, want to know it

as something more than crimson,
purple, yellow—phlox, maybe, or

gaillardia or oxeye or aster, all of us
with our names intact

on our way to becoming the earth that
earth alone can touch.

Meanwhile, let us touch. Meanwhile,
speak my name.

Purple Iris

FOR ELOISE ANN, AFTER FIFTY-FIVE YEARS

Now the purple on the first iris of Spring makes
you want to hug something. Pillow.
Cloud. Reflection in the window

of a figure standing beside you. You turn and
hug it, saying Look! Just look
at the purple on that

iris beyond the window! You point. Your
finger takes the eye to the purple on the
iris that now is moving in what

you assume to be an easy breeze. The one
beside you is the one you fell for in the
classroom when no one except the

one you were looking at was looking. Now
both of you stand admiring the purple
on the iris. You met her then

at a designated location after school, the iris
meanwhile waving. You and the one
beside you wave back. O it is

a good day to be alive, to be in love! At the
designated location you sealed the
future with first a touch, then

just one more. Holy smoke and easy does it. It
is the feel of something delicate against
the fingers' tips. A modest

breeze. Petals on a purple iris moving. And the
feeder near the window where suddenly
a burst of fire alights, its beak

breaking open one seed, then another, seeds
you will need to replace tomorrow,
the one beside you taking what

you must never fail to offer, an open hand.

||||||||||||||||||||||||||||||||||||||||||||||||||||||||||||||||||||||||||||||||||||||||

Dying to Get by with Everything

> . . . this is a Mormon cow, one of the twelve lost tribes
> of cow, eating her way through the meadows of Zion,
> grazing this bare gray gravel, empowered to dine at last
> on the spiritual grass that springs from the rocks in this
> moony tabernacle of cow.
>
> Bill Holm, *"Driving from Boulder to Hanksville, Utah,"*
> *in* The Dead Get by with Everything

Now you too, my dear friend, are one of them, not
one of the cows, perhaps, but one of those others, those
who are dying to get by with everything, except that

in your case you'll not, because the immeasurable herd
you left behind, you lovely persistent mastadonic rosy-
cheeked son-of-Iceland icon, is holding you accountable

for having lifted us to the branch where, like
children—as you told us—we are waiting *for the sound
of something climbing up from the hole nothing*

should ever get out of. This much I know: Already
you are free of the hole that some nearsighted god
devised, your presence outflanking all concepts

of containment. Look, this morning in the kitchen
I thought of your kitchen in Minneota,
of the pots and pans of its traffic, of you with your

sidekick Whitman breaking eggs for an omelet,
Walt and William so blessedly inseparable
I could hardly tell one from the other, you quoting

him, he quoting you, and as the eggs popped and sizzled
both of you singing symbiotically the body electric, both
of you in your kitchen and in mine—oh, how the hell do

you do it, anyway, Bill, such wizardry, such sleight of hand,
such remarkable compassion! Look, time at last means
only the following: on the one hand, everything. On

the other hand, nothing. And what of that space in
between? It is filled with cows and tribes and gravel
and spiritual grass and the likes of me and thee and

clocks that always and forever are winding down—that
one there on the stove, for example, telling us
the omelets for the orgy are ready, telling us to grab

our partners before somebody else does it for us, that
the dance we don't know but should be willing to learn—
the rhumba, say, or the Bulgarian stomp—is about to begin.

Bringing Up the Rear

I'm the one in the caboose, that happy fellow
bringing up the rear,
waving to the weeds and the clouds and the

children, with my lantern at dusk waving to the
engineer to say that
back here, far removed from the awful piston

and steam, all is ready, the tracks back here all
polished and parallel,
lantern saying this with its wide greenish arc as,

with the familiar *whummp whummp whummp*
of couplings, the cars begin
to move, and I move with them, trotting easily

beside the caboose until it's time to step aboard,
beneath me the world gaining
momentum, and here I am in the first moonrays

of evening sitting on a high wooden chair waving
to a bird I believe I see
trailing what surely it doesn't understand, wondering

perhaps where all I might have been, wondering
as it returns my wave
where, on this unlikely earth, we might be going.

There is always the rock:
That, first and last, to remember.
The rock, at times at dusk the rabbit,
Robbing the garden in its own leaden way.
And I remember how once
I lost time deliberately,
Reining the team to a stop
And raising the rock high to crush it.
Underhoof it had wanted to trip
Even the full-rumped mares,
And I stood there in the furrow
With the rock raised above my head,
Powerless at last to reduce it
Or even to lose it to sight.
Yet I tried. (For in those days
I had not learned to say
There is always the rock.)
I threw it into the soft-plowed ground
And dreamed that it disappeared.
How many times then it rose with the rain
I cannot say, nor can I boast
That ever its usefulness
Was fully cause for its being:
The fences failed to deplete it,
And it collared the hogs but partially.
Yet somehow I expected yesterday's blunted share
To be the last. That part of me which I cannot see,
I said, cannot reduce me.

i'm sorry
i fussed so
much about those new
organdy curtains they
don't seem nearly so
expensive now
filled as they are
with this wild september
air you know
if i wouldn't have to push
our sheet away
and put something on and
if tomorrow wasn't
a school day
i'd wake the boys and
bring them in to see it
priceless!

So pshaw! the hogs went loose again,
And I can't blame a woman for saying
She is sick to the death of manure.
At a time like that even the mind
Goes muddied. (But she did very well,
That woman, hip-deep in muck,
Circling those hogs like a snake hunt
Closing in. And all the while
Going to the mud on her apron
To wipe the mud off her hands.
Manure, she calls it, and I don't argue.)
At such a time
The lifting of a single thread
Unhems the world.
The price of corn is up.
Hogs are down.

The next thing you know
The government will place a tax
On prayer. All this, and more,
As we change our socks
And put on new faces for supper.

―――――――――――――――――――――――――――

I am ready now to admit
That I failed at everything
Except perhaps at one quick span
Of crisis, when I said yes
To my dying father and
To his only piece of acreage.
Gifts are not easy to accept,
Not when they nudge you to
The sudden wall of your stubbornness.
But at thirty I lay awake, alone,
Dreaming growth. I had failed
At everything, but when
I touched the land again
And heard my father's voice
I saw but one image:
Not the pondless pasture
Or the unpainted house
Or even the rock,
But a single seed.
I said, *Yes.*

―――――――――――――――――――――――――――

The baby's cough was still in my ears
When I shot the rabbit.
Maybe that was why I found it so easy
To pull the trigger. We needed
Every peavine our plot could muster.
I don't know, maybe I

Should never have started farming.
I just don't care to see blood
On the lettuce. But the baby's cough
Was deep and going deeper,
And more than onion soup seemed necessary.
So I shot the rabbit again and again,
Sliding a deheaded stove bolt
Down the barrel to dislodge
The smoke-smeared casing. Then
In winter the blood was bright
Upon the snow as I anticipated
Spring. But the rabbit
Was always there,
Singular as buckshot. Still,
I did what I could to save the garden,
Even long after the baby was buried.
We needed its savings for other ailments,
Other medicines. So into the seasons
I fought the rabbits,
The chamber of my .12-gauge
Like a little throat, coughing.

||||||||||||||||||||||||||||||||||||||||||||||||||||||||||||||||||||||||||||||||||||||||||||||||||||

This morning I am dizzy
With the plump brown evidence of fall.
The granary is full.
The bucket at the cistern glints its use.
The baby is solid as a tractor lug.
In the kitchen
Martha glows fuller than her cookstove's fire.
I want a dozen pancakes,
Ma'am,
A ton of sausage,
Half a crate of eggs,
Some oatmeal and a loaf of toast.
Feed me,

Woman,
Then kindly step back!
I intend to do some pretty damn fancy whistling
While I slop the hogs.

||||||||||||||||||||||||||||||||||||||||||||||||||||||||||||||||||||||||||||||||||||||||

Martha says that all the rivers
Run to the sea,
Yet the sea is not full.
I have trimmed a new wick,
And beside its even flame
Martha reads aloud,
Her voice clean as mopped linoleum.
Pshaw, I say, needling,
What has that to do with downspouts?

> (I know that she wants the baby baptized,
> And I don't really care, one way or the other.
> Our first child took her rebirth
> With her to the grave,
> So that I'd personally rather see
> The water on the corn, or not at all.
> But I'll not be muleheaded.)

She looks up briefly, not answering,
Then reads that there is no new thing
Under the sun. I nod,
Meaning that I shall arrange the baptism
For the earliest Sunday.

> (I wouldn't mention it
> In town at the feedstore,
> But Martha's voice by lamplight
> Is worth at least one waste of rain.)

I am a dirt farmer
Who dreams of poetry.
Is that so strange? Is anything?
I have bent myself thankfully
Over the heat of cowchips.
When the lespedeza flowers
I breathe its blooms.
The calf I winch to birth
Grows legs like oaks to graze on,
And stuck hogs bleed for breakfasts.
This morning at milking
I kissed the cow's warm flank
And she kicked the milk to froth beneath my knees.
I forgave her,
Then cried with the cats.
Now the manure is in bloom,
Thistles defend the driveway,
And corncobs gird the mud beneath my boots.
Plotting harvests,
I roam my acreage like a sweet spy.

After a difference
We go together as
We fall apart: with words.
They are clear and clipped and
Gently strange,
And hearing them I think
Their sound is like the little noise
Of needles, knitting.

Perhaps one of Ecclesiastes' rivers
Does somehow begin at our downspouts,
And if I mended them as well as I meant to
The cistern should be bursting.
I have never seen such rain, the rocks so clean.
Because I prefer not to think of mire,
Of the chores of evening,
I'll settle back
And contemplate the woman.

I see her with a dishpan
Catching rain. She wants the water
Straight down from heaven, untainted even
By my soldered tin. With it
She will wash her hair,
With it rub her clear face clearer.
She has a small nose,
Active eyes,
And a high forehead that
Under a wrap of hair shampooed
Will smell like rain.

Later I'll use a kiss. But
With words I reach to touch it now:
Lightly, like the skimming of cream.
My hand to her brow,
My fingers,
Tipped in butter,
Suddenly rich and unpalsied and newly nerved.

||||||||||||||||||||||||||||||||||||||||||||||||||||||||||||||||||||||||||||||||||||||||

look boys
i don't honestly know
whether jesus wants either of you
for a sunbeam you'll
have to check with your
mother if you must have
my opinion though
i'd guess he has
plenty already like
for instance that one
there on the knifeblade
which by midnight
just might be
sharp enough to saw
lard if you two bandits
will keep the grindstone
wet
you hear me?

||||||||||||||||||||||||||||||||||||||||||||||||||||||||||||||||||||||||||||||||||||||||

Our latest calf has found its legs.
Behind a slatted gate
The boys look on, laughing.
Today the world is upright,
Blue-headed and fine and clear as quartz.
Don't all men, some time or other,
Deserve such openings?
The milk has gone its rounds,
From cow to separator to calfbucket,
And the boys, who steadied it
Against the calves' impatience,
Have gone glandular with advantage.
They are both old men now, and wise.
They cannot remember ever wobbling.
They spread their breakfast sorghum by themselves.

Barefooted, their leaning into life
Is like a breeze to cheekbones,
And watching them I feel my strength
Go doubled, my shoulders rippled
With cords toughskinned to time.

                              O Lord,
How sweet to be free of the cradle!
To walk cocksure a furlong of bunch grass
As if it were boundless, and bottom land!

ııı

The cats too congregate
At milking time,
Discovering their own
Firm ritual in mine.

Together we make a church of it:
I and the cows and the cats,
And the flies that swarm like music
At the worshippers' backs.

          With careful hands
          I direct a stream of milk
          Into the mouth of
          One soft beggar.
          In the midst of steaming dung
          I am more than priest:
          Confessor to cats,
          I sit in total ignorance,
          Intermediating only substance.
          Alpha and Omega are
          Somewhere in the pasture, perhaps—
          Perhaps playing brackets with lives.

I couldn't care less.

> I have my cats and my cows,
> My horde of bandied flies.
> Barnlife. Shinglesmell.
> The thick slobbering of grain.
> And the milk that squirts
> From one mystery to
> Another, and back
> Somehow
> Some way
> Some time
> Again.

O brothers and sisters!
The meaning all is here—
Here in the barn and the milk.

|||||||||||||||||||||||||||||||||||||||||||||||||||||||||||||||||||||||||||||||||||||||||||||||

Outside the kitchen window,
On the unpainted seeded shelf
Of this year's feeder,
Lies a dead wren. I see it
Incidentally
Over an early winter breakfast.
A north wind spreads the feathers
And animates the grain,
Of which no single seed
Is larger than a bird's eye.

I hurry with egg on my chin into the bedroom.
Martha!
I cannot soon enough uncover you.
To watch you blink again.
To hear you fret. To part your hair.
To kiss the stretch marks on your stomach's skin.

friends that
fresh-braised pork
you're licking chops
to was on the
hoof a week ago
rooting rubbish
with the same
nostrils i chose
to fire the rifle bullets
into that act being
only one of god's
manifold mysterious
ways for which
on this november day
we all should probably
give thanks
amen!

||||||||||||||||||||||||||||||||||||||||||||||||||||||||||||||||||||||||||||||||||||||||||||

When the sap starts downward
Farmyards sigh,
Their sound the drone of deliverance that moves
Like half-slept moments
To the first shrill hour of Spring.

It is the relief of closing in,
The disconnection
Of leaves that echoes human sighs:
The time for living,
Both say, has been survived again.

Though Martha is small
I have yet to have to shake the sheet to find,
Or rouse, her.
Sometimes on an icy Saturday morning
Deliberately I calm her animation:
At such a time I view my hand as anvil,
And leaving it poised gently on her breasts
I slip away to do the chores.

And sometimes, sure enough,
I reappear to find the anvil holding,
With Martha's form beneath it, warm as cowflanks.
And O! these are the truly sweet, the sacred times.
The anvil gone,
The boys asleep,
The smell of milk and breath and chill
Against my woman.

To say *There is always the rock*
Is not to forfeit the harvest.
Below, beside each hard place
Lies the land,
Though I remember how one summer,
Wanting rain,
I watched my topsoil disappear in wind.
I called Martha to the south porch,
To the screendoor,
And told her the future, and my plan.
When the end arrives, I said
(And it is just around the corner),
Only rock will remain.
So I told her I'd fight it no longer:
To the conqueror goes everything.

Walking out and into the dust then
I released my hat,
Intending myself to follow it
To the remotest end of oblivion.
But my bootstrings,
Pesky with sandburs,
Snagged the treetops,
So that when the ceiling cleared
I tumbled to rest in a plowseat,
And hitched to familiar mares.
After a recent shower then
The soil turned comic and dark.
On and within it the rock chuckled,
And no longer believing in wind
I joined their joke.
Now late into each year I work the ground,
Burying seedling and seed,
Stubble and husk and leaf.
That,
And the crushed dusty felt
Of the hat.

Uncertain the Final Run to Winter

Summer,
a fat horse
tender against the spurs.

Now as the last edge of autumn
hangs precipiced in yellow on the trees
the animal sees the sudden space and shies.
I sense the ropy girth go loose:
uncertain the final run to winter.

Between the halt and the beginning
lies the gap,
familiar to the eye
as palm to pommel.

My lean horse balks: ahead,
the wide white skylessness of space.

Not knowing where mount and rider end,
or where they come together,
I see myself as statue weathered,
sitting its saddle like an Ichabod.

Country Boy

Today a south wind rises,
bearing boyhood's grim effluvium.
(Once I was invited to a posh estate
reigned over by him whose head
has since been bronzed, and there
I reached for the wrong fork.)
It is that sort of day:
the warm wind, up from Kansas,
has bad breath.

(And I remember the night
I failed to wet the bed,
but at the height of pride
discovered urine, stout as cateyes,
in a dresser drawer.)
It is that sort of August day,
precisely:
bedsheets snapping on the line,
the scent of oxblood, tart as ensilage,
rising from the spitshine
on these Saturday night shoes.

Cleaning Out My Dead Grandfather's Barn

A sudden flash of light
No larger than a dime
Told me that human hands
Had worn the pommel to newness
Where old leather had been.

But today the human hands
Went dead a final time.
Piling harness and saddle away,
Cantle and stirrup, singletree,
Checkrein, blinder and hame,

I saw the sudden flash
Of Granddad in the coin
Of light: his hands without
Splotches lay like the power
Of horseflesh tugging to join

Gray seasons to this fresh September.
Then heartlessly the hands
Went dull: no more. Just the
Heavy hide of cracked
Harness, a broken bellyband,

And cruppers rubbed with the brown
Of fifty years of dung.
I piled it all in the pickup
And drove it quickly away
From the low-angled autumn sun.

||||||||||||||||||||||||||||||||||||||||||||||||||||||||||||||||||||||||||||||||||

Dec. 8, 1941

Sound travels to tell us
Not of something ended
But of something begun.
So in the early morning,

During the hour for arithmetic,
Jackie Dellman stands alone,
Privileged in the cloakroom,
Crying without raising his hands

Before a clear bright pane
Of window. Yesterday the Japanese
Bombed his big brother at
Pearl Harbor; today the sound of the

Rising Sun is rich with bravado
And fear and the slight vibrant
Embarrassment of seated schoolboys
Calculating their new classmate,

Who only two days ago celebrated Friday
By bloodying the taller nose
Of a red-haired confident
Fifth grader, but who now,

On this peculiar Monday morning,
Weeps at the window with the
Cloakroom door open, weeps
With his victorious fists

Dangling like bandages at his sides,
His bare grief confounding all
Human equations. Yet I with others
Hear and work with it; it

Enters my wooden desk
To travel up my spine
To finally force a whiteness
Upon the foreign fingers that

Clutch at pencils. There seems
To be no stopping it,
It that rose how long
Before the rising of the

Rising sun, that slid inviolable
Over calm international airways
At how many hundred feet-per-second
To tell the Emperor that he owns

The world and must dispose of
Jackie Dellman's brother,
To become the whistle of bomb-fins
On a soundless Sunday morning,

To be the keen of boyhood
And the wail of silent
Bewildered mathematicians,
Their long division growing forever

Longer: who in this conflagration
First spoke of fire? And who
Will be the last to shout its heat
Into the cool quotient of emptiness?

Prime Moving

I think of scrap lumber
Going warped behind our toilet,
And of Father, bent like bad pine,
Putting a pipe wrench to plumbing strange as neckties.

Of unlikely pieces that make all linkage possible:
Of the toilet, August dry—
Like Kansas creeks puffed white with sand,
Parching, twisting, waiting for water;
Of the lumber, scrapped but handy,
Askew like fiddlesticks;
Of the match I threw that day,
Its tipend hot as the high sun;
Of the rabbit that startled bounced away
From the accidental flame,
And of Mother, big eyed,
Blowing into her apron a nose
Bereft of its family convenience.

Until by evening, when the smoke
Had cleared and Mother felt God's hot hand
Gentle upon her brow. It all means indoor plumbing,
She said, and *now*.

Even today I hear the words
And think of matches,
Of the fleeing rabbit,
Of scrap lumber and the tiny tilted shed,
Of Father, bent like bad pine,
Putting a pipe wrench to plumbing strange as neckties.

And of the new porcelain bowl
So beautiful
It might have been Christ feeding the multitude.

LTL

Carry A. Nation came into our house and filled it
With her meagerness. She was hung full-fleshed
Against the flowered wallpaper of our living-room,
And Mrs. Wilma Hunt, who brought her, gave each
Of us a little wooden hatchet. "John Barleycorn
Is the Devil," Mrs. Wilma Hunt said. And
By dropping worms head-
First into alcohol she taught us
To hate him. "Now let me tell
You," she said, "about the LTL . . . "

She taught us the Loyal
Temperance Legion song, all of it, then killed
Another worm and served refreshments. Our house
Had never been so full. There were all of us, with
Carry on the wall-
Paper: Kool-Aid, Cookies, Song,
Something-New-to-Hate—
And several dead worms
Curled in alcohol.

||||||||||||||||||||||||||||||||||||||||||||||||||||||||||||||||||||||||||||||||||||||||||||||||||||||

Town Team

The local jocks back home in Attica
seem more than amply snugged.

At first base a stomach extends itself
to scoop a low throw, like a gunslug,
from the dust.

The shortstop moves like a sweet fat fairy
to his right or left,
his sneakers leaking ballbearings.

Outfielders jog for several days to their positions,
pivot like bloated ballerinas,
doff their caps,
then jog for several days back to the dugout.

The infield is a squat and pussel-gutted chain.
Round faced and red, it
chews its tongue and
spits practically perfect daisies.

The pitcher trembles the mound with a headshake:
he wants another sign.
The catcher, wide as a sandcrab,
sweats marbles.

At the plate
a batter settles into his stance
like a tender, untapped keg.

|||||||||||||||||||||||||||||||||||||||||||||||||||||||||||||||||||||||||||||||||||||||||||||||||

The Spring House

Seeping upward from some deep sense
Of purity, our spring gathers
Itself like the shaping of a birth
Inside the damp hush of unweathered

Stone. It rises to fill the basin
That Grandfather poured, to flow unrippling
Down a concrete trough toward sunlight
And a vast world's deeper swifter stream.

The square brown stones that shape the house
Speak our respect. Under rockless skies
They shelter what we have to need:
The pressing of an open eye

Onto clarity. I kneel beyond
All kneeling to see what seems to be
The source, its shade the gravelled sand
Scouring my impure memory.

Inside the soundless house I touch
The water with dry lips, drinking
The cool life of an unborn catfish
That in our pasture on a winding

Muddied stream sleeps belly-buried
At the bottom of a hole. The coolness
Is like a sudden flushed repose
That drives even sweat before its rest.

There is no wind in the spring house,
No weather; the air is water rising.
With it I rise, fulfilled. The sun
Is a network of screen-door, glaring

Upon all deeper swifter streams.
But it cannot change the stone spring house:
Memory stands inviolate in
The shaded place where all times pass.

I leave the spring house only to
Return, to breathe barefooted
Upon the clarity that joins
The muddy miracle of uprooted

Universes. For it is the source
Of Afton that I seek and dread,
Compelled to marvel at movement and
To worship visible fountainheads.

Unloneliness Poem

FOR MY WIFE,

AFTER 20 YEARS

Let us shake hands.
Rub noses.
Press unshod feet.
Skin of skin,
we seek
the impervious covering
to wrap our isolations in.

And though it is
as always
only tissue,
brief as morning,
we go at least that
single span unlonely
in the joining.

Call me loony,
who spent most of his night in the outhouse,
counting rocks.
Listen:
the young folks hereabouts
steal them free from the railroad,
then trap me inside my toilet.
They know that at least in bathroom matters
I am a little like them,
though in things of substance
I am alone.
For listen:
I am the loony,
my tongue so thick
it has no space to speak in.
And at my angriest sometimes I grin.
Each Fourth of July
I do my dance for the children,
yet no one seems to care or to remember.
Last night, for example,
I sat for hours and hours in the dark,
counting rocks.
They hit the sides and the roof
like short jabs to the loony's groin,
and he was so afraid and so angry
that he must have smiled
well into dawn.

‖‖‖

I confess
that I am guilty,
that I am the one with fits,
that when the spittle and the blackness come
I am at the mercy of this gentle town.

I must have chosen
to make a wrong turn in the womb,
and of course there can be no cure:
what I must have done
must still be bouncing
somewhere.

Is it any wonder then
that everybody and his dog
calls me only
by another
name?

‖‖‖

The preacher squatted me
into the water and said
In the name of the Father,
and of the Son,
and of the Holy Ghost,
Amen,

and I did feel different,
we both naked
in a stream in a pasture,
a brown cow
chewing its cud at us
from across the
clear rocky water.

And even later,
drying in the sun,

I did feel different,
as if I had just waked up
on a cool morning
to find myself
not alone.

‖‖‖

When Lloyd Fetrow's picture show burned flat
I was the last to leave,
uncertain where John Wayne ended
and the fine bright flames began.
And folks are not always gentle,
ripping me as they did
from my seat, my popcorn:
even today, under the arms,
I can feel their handholds,
bruises thick as thumbs.
And with each snowfall
the wasted popcorn returns,
white flak upblown, arrested,
exploding the eyes.
Later they said they had to,
that one second more
and the tip of my nose
would have gone ablaze.
Because they said that
even a mongrel has feelings,
and that no respectable
God-fearing Nebraska town,
without a fight,
lets its loony die.

Sound of the loony is a sound
inside the mind,
cannot be sung.
Loony's ears collect the music
thick as tar
on loony's tongue,
sending loony's heavy head
beyond the hatbrim
overcome.
Then does loony close his eyes
and smile his lips
and hum.

That hot August night
I was the first to reach her,
her face laid open like a movie.
There was rubber in the air,
and the driver of the car,
not able to ungrip his fingers,
stuck like a fly on glue behind the wheel.
And the girl seemed not much heavier
than a scrap of pine,
her little blood
a warm uneasy tickling at my hands.
And someone said later
he had never noticed them before,
the hands,
how brown,
how big as buckets.
And the child hung on,
its face full grown now—
saying *hello hello* to loony
from its twisted smile.

I know something I might tell:
the youngest Cunningham girl
is a tease and a thief,
she very pretty
sneaking the sweetest of smells
from the Rexall Drugstore,
swinging herself then
south past the pool hall
toward Selma's,
both her sweater and her handbag
heavy with what I know
and just might
one of these bone-lonesome evenings
spill:
that some of us here
in the heat of this jungle
are being burned very badly
by the youngest Cunningham girl.

Warm is what the Gypsy Wine is,
it having bled in bottles
from the broken train.

Warm is the rosy water
at the knees,
at the brain.

Until the rosy nectar
fires the engine,
starts it up again.

Then the wreck begins to move
in circles,
and the eyes to rain.

Warm is what the loony's breath is
on a pillow
after pain.

How what we have
and where we go
and what we do
and the hours
and the days
unwind

as from
a bolt of wire:

with money from his brother's letter
loony has a mower,
cuts the grass of Lloyd Fetrow
who pays his labor off
in passes to his picture show.
And how the wire unrolls:
loony near the front row,
his lips aflame with salt and popcorn,
and on the screen
a German spy
about to jump
a nice American lady.
But listen:
I am not afraid.
I have seen this reel before.
The lady will not die,
and the German will be helped
across the water.
And loony will go to the drugstore
for the chocolate malt
that lies like thick sweet dust
along its inch or so of wire.

Selma says *Good morning*
and tests my coffee
with her finger.
Harvey Crenshaw says this time

to rack the God damn 8-ball
squarely in the middle,
mister loony.
Shorty Coleman
calls me Dogears
and asks after the 8:40.
Butch Miller nods and shows me
another busted cuetip.
Pete Corser wants to arm wrestle.
Delbert Garlow's eyes are so crossed
they seem to be asking
the bridge of his nose,
instead of loony,
for another cold tomato beer.
Troy wonders if there is anything
I need.
Mr. Terrell calls me Senator
and wants to know
what's new at the White House.
Preacher says *Evening, Larry,*
and returns my hand.

IIIIIIIIIIIIIIIIIIIIIIIIIIIIIIIIIIIIIIIIIIIIIIIIIIIIIIIIIIIIIIIIIIIIIIIIIIIIIIIIIIIIIIIIIIIIIIIIIIIII

The good folks at the camp meeting
are singing and shouting
and clapping their hands,
and some are crying,
and the right little, tight little
Mendenhall girl
is on her knees at the altar,
praying to the top of the tent.
Last night old Mrs. Carlson
won the victory in
her right ear,
where now, she says,
she can hear a smattering

of the highest parts of the sermon.
The preacher says that he has
never been to college,
but that he has a sheepskin
from the ivory towers at Jerusalem,
and that more than once
he has trod up Calvary,
stepping where Christ himself stepped,
and that he felt His presence there.
The preacher says that
he would rather be just a poor beggar,
and live in a shack
by the side of the road,
and know Jesus,
than to be as rich as Rockefeller,
which the preacher says
is like a boat without a rudder
or a fish without a tail.
And listen:
tomorrow night, for sure,
Junior Ogden's mother
is going to throw away
her crutches.

And the August air is hot and still,
full of tentpoles and ropes,
sweat and sawdust and straw.
And more and more,
as the night wears on,
the good folks at the camp meeting
warm to the hand of loony:
all of us, it seems,
full of wrath and worms and vinegar,
all slightly disconnected in the head
and needing mercy.

In his toilet sometimes
does loony spend his life,
trapped by the stones
that slip from the hands
of little sons
and daughters.
And once upon a midnight
loony had his radio,
and listen:
bombs like little drops of death
on London,
and at this very
point in time
exploding.
Then into the night
does loony count the stones
and listen for the planes,
and look:
here is the dawn,
here is the high, uncluttered sky,
as harmless as the rockpile
left by children.

I would learn from my friend Troy
the art of battle
so that I might do more
than throw myself unguarded
against the night.
For darkness is what is at the middle
of the Devil's head,
and I would be a good boy
all my life,
and then some.
But the blackness keeps on coming,

sometimes even when the sun
is like an unspent coin
atop the bank building.
Then do I throw myself
full body in its path,
flail and fall and flail,
me no more nimble than a kitchen towel.
Then is the Devil at me,
heavy on my chest and at my throat,
his breath like ether.
And that is why
I would learn from my friend Troy,
who is quick and strong and kind,
the art of battle:
then I would stand on both feet
like a normal god,
grinning my forward fist
into the deep dark hole
of the enemy.

||||||||||||||||||||||||||||||||||||||||||||||||||||||||||||||||||||||||||||||

Sure as kingdom come
the long dark ends.

Sure as Shorty Coleman
has the time of day
the light begins.

And this familiar juice
that drools the lips and chin
will soon be over,

sure as the weld
that keeps the back
of loony's head

together.

Clifton Berry,
night watchman,
trails the beam from his flashlight
as if it was a big dog on a chain.
How the dog goes up one street
and down another,
and into the darkest alleys,
sniffing out doorlocks
that rattle like a train
when Clifton Berry tries them.

And going home too late
sometimes I catch the beam,
it like a dogeye
dancing in the dark,
and listen:
even on the coldest night of all
this dogeye warms.
That is why loony
is so soft upon his bed now,
safe as a silent store
against the bright fur
of his dreaming.

||||||||||||||||||||||||||||||||||||||||||||||||||||||||||||||||||||||||||||||||||||||||||||||||

It is when the wind comes
hot and dry from the south,
and when the wheat comes
rolling fast as truckwheels
into town:
then would loony be
beyond these little streets,
would loony let his long
and loony hair down.

For on the wind
smells something else from somewhere,
and from their bins
the little seeds are whispering.

Listen:
loony should not care who cares,
or be afraid.

Listen:
loony should stand wide and tall tonight
and blow away.

For on the wind
smells something else from somewhere,
and from their bins
the little seeds are plotting.

|||||||||||||||||||||||||||||||||||||||||||||||||||||||||||||||||||||||||||||||||||||

Urie turns from the bunched-up hair
of his customer
to say how Pistol Pete Reiser,
centerfielder for the old Brooklyn Dodgers,
used to bang his body
against wire and wood and concrete walls,
chasing fly balls.
Urie says that old Pete broke his head
at least a dozen times,
one time so bad
they had to hire a welldigger
to drain it.
Urie says that Pistol Pete
was one of the most dedicated men
that ever filled a jockstrap,
he no more nutty, Urie says,
than the rest of us.
Urie, who drinks,

says shitfire it takes all kinds:
how there are a lot of things
we aren't supposed to understand,
and how the good Lord,
after all is said and done,
draws straight with crooked lines.

||||||||||||||||||||||||||||||||||||||||||||||||||||||||||||||||||||||||||||||||||||

Always on the darkest of nights
she fills the upstairs window,
and once I tapped old Clifton Berry
on the elbow, and pointed:
but there's no law against
a wild woman brushing down her hair,
Mr. Berry said,
and loony thinks that loony paused
and nodded.
Yet always she performs
half naked in a bath of light,
herself so smooth and slow and unconcerned
I sometimes wonder.
As if she is always on the edge
of being absolutely ready.
And one time from the alley
back of Bert's Garage
I made myself to watch her
long into the night,
until I turned and ran.
O wild woman,
do not feed your long arms
to the animals!
Who gag and spin
and suck the heavy air,
clutching for dear sweet mercy
at they know not what.

Early each summer evening
the gang from the Santa Fe
moves slow as syrup
from the toolshed
to the depot
to the main street
to the pool hall,
its legs always the same,
its face and dirt and grease
and cap and watchchain
always the same,
always the same slow stretch
before Butch Miller at the bar
and the same word
that brings the same cold beer:
and the gang is not happy
or much for crying,
not done in
or anxious for the evening,
but steady,
as if that constant space
between two tracks
had told them something.

And loony watches them
and hears it,
and sure enough:
the moon is coming up
as slow as syrup,
sleep in its opening eye,
a timetable in its left hind pocket.

In the early morning
on a stool at Selma's
I can smell the hashbrowns and the bacon,
and the countertop as clean as new linoleum.
Everything is in its place at Selma's,
even loony:
how when he sits down
the puzzle comes together,
and will again tomorrow
and tomorrow.
Listen:
this is something not so small to have,
and something very large to look for:
cup and spoon and coffee steam,
the hands of Selma from behind the counter.
And he must be the loony
who cannot be thankful
for the merest order:
who can only know that
life is good
when life is over.

I whittle a bird
to fit the flowers
that sweeten the form
of Junior Ogden's mother.
And look:
how dry and tight
this square of wood
from Dickman's lumberyard,
its smell a winesap apple.
For Junior Ogden's mother
is holding very still,
no more the cripple,

and Junior Ogden,
not so young or sure of foot himself,
has eyes like something wild
that's sniffing freedom.
How else explain
the empty lot beside my porch
that's smoking?
Junior Ogden,
burning his mother's canes and crutches
and walking sticks,
his poor dead mother's clothing.
Yet in the night
does Junior Ogden
rise above the fire
as if wooden,
as if his wings
were just as surely pine
as what the loony whittles on:
O little bird,
O small, unfinished man!

|||||||||||||||||||||||||||||||||||||||||||||||||||||||||||||||||||||||||||||||||||

Delbert Garlow talks
on and on and on
about the rain,
says that already the mud is so deep
that all his shorter hogs
are disappearing.
Delbert talks with his eyes crossed,
as if for luck:
says where is that
God damn Noah, anyhow,
now that we need him?
Delbert sits
far tilted back
like danger

in his chair,
eating a new cigar.
In front of him
his hands are placing dominoes
in the shape of a tapered wall.
Delbert, who is keeping score,
says that the only thing
a man can do,
unless he's a duck,
is stick his finger
in the nearest hole.

|||||||||||||||||||||||||||||||||||||||||||||||||||||||||||||||||||||||||||||||||||||||||||

I plant geraniums and four o'clocks.
They will say *How lovely,*
how green the loony's thumb is!
They will be drawn off the gravel road,
across the patch of lawn.
They will bend themselves far down,
seeing, touching, smelling.
They will note the color of the soil,
will pinch it, sift it,
memorize the texture.

They will dare to pick the choicest cluster.

Then will they retrace their steps
across the grass,
looking back over their shoulders.
They will show the flowers to their friends,
who will need some of their very own.
They will come in the night,
while I am asleep,
and take them.

O sweet as malt sometimes
the space we move in,
trunk and arms and legs
like noses, breathing.

The ears on the face
in the chair
in Urie's barber shop
are splashed with Sweet Pea Talcum.

In Bert's Garage,
the popping of a brand new oilcan.

Into the east a freight train's sound
is nothing more than smoke now,
a veil of coal, and settling.

In Vernon Potter's unswept store
fruit and meat and vegetables,
exhaling.

The chicken mash
from Cecil's hatchery
is falling fine as sawflakes
from the transom.

There is heat the color of honey
from the newest breakfast biscuits
stirred by Selma.

Butch Miller sets free
another bottle of beer.

And back in the drugstore
the easy whir
of the malt machine
has loony watering.

Loony has no card, no badge, no age.
Loony happened long ago,
or maybe yesterday.
Tomorrow loony
is burning out his bootheels
on the sidewalk
not so very far away.
Look:
he is under a streetlight,
eating a toothpick.
He is racking pool balls
for a game that
always has been,
always will be,
played.
He is stuffing the loose ends
of his workshirt
into the empty gaps
that bag his pants.
And look:
he is bending his nose
into the cup of his hands,
washing himself
and hiding himself
and peeking between the cracks
and giving thanks.

**ludi jr invites the reader
into the ripening of his garden**

come:
into the mulch of ludi jr's mind

hear there such sounds
the mating of worms
the call of the coyote
the pecking of small birds

and in the spaces
between the sounds
the germ of silence

into the mulch
of ludi jr's mind

dip down the hand:

know that something
only partly sour
is working there

with ludi jr
touch the fingers
to the dark wide flarings
of the nose

catch then and hold
the outsniffed air

and turn it turn it turn it

oh trying
with ludi jr
to understand!

**during the sermon
ludi jr dreams of the girl
in the next pew**

how her long blonde hair
must follow her
everywhere

when she sits down
the hair settling itself in place
not daring to move
until spoken to

when she enters the dimestore
the hair reaching out and down
to examine the cold cream

in potter's grocery
the hair polishing the apples
catching their fire

and at night

oh at night!

the tipends sparking the linen

**ludi jr as conductor,
by which means the cow and the milkstool
are however briefly united**

grant these:
sky above   earth below

how then the tits on the milkcow
hang down as if a part of
something cumulus

the milkstool up from the soil
like the very solid throne
that the wide almighty lord himself
gives orders from

and in between
the feet   the head   the bended knees
of ludi jr
his fingers drawing ropes of
milk like nectar
from the bursting udder

between the sunlight
and the shadow
sits ludi jr

between the swallow
and the damp compacted dung
sits ludi jr

between one substance
and another
sings ludi jr

isn't this the way
that the world begins
world begins   world begins

isn't this the way
that the world begins

with two bloods joining?

every day ludi jr
eats a package of lifesavers,
just in case

thus he alone
bobs like a cork
on this ocean of pillage and blood

from the height of his buoyant throne
hears he the wailings of the doomed
the gnashings of full-grown
men and women

he alone
is not consumed
in the forest of ash and fire

from within the protected circle of his room
smells he the hair   the flesh
the sweet stench of the last blackened tongue

and what of the wind?

tomorrow or tomorrow
the tornado touches down

he alone only escaped to tell it

ludi jr runs all the way around
his paper route without stopping

opening the door of urie's barbershop
without breaking stride

tossing a paper into the hollow
of andy martin's lap

and circling the barber chair
and out the door

and over the cracks in the sidewalk
to each of the businesses

with the same precision
except for moulton's grocery

where old lady hostetler fills the door-
way her tough luck her groceries

splayed like so many soft potatoes
over mr moulton's oily sawdust floor

the world of mr moulton
and of old lady hostetler

like the flutterings of so many songbirds
at ludi jr's ears

who is full in his stride now
the bundle of papers bumping bumping

bumping at his ludi jr side
and the soles of his plastic boots

ablaze as he sends a paper
through mabel cleveland's front

screendoor which is nothing compared
to the sound of glass that comes from

charlie fenton's window
another songbird until

some gravel drops into ludi jr's shoe
and the running is now not so even

but steady enough
urged on by the sound of boys

at basketball and without breaking stride
without shifting the bundle

ludi jr is in the middle of things
faking snatching dribbling jumping

and pop like a cork shot from a bottle
out of things and back on the

route worrying just a little now
about crocker's old leather bulldog

thinking of how best to kill him
without breaking stride

without slowing
without losing a pantleg or a leg

and when the time comes
feeding him the hard end of a paper

pushing it so deep into his throat
that he rolls over gagging

another songbird
and ludi jr soon far out of range

the gravel at home now in the softer spots
of ludi jr's foot

and fannie young standing on the front porch
with her hand out

saying songbird songbird songbird
as ludi jr passes the paper like

a baton while seeing ahead the tobacco pouch
that virgil shannon leaves his money in

it dangling from a nail on a gatepost
three quarters and one nickel old virgil

the most honest injun
who will just have to wait until tomorrow

for the return of the pouch
ludi jr flicking it from the nail

without breaking stride
without slowing

tossing old virgil's paper with the left
hand over the fence and toward the back porch

old virgil's greeting
the faintest of songbirds

until the end of the circle is in sight
and ludi jr picks up the pace

the gravel now worked up and into the knee
the bundle at ludi jr's side

now limp as the pelt from the rabbit
that newberry skinned this

morning he in a red rubber apron
peeling off the skin in one amazing upward movement

and saying to the rabbit
now how do you like that leroy

all the rabbits in all the world
that newberry ever skinned being leroy

all of them sooner or later
as newberry himself used to say

naked as the rest of us
until already the long jackrabbit legs of ludi jr

are fanning a breeze beside the south porch
of ludi jr's final customer

eldon bateman the town catholic
whose paper hits the top of the house

with a thud
rolling then like a shot songbird

down the shingles
and into the guttering

and without breaking stride
ludi jr undresses the paper bag

from his side his shoulder
holds it high it catching the wind

trying to brake the ludi jr's incredible pace
but not doing its job

so that when ludi jr takes a sudden left
at the main street

the paper bag billowing
hurries like a dazed dog to catch up

old ludi's body now a slow blur
in the bank the barbershop

the drugstore window
and across the railroad and past

the grain elevator
the smell of wheat in the nostrils

like a second wind
and due east then

toward the city limits
toward the city limits sign

which ludi jr kisses
with the outstretched palm of his left hand

another songbird
the sweetest of them all

saying so long so long so long
all you lovely nitpickers

ludi jr will not be born again
born again born again

until the fall

**plowing the north forty,
ludi jr unearths the remnants
of his paternal grandfather**

who lived on sourdough and dock
grubworms and milfoil
and the breasts of small birds

who lived day in day out unaware
that he could not kiss the overgrowth
in his own ear

who heated both himself
and the scirrhus in his wife
with what the milkcows hourly
walked away from

who wore both lobes to the bone
listening for the word
of the lord

who heard it:
old man lie down

who stretched himself out in a furrow
pulling the dark moist soil
over him like a comfort

who without further comment
is becoming something else
the process a kindness to him
that these bones these bones
these dry white bones
shall never walk again

disguised as a square knot,
ludi jr infiltrates the boy scouts

now I know all their secrets:
the handshake the bowline the survival hike
the meadowlark the history of flint

ask me a question
any question   anything
go ahead   ask me

the answer is poland china

the answer is eagle

the answer is beanhole beans

you begin with north
and you box your way clockwise
back to there

between the beginning and the ending
are directions for everything

and with new binoculars
you too can see that cindy kohlman
has hair

that's what larry schmidt said
on his honor

black as a crow
go see for yourself

you jump don't dive into the water
one hand over the nose
the other hand
over the place where the crow goes

the answer being dot dot dot dash

and you lose the limb maybe
if the pressure on the tourniquet
is too long or too severe

there are pressure points
here here here here here
here and here

there are only these
precise pressure points

there is no
other

the answer is be prepared

〰〰〰

**ludi jr, nipped at by crocker's dog,
plans revenge**

when?

when he is asleep
dreaming of ludi jr's ankle

when in the dream
his teeth are so deep into bone
that the lips drool red

where?

at crocker's house
under the front porch
atop the damp sifted dust

how?

with that part
of the new blue blade
so fine it cannot be seen

for how long?

again and again and again
or until the hind legs
stop jerking
why?

because
no matter what my father said
blood for blood
is sweetest

‖‖

**ludi jr bounces his basketball
on an anthill in a crack in the sidewalk,
inflicting heavy casualties**

some of the little backbiters so flattened
so much reduced to ooze
they serve only as the ripest of rosin
others unmarked roll with the wind
tiny weightless gumballs too late to grass

all in a day's work the pilot says
I didn't come to this here hellhole
to pick shit on the sideline
I came here he says to dance

and his bombs strike with a smart curt clap
each a dead or blind or crippled enemy

until the anthill is leveled
its grains humbled and dispersed
its inhabitants scattered to the four corners

on such a day the blade that juts
from the bare shoulder
like a wing
dances and dips its victory
sends the sharp flashes of its semaphore
back like bullets to the sun:

mission accomplished hightower two
hightower two do you read me?

this is hightower one

||||||||||||||||||||||||||||||||||||||||||||||||||||||||||||||||||||||||||||||||||||

**ludi jr announces the name
of his lady fair**

it is what only the ear
can understand

the name circling the rim
like the dark sweet wine
that ludi jr
strained among his teeth

and strained again

that sunday morning
at communion

it perfect in every way
but one:
not enough

my girl like the small cup of crystal
that holds the small dark wine

she the salt
that leavens the pomp
that the preacher whines

making it betty jean betty jean betty jean

to the ear   on the tongue

I am sure of only one thing:
when I die I will live again

ludi jr turns cartwheels and backflips
from one end of the gymnasium
to the other

as if some sleepy caretaker
had left the door
to the monkey cage
wide open

as if tarzan
had tossed a bunch of bananas
against the distant backboard

ludi jr in his leopardskin at night
enchants the multitudes

in his nose the aromatic mist of
floor polish and sawdust

sweat flicking from his forehead and chin
like water off a saltlick

and all the time the chosen one
not missing a single beat

hell you know he's plenty good
you can tell it in the way
the muscles at his back
and on his legs
are bunching

and look see the shadow in the balcony
with both thumbs pointing upward?
it owns the place
it's god

it means that business is so good
that for the moment most of us

can go on turning

**from an easy chair in the living room
of his treehouse, ludi jr
attends a prayer meeting**

through the space where a window should be
I can hear the singing

      have you been to jesus for the cleansing tide?
      are you washed in the blood of the lamb?

beneath me a squirrel
with a walnut in his paws
pauses cocks his head
looks up
winks

      are your garments spotless?
      are they white as snow?

a bird no heavier
than a soapchip
settles on my shoulder

      are you washed in the blood of the lamb?

through the space where the door should be
I can see other houses
other spaces other eyes

      are you washed—
      in the blood—

at the corner
under a streetlight
crocker's bulldog stands
making friends with an elm tree

      in the soul-cleansing blood
      of the lamb?

the leaf I position
in my hands
flutters like a green kiss
against the tongue

      are your garments spotless?
      are they white as snow?

through the space where the roof should be
I can count the stars
more than a million
more than a thousand
more than a hundred
more even than one

      are you washed in the blood of the lamb?

and all the time
under the space where the floor should be
the answer:

as sure as walls are made
for breaking down

I am I am I am
I am I am

||||||||||||||||||||||||||||||||||||||||||||||||||||||||||||||||||||||||||||||||||||||

upon the death of crocker's dog
ludi jr takes it all back

because ludi jr has healed
has lived to tell about it

because the scars on ludi jr's ankles
are bluer far
than any other part

because the silence in the throat
of anything
repels

I say to crocker's dead dog:

I take it all back
the sticks the pellets the words
the rocks from the railroad
the boot whose toe went lost
in the only soft spot
on your belly

rest easy
be gentle with the worms
and in that space
behind the holes that were your eyes
remember:

do not return

||||||||||||||||||||||||||||||||||||||||||||||||||||||||||||||||||||||||||||||||||||||

ludi jr, as the hired hand,
pays dearly for what
he is paid for

beginning the task spic and span
spitting like a lumberjack
into the cup of his bare calloused hands
ludi jr jumps over the gate in a single stride
to confront face to snout
the hog that he has been hired
to stalk and bring to his back and bind

but after more than one lunge
after half a dozen frenzied dives
the palms the arms the boots the bib
hang heavy as sashweights with dung

and he takes a break
several long deep deliberate breaths
before plunging in again

the hog meanwhile
wide and low and apparently immobile
watching the hired hand resting
watching him

until with a fresh vigor
ludi jr begins all over again
hogshit and corncobs and mudchips
like the devil's own
dark flurry of divots
storming the pen
neither hog nor man
willing to back down
the sounds from them
frequent and short and gutteral
the face now of the hired man
aslop with that square of space

where only a second earlier
the hog had been
a crust of hair only
in the hired man's fisted hand

and he takes a second break
this time not simply to breathe
but to think things over

while the hog
wide and low and all at once again
apparently immobile

guards his ground
grunting
watching

and here is what the hired man knows
but cannot think:
the essence of hog

in the boots hog
in the hair hog
in the nose hog
in the eyes
down the back
between the lips
against the tongue
adrift all up and down the spine
hinged in the knuckles
in the elbows in the knees
in the bend and snap of the ankles

hog

knowing but not thinking that no word
not even hog hog hog hog hog
can backflush the bowel that is truly hog
like brother cannot itself
as either sound or squibble
be what the brother knows
under the skin in the bone
to be

that no smell however stout
can do it either
no snort no grunt no squeal
however deep and short
however shrill
the syllable

yet something in the belly
bristles with the same blood:
that will   hot and barbed and defiant
not now or ever to be laid hold of

which means that ludi jr
no less than god
must earn his keep:
must become the essence of hog
before he has the right of blood
to bind the feet

and when all of that has come to pass
and the snout is seized
and the head is forced back
and the quaint taut throbbing throat
gushes red

must drink as if elixir from the very well
he dreamed and planned and dug himself

and filled

||||||||||||||||||||||||||||||||||||||||||||||||||||||||||||||||||||||||||||||||||||||||||||||||||||||

**ludi jr kills one cow, seven frogs,
and fourteen toads to make a fur piece
to adorn the shoulders
of his lady fair**

armed to the teeth he approaches the pond
the singing at the banks hushes

he looks across the lily pads   the moss
speaks his plan slowly and clearly
into the eyes of a thirsty milkcow

and the cow itself approaches first
its udder made light in the water

then the frogs
then from the edges of the pasture
a skirmisher of toads

all in a heap throwing their little lives
at ludi jr's feet

who kills them and skins them
cures and stretches and stitches them
leaving one set of eyes
one tongue
to keep the flies from groveling
at her bosom

ah my sweet ambrosia
can't you hear me?
I am what I skin
love is in me like a .22 long
it smells of powder
it is always green
kiss its unlikely mouth and
behold!   the prince

||||||||||||||||||||||||||||||||||||||||||||||||||||||||||||||||||||||||||||||||||||||||||||||||||||

**after spending 97 years
with his nose to the grindstone,
ludi jr admits that he has failed
in his effort to invent the wheel**

the task demanded too much
the imagination of ludi jr
racing leagues ahead of his
enfeebled fingers

yet a couple of times
he very nearly had it
this end to that end
very nearly joined

and the length of cane that lay between
so very nearly perfectly rounded
eternity so very nearly
in a nutshell

that to think of it as if quintessence
very nearly takes the breath away
the heart very nearly
misses a beat

and I am sure of this:
that ages hence
we shall yet be at it
this end to that end
very nearly joined

I have not lost faith
children do not be put down
at the tipends of your fingers
the polished pearl the paragon
rotates its lure

an end to death
is
just around the corner

Fairport

According to Stocker,
most of the people
that do their serious shopping here
are too muleheaded ever to pass on.
That's why sometimes at night
you can hear a rattling from the graveyard:
Republicans and Democrats, Methodists and Baptists,
all at each others' empty throats.
In the oval frames
that decorate the bank
are faces of the first fathers,
and when an old man dies
his son, or someone's,
rises full-blown from the ceremonial dust.
Bones and eyebrows everywhere,
according to Stocker,
some of them still alive and lifted,
wearing out the storefronts
on a Saturday night.
They stretch as far south
as the mind can see,
Stocker says,
then two days west:
from Maine to Medicine Lodge,
from time to Timbuktu,
from hell to breakfast.

Elsie Martin

She's six of one, half a dozen of another,
According to Stocker:
Not a bad looker, for a widowwoman,
But her face so knobbed with indecision
You'd swear she has hemorrhoids.
Heard of another case just like her,
He said,
Who starved to death in a grocery store,
Comparing labels.
Always and forever between a rock and a hard place—
Not fishing, quite,
And not quite cutting bait.
So precisely between the devil
And the deep blue sea
That she lives with one foot in heaven
And the other in hot water.
Split her right down the middle,
Stocker said,
And it wouldn't make a dime's worth of difference
Which half you reached for.

||||||||||||||||||||||||||||||||||||||||||||||||||||||||||||||||||||||||||||||||||||||||||

Mrs. Wilma Hunt

Stocker said the air that came from
Mrs. Wilma Hunt
Had no more teeth in it
Than Prohibition.
He knew more than one woman just like that, he said,
Most of them sired no doubt
By dreams of cyclones.
Mrs. Wilma Hunt knew everything
There was to know
About nothing,

According to Stocker,
As if someone some time or other, he said,
Had twisted her one notch too tight,
Stripping the threads,
So that now she's like a cattle truck
On its way home,
The wind whistling Dixie
Through the slats of her sideboards,
The whole kit and caboodle
Going hellbent for election,
As Stocker put it,
But running empty.

|||||||||||||||||||||||||||||||||||||||||||||||||||||||||||||||||||||||||||||||||||||||||||||

Sonny

The boy had bad luck written all over his face,
According to Stocker:
Something about the tilt of the eyes,
The way they saw but never could quite focus.
Stocker said that sometimes people come that way
Straight from the shell,
Jostled too much by the hen, maybe,
Or the membrane scared loose by coyotes.
But in any such case the sign is there,
According to Stocker,
And clear as sin to the one with wits to read it.
So Sonny should have stayed in the egg,
Stocker said,
So poor in luck he'll bust his back one day
Picking shit with the chickens.

Urie

It was general knowledge
that most of Urie the barber's body drank,
maybe even to excess—
this speculation an embryo
that one hot August afternoon
grew legs and lungs,
as Stocker said,
and stood up and declared itself
a full-blown human.
It happened when the hot bourbon
reached at last the delicate tips
of Urie's business hand,
causing the razor to decide itself
its most indulgent course.
And very naturally it chose the knob
at Leland Corser's throat,
halving it, as Stocker said,
like a tall tomato.
Corser, moments before he died,
vowed that for such sorry slipshod work
Urie should not be paid.
Whereupon the barber closed his shop
and went fishing,
went to sleep night after night,
as Stocker liked to guess,
to the thrill of old corks,
bobbing.

The Rearranging

Stocker used to say that something
is seldom reduced to nothing
by the wind. Chiefly, he said,
it's a matter of rearranging.
That's why sometimes you see a leghorn
shivering down Main Street,
naked as a needle,
or a phone pole growing feathers.
What the wind picked up an hour ago
it'll deposit tomorrow,
according to Stocker,
and sooner or later it picks up
damn near everything:
bedsheets and shingles
and hubcaps and small children
and the spoken word, even,
and the remotest odor.
Stocker claimed that on a clear night,
when the wind goes suddenly calm,
you can hear the pyramids being built,
can catch with the flaring of a nostril
the brief, sweet stench of kings.

Stocker

Said himself
he was planned laid out and constructed
on that green bench
in front of the pool hall,
that he had neither first name nor kin:
and no matter where you found him—
playing dominoes in the pool hall,
at breakfast in Bake's Cafe,

picking his teeth at the streetcurb,
whittling on the familiar green bench—
Stocker looked as if he had always been there
and had no intention ever of leaving.
For he was a huge man,
giant everywhere,
especially in the calves and belly,
looking a lot like a baby building.
Said as much himself,
and more than once,
each time grinning like a sophomore.
Even in his casket he seemed larger
than those of us looking on,
as if even in death
he had been given
the last word.

Beginnings

This morning the leaves on the cottonwood
made their first apparent move,
the new blades of grass,
timorous and delicate,
presumed to breathe.

And all morning I loafed beside the house
to watch them.
I figure this,
that someone has to mark such things,
someone know, beyond all other knowing,
that recurrency is something more
than a primate's dream.

And this:
that evidence of the most essential type
is what we break our legs for,
the bud about to burst,
the grassblade rising
from its dram
of water.

O I have been in the earth too long, too long!

Yet I am not so much amazed
as I am dumb
to fill again this space
expired from.

New Year's Eve

an hour from now and Shorty Cleveland at the power plant
will make it official, will blow the whistle to say
if you didn't know it before you know it now

time if not chance happens to all

meanwhile I play Parcheesi with my grandmother
she is laughing and weeping and moving her buttons
around the board too quickly   she is cheating

she has everything her way tonight and knows it
on schedule her prodigal grandson has returned
for the popcorn and the games, for the whistle

and for eventually the smell of breath and bedding
grandmother's most recent spoon of codeine
like a stout unending benediction in the frozen room

always the time draws nigh

her large German breasts heave and fall with her laughter
I am in bondage now   the dice have the little eyes of lizards
later as a man I will imagine this explosive woman

receiving the news that the son of the son of her brother
was bombed dead by Americans less than a month
before the ending of the second great war

her false teeth meanwhile are the clicking of small
bayonets   she moves her last button up the ramp
and, cheating again, miscounting, into home

cut down again, sweet baby, out of time

and her triumph moves her into a fit of coughing
that sends her back to the cupboard and the codeine
she pads the linoleum in brown cotton hose,

a sack for a dress, nodding a head of white thick hair
in the direction of begonia and fern and violet,
the unlikely flare of row on row of Joseph's coat

well she wants another game, change buttons and chairs
for the little fellow's luck   after that, hot cocoa and bed
and the dice begin already to sing only to her

this moment is the time of love

and I love the moment for her loving it, her
cheating the buttons home, her face broken and brown
and glorious in silence when the whistle blows

||||||||||||||||||||||||||||||||||||||||||||||||||||||||||||||||||||||||||||||||||||

Jubilation

FOR MICHELLE AT 17 MONTHS

In the nude in the living room
she dances,
her hands now clapping,
now at her sides, now swinging,
her small perfect body
fresh from its bath,
her white to yellow hair
a cowlick drying.

In her eyes
the music glints
to a pirouette,
and she falls
like a brisk sweet-scented drunk
into the carpet

only to be up
and about
and around again,
and with a kiss and a shrug,
a show of gatted teeth,
a jut of chin,

she finds her way
back to the heart of the heart
of the rhythm.

And we who have spent
the larger portion of our days
north-northeast of Eden
let loose encumbrances
like something silk
to join in:

O Grandma is going topless,
Parson,
this heel to that brief toe,
this canker, cured,
to that unsullied skin!

||||||||||||||||||||||||||||||||||||||||||||||||||||||||||||||||||||||||||||||||||||||||||

Out-and-Down Pattern

FOR JOHN

My young son pushes a football into my stomach
and tells me that he is going to run
an out-and-down pattern,
and before I can check the signals
already he is half way across the front lawn,
approaching the year-old mountain ash,
and I turn the football slowly in my hands,
my fingers like tentacles
exploring the seams,
searching out the lacing,
and by the time I have the hands positioned
just so against the grain-tight leather,
he has made his cut downfield
and is now well beyond the mountain ash,
approaching the linden,
and I pump my arm once, then once again,
and let fire.

The ball in a high arc
rises up and out and over the linden,
up and out and over the figure
that now has crossed the street,
that now is all the way to Leighton Avenue,
now far beyond,
the arms outstretched,
the head as I remember it
turned back, as I remember it
the small voice calling.

And the ball at the height of its high arc
begins now to drift,
to float as if weightless
atop the streetlights and the trees,
becoming at last that first bright star in the west.

Late into an early morning
I stand on the front porch,
looking into my hands.

My son is gone.

The berries on the mountain ash
are bursting red this year,
and on the linden
blossoms spread like children.

||||||||||||||||||||||||||||||||||||||||||||||||||||||||||||||||||||||||||||||||||||||||

My Love for All Things Warm and Breathing

I have seldom loved more than one thing at a time,
yet this morning I feel myself expanding, each
part of me soft and glandular, and under my skin
is room enough now for the loving of many things,
and all of them at once, these students especially,
not only the girl in the yellow sweater, whose
name, Laura Buxton, is somehow the girl herself,
Laura for the coy green mellowing eyes, Buxton
for all the rest, but also the simple girl in blue

on the back row, her mouth sad beyond all reasonable
inducements, and the boy with the weight problem,
his teeth at work even now on his lower lip, and
the grand profusion of hair and nails and hands and
legs and tongues and thighs and fingertips and
wrists and throats, yes, of throats especially,
throats through which passes the breath that joins
the air that enters through these ancient windows,
that exits, that takes with it my own breath, inside
this room just now my love for all things warm and
breathing, that lifts it high to scatter it fine and
enormous into the trees and the grass, into the heat
beneath the earth beneath the stone, into the
boundless lust of all things bound but gathering.

|||||||||||||||||||||||||||||||||||||||||||||||||||||||||||||||||||||||||||||||||||||||

If Only I Can Shake off This Dream
All of the Others Should Follow

I am back at the farm
talking to the man who bought it
the man who with his plethora of sons
is busy razing it   he is a large gentle

man in his eyes the running feet of virgin
lumber the multiplication of studs
into granary and henhouse and barn
into house the product at last

what these busy strangers will deign
to call the home place   the man is
impatient to return to his work
yet with the edges of his eyes

he talks to me   he does not understand
that those small weathered hulks
were one day large enough for all of us
at the hands of his sons they are pasteboard

well no matter all I want is a little time
to stand here a final time   some things
after all exist beyond the crowbar
and the sledge   I am thinking of

rock and gumbo and bunchgrass
of the angle of the house against the hill
these mister and the water
that cooled the cattle in the pond

just over there are what my nights
alas are made of   and he nods
but he does not understand
he believes in the future   the poor

demented bastard believes in the future
and I want to explode I want to bleed
and quarter him on the spot I want
to throw my arms around him

and crush him to the earth
and call him father father father

||||||||||||||||||||||||||||||||||||||||||||||||||||||||||||||||||||||||||||||||||||||||||||||

I Don't Like Having a Grasshopper in My Hair

Things happen in General Science
and the world is tremored but moves on.
An apple speaks of gravity
while a grasshopper defies it,
choosing my daughter's hair
as a hiding place.
Where did it come from?
Why is the child screaming?
(Who poured the first pint of oil
on the original troubled waters?)
Anyway, don't anybody leave the room.
Jimmy, rescue Tracy Ann.

He does. He kills the grasshopper
and the mysteries are quieted,
until evening.
"What did you learn in school today?" I ask.
"I don't like having a grasshopper in my hair," she says,
her voice her proof, empirical as a ribbon.
And when she sits on my lap,
and my hand hops upon her head,
I grow grasshopper legs for fingers.
They are slim and hard,
and though they mean no harm
they touch the fair small scalp defensively,
aware of Jimmy.

||||||||||||||||||||||||||||||||||||||||||||||||||||||||||||||||||||||||||||||||||||||||

Daddy (Drunk) Mows the Lawn at Midnight

FOR THE MEADOWLANE CHILDREN

Daddy drank too much,
then mowed the lawn.
From my bedroom window
I could watch him
going round and round,
his mouth wide open
as the mower's,
singing:

Crrrr-ank! up the mower,
We'll have a barrel of fun!
Crrrr-ank! up the mower,
We'll have the weeds on the run . . .

Daddy drank too much,
then mowed the lawn.
In the moonlight
he marched up and down,

the motor joining
like a goofy friend
my daddy's
roaring:

O zing! boom! tra-la-la,
Sing out a song of good cheer!
Everybody crrrr-ank! his mower,
'Cause the gang's all here!

Daddy drank too much,
then mowed the lawn.
But in the moonlight
Mother, in her nightgown,
came along.
She put a finger to her lips,
and Daddy first,
then Daddy's mower,
hushed.

And I watched Mother
take my Daddy's hand
and press it,
then silent as
the very smallest mouse
she pulled him like a
toy on busted wheels
back to the
house.

Benediction

FOR TERRY AND DAVE

We open our hands
to discover them empty,
the fingers small birds
ecstatic in their flight.

Let them fly.
From their vantage point in space
let them see both the measure
and the worth of distance.

Let them see.
Let them lower themselves
to gather all the tidbits
all birds gather.

Let them gather.
Let them fix the pieces,
end on end,
delivering at last the shape of hands.

Let them deliver.
Let them bring their own creations
back to those places
where the touch had been.

Let us touch.
This skin to that skin,
let us join
these hands.

Let us open them
to discover them full again,
these bones, these bones,
these wild and delicate bones

alive with children.

Mid-August, and something
hot as Kansas wind
is at me.

O I am done with the memorizing
of initials in the bench
outside the pool hall!
I don't care whether what loves who,
or when.
I am not excited even
by the span of Wilma's bosom.
The stories in this bench
irk and depress me:
so deeply-grained their lines
not even Jesus Christ
the Lord of Hosts Almighty
could undo them.

That is why I am leaving town.

I want to carve myself a place
too wide for wooden histories.

Thus I stuff some bare belongings
in a feedsack—
then looking back
spit stoutly on the sidewalk.

There is a sizzling.

So long, suckers, I say.
I'll see you in the funny papers.

|||||||||||||||||||||||||||||||||||||||||||||||||||||||||||||||||||||||||||||||||||||

I pass one hand over the other,
surprised to find no strings attached.

To the east a mist is rising
from the bottoms.

My bones, some of them yet in the blanket,
make little morning noises.

Stockpiling the lungs with unsung air,
I volunteer a yodel.

For two cents I'd kick my underpants
into the adjoining pasture.

The sky is so vast, so deep
the nose bleeds.

I am free, white, and at least sixteen.
Thus with my Barlow I notch only every other tree.

|||||||||||||||||||||||||||||||||||||||||||||||||||||||||||||||||||||||||||||||||||||

The early, good-natured smiles
on the faces of the farmers
have gone flaccid and grim,
the mouths of unrequited clowns.

Drought like a lanky locksmith
has let itself into the house
of the midlands.

A jackrabbit no thicker than shale
is wearing his teeth to the gums,
gnawing an epitaph.

Rocks are rising in the plowed fields
like the tops of small,
solid skulls.

Before an open cistern
a woman with big eyes and a hatpin
is about to drop a doll.

Sweat sizzles like bacon grease
on the high, receding forehead
of the local John Deere dealer.

Beneath a cloud
the size of a dime
the last of the feathered birds
is circling.

In Orange City, Iowa,
a carhop with Scotch tape in her hair
sits like an ornament on the hood
of a red Volkswagen,
watering the flies.

||||||||||||||||||||||||||||||||||||||||||||||||||||||||||||||||||||||||||||||||||||

All morning I have practiced an ancient art,
testing nickels against the heft of freight trains.

Not once did the victims whine.

Amid the din of loaded cattle cars
they fell from the rails as trim as rummies,
and as malleable.

But when I give them to the blind man
he consults his broker,
who shakes his head.

When I throw them into the river
the carp die,
laughing.

When I join them into
necklaces
the lovely ladies
shred their breasts.

When I box and bury them
the pirates all retire,
tickled pink with social security.

That is why tonight
I lie flat on a busted back,
biting a silver bullet
and reconsidering.

||||||||||||||||||||||||||||||||||||||||||||||||||||||||||||||||||||||||||||||||||

In New Orleans
there is bourbon in everything,
even the ice cream.

I buy a bourbon sweetheart,
cross her bourbon palm with bourbon bills.

She has black bourbon hair,
wears a bourbon blouse,
bourbon underwear.

On a bourbon bed I undress her.

She has bourbon breasts,
etcetera.

Amid bourbon breath
we dream on bourbon sheets.

Next morning
I brush my teeth with bourbon toothpaste,
having confessed everything to a bourbon sink.

||||||||||||||||||||||||||||||||||||||||||||||||||||||||||||||||||||||||||||||||||

Clock is the sound the punch makes.
It is trying to tell me something,
and I am all ears.
Thus I spit on my hands,
then serve the wise contraption faithfully.

A whistle
interrupts our talk.
I stand beside the Coke machine
and count the empties. I am amazed
that the total does not mean anything.

In the afternoon
things are pretty much the same.
Clock is the sound the punch makes.
Still trying to tell me something,
and I am still all ears.

Mr. Lincoln is square
and solid as a John Deere tractor.
He sits upright, not quite at ease,
in his eyes the glint of small slaves.
Mr. Washington is as I thought he would be,
at attention.
How many others then
landmark this sacred city?
Impossible here to stay lost for long,
though yesterday, at Arlington,
I had to bother a guide.
I had been going in circles since sundown,
trying to memorize the crosses.
He took me by the shoulder,
showed me the way out.
Also said that I should not again,
without written permission,
disturb the dead.

Today I plan to learn more,
to talk with people I have never met
as I watch my step.

In the dead center of Cement City
an unlikely smell of sorghum
grabs at something in me
like a moletrap sprung.

O I would like to be
a Red Man ad
on the side of a
South Dakota barn!

I would like to be
the easy heat
inside a moot
Montana roadapple.

I would disappear into the
land-level silo,
close and secure the lid
and there share juices.

But I am merely here,
a left-handed boy
with a pinched nerve
and shit on his Sunday shoes.

This year, in Casper, Wyoming,
they are wearing the hemline
precisely half a hand above the knee.
This year, in Dillon, Montana,
they are crowding
all the brightest flushes of the rainbow
into their undergarments,
and much of the color this year
is spilling over and up and into
the thick fine arches of the eyes.

This year, in Henderson, Nevada,
they are carrying themselves
on high, enduring heels,
and the hair this year
is long and blown and light as lace.
Next year, when the graves are opened,
men with orange gloves will say
how they remember:
that turn of shoe,
that twist of hair,
that cast of purple eye.
And the men will hoist their shovels
and look away quickly
from the little knee
below that rage
of hemline.

||||||||||||||||||||||||||||||||||||||||||||||||||||||||||||||||||||||||||||||||||||

There is a beer can bobbing on Walden Pond.
Also a duck.
Not far from Oshkosh, Wisconsin,
a young man in marshmallow pumps
is drop-kicking a football.
He is unaware of the girl in the yellow smock,
in Tallahassee, who is reciting First Corinthians 13:3,
or of the lass in Sandy Springs
who has chosen the school custodian's closet
as the setting for her first pregnancy.
Meanwhile, a jet drops from the air
like a deceased quail,
a length of its instrument panel
blooming like curious grass for the milkcows.
Along the main street of Timothy, Wyoming,
a rodeo queen is aware of her measurements,
while in a cemetery west of Waterloo
the Republicans and the Democrats
are at each other's bones.

Even in Chicago the various world drones on:
a pimp on State Street peddling leftover liver,
a man not more than half a mile away
dancing with his only wife,
and that a woman.

||||||||||||||||||||||||||||||||||||||||||||||||||||||||||||||||||||||||||||||||

Snow upon a peak in Colorado:
and along Larimer Street
the heat of bootheels worn to skin.

For the price of a pint of Thunderbird
I can whip any man in the house.
For two bits I can earn the privilege
of watching Slim Jimmy pee beyond his shoes.
For an extra coin
he'll try it standing on his head.

O I have more friends here than a dog has fleas!

Yet something about their anxious breath
unnerves me.
That, and eyes that comb
my haircut's gaudy rum.

Thus I head for the hills.
It is untracked snow I covet now,
rare air and an overview.
Then later, maybe, a good solid woman
I want to sit down with to ham and eggs,
to a plate that looks back
for something more than cheap mercy.

||||||||||||||||||||||||||||||||||||||||||||||||||||||||||||||||||||||||||||||||

Back home it is ten o'clock at night,
and elfish men in flawless coveralls
are surfacing from indiscriminate holes
to roll the main street up
and tuck the town into its daily death.

The little men are anonymous.
They move efficiently, and without
the slightest sound,
overhanding the pavement into perfect folds.
They are Eagle Scouts over a long dark flag.
Finished, they tumble the huge package
to the east brick wall of the Post Office—
there, with bootheels spiking the sidewalk,
they push enormously until the package
is no larger than a blackened brick.
At attention then, the detail
dances itself across the undone street
and through the lettering on the plate of glass
that marks the bank. They are inside now,
at the back of the bank, among the vaults.
They will choose one, pick it open with a hatpin,
then place the main street carefully inside.
How it will manage to escape,
to unroll itself like a runner of rug
under the feet of the earliest riser,
is everybody's mystery
but its own.

Three-legged dog appears from nowhere.
When I tell him to go back home,
he rolls over and plays dead.
When I run through the thick catalpa,
he attacks from behind the next tree.
When I grow stern,
he offers me the sorry stub.

He must have been assembled
by a Baptist:
wayward ears, unmatched eyes,
a tail shot skyward like a sudden steeple.

So I pick the cockleburrs
from his unholy hide
and buy him supper.
Long into the night then
we sing our stories of lost legs
to a convivial moon.

||||||||||||||||||||||||||||||||||||||||||||||||||||||||||||||||||||||||||||||||||||||||||

Back home the people
some of them not yet strangers
walk on two legs.

Between dirt roads and skyways
the leaves on the trees hang green.

A Minneapolis-Moline
squats on dual haunches before its springtooth.

Back home the people
some of them not yet strangers
walk on three legs.

A southwest wind is rising,
scattering rain.

In the pool hall
the air is damp with tomato beer.

Farmers at dominoes chalk their scores,
hug the center of the highway.

Back home the natives
some of them not yet strangers
die unattended in their sleep.

Still thinking of unsettling down
I see myself beside wild rivers,
gigging mushrooms.
In a boxcar I am clickety-clacked to sleep.

Still thinking of unsettling down:
and in another town
I throw another kiss,
shattering (alas) another life.

Still thinking of unsettling down
I go threshed with the treetops.
An Arapaho finds me, heals me,
teaches me everything.
I am to be called Little Restless Spirit.
Thus I break an arrow, leave the tribe.
The tepees run deep with the water
of many maidens' grief.

Still thinking of unsettling down
I hop the first rocket up.
The moon is blue, as silent as sugar.
Below, a green configuration.
It is called the world.
I spy upon it,
identifying whorls.
Can they be fingertips, an untouched face?

Still thinking of unsettling down
I see myself as lifted off:
I am jogging now in sparse, unsullied space,
weightless and bemused and continuing.

Not Such a Bad Place to Be

True, the wind in the elms
is sometimes enough almost
to tip the scales
in the wrong direction,
and when the water gathers itself
into an onslaught down the big branch,
even Christkiller Burhman
goes to his knees in the pool hall,
pleading for fins.
And the soil:
true, it often takes back
more than a portion
of that which it gives,
it being in cahoots, one suspects,
with the water and the wind.
Which leaves us with
the daily vexation of fire:
how it can warm to madness
that very same skull
it enlightens.

Even so,
it's not such a bad place to be.
At certain moments
an element swells the lungs
with something akin to faith:
and all else falls away
as if dark appendages let loose
when the child stops dreaming.
And we know what we know so clearly
that not even the heft
of whatever follows
can altogether obscure
the meaning.

Teenage Halloween

Under the girders of our old garage
The gang joins without quite touching,
Exchanging energies
Amid the flutter of crepe
And grinning gat-toothed lanterns.

The girls, new breasted,
Smell of popcorn and cider.
The boys are apple red,
Tight belted and firm,
Like pods about to burst.

A cadenced thump backgrounds the sight:
The beat,
Pulsing its way into the rooted rafters
Like warm spikes gently malleted.

The party soon is butter rich
In Nehi and Root Beer,
In dancing everywhere:
At basketball and ping-pong,
In the shuffle of peanut hulls
Under ankles
Weightless as October air.

Hairswirling. Applecores.
The catshine of quick eyes,

As into the night the revelers
Cavalier their attitudes,
Handling life like extra saucers.

The huge orange evening throbs toward curfews.
Cyclical as old cisterns.
Philosophical as trick or treat.

For My Wife's Father

More and more my wife's father
sleeps in his chair,
as if practicing.
But I am not deceived.
I have seen him
at the muting of a single word
revive,
his osseous hands toss off
their fitful tics.
I have watched his eyes
return from the water's edge,
become sharp as spoons.
Those who catch him in his chair,
at sleep, should not be deceived.
He is not practicing.
He is at the water's edge,
listening to the sucking of the carp
and with them gathering.

Braces

The gentle doctor called it
hardware
the gear he used to wire
my daughter's doubting face
toward beauty.
You can't even tell
I have them hardly
unless I smile, laugh,
talk, or yell,
she says,
and I see a thousand ships
shining in Aulis Harbor,

their masters' hopes,
hard as fish fins,
fixed on Helen's wayward teeth —
and in the near distance
Iphigenia,
bleeding at the gums.

Dear daughter:
Smile. Laugh. Talk.
And yell this poem
if some day I should
promise you Achilles.

<hr />

Returning to Caves

I lie on my back beneath the house,
cool and damp as the clay
that shaped the four sudden sides
of my first hand-dug cave.
The plumbing has come unglued,
and the dripping has sent that smell of cave
all the way up to the bedroom.

Boy, where are you?

It is the only way to repair,
to get things done:
to crawl like a child
from what seems almost certain
to what is dark and moist,
quiet and enclosed and unknown.

It is late, and the clouds are gathering.

The handle of the pipe wrench
describes that place where the fingers end,
where something cold as night rain begins.

The heavy wrench sends a shudder
through the length of pipe,
and I run a finger up and around the joint,
tight now as the chinked and weighted roof
of that first cave.

Finish whatever it is you are up to,
then hurry in.

I wait for several minutes,
just to make certain.
I have plenty of time.

The taste of caves is in me,
damp and old and heavy,
compelling as the closing of an eye
and sweet as sleep to the tongue.
I am lulled to remain.

Boy, where are you?
It is late, and the clouds are gathering.
Finish whatever it is you are up to,
then hurry in.
Already your mother is at the supper table,
eating her hands.

||||||||||||||||||||||||||||||||||||||||||||||||||||||||||||||||||||||||||||||||||||||||||||||||||||

Thanksgiving

Aunt Vivian leads the charge
against the paper plate:
eat noodles off something like that
and you deserve
whatever brand of scurvy it is
you pass away from.

Steam above the platter of roasted turkey
portends an eruption:
Vesuvius in fullest flower,
all over again.

Uncle Howard's new blue shirt
gapes like a goldfish
shortly above his beltbuckle.
Pass the potatoes, sweet William,
and while you're at it
throw in some gravy
and a fistful of hot rolls.

The flesh on Beulah's upper arm
hangs so low it
brushes the broccoli.
Iced tea gurgles like a busy drain
in the small arid throat
of Cousin Eileen.

Eldon remembers when ham and beans and Monday
were the same.
Slim Jimmy, attempting once more
to chink the gaps
under the slack of his nettled skin,
devises a totem of apple pie,
sliced cheese, chocolate cake,
vanilla and butter brickle
ice cream.

Easy there on the rum, Grandma:
Marvin the Would-Be Missionary
likes his strawberries
tart as a sermon.

You can do the dishes, Vivian.
I'm going outside
to dropkick a football
through the Virgin Martha's window.
Curious I am, and lonesome,
to know the sound of something trapped
escaping.

Final Scenario #6

The dresses of all the girls we ever loved
are reappearing,
are in the breeze suspended:
blue and yellow and green and white and rose,
all the substance and texture of gauze.
They are in the air
suspended,
attached to God knows what,
loose and light and billowing.
And look:
they all are empty.

The dresses of all the girls we ever loved
are empty,
are dangling alone
like silk or crepe
or cotton or linen or gingham
pared free from bone.
Now and then they catch
the fitful breeze,
but cannot hold it.
And look:
they all are leaving.

The dresses of all the girls we ever loved
are leaving,
are bending away so slowly
and so demurely
that what we never saw
and never knew
are all that we remember.
Until the dresses
at last are clearly gone,
and look:
they all are reappearing.

Epitaph for a Grandfather

Fifty paces short of the designated grave
the hearse takes a wrong turn,
and the driver, drenched and apologetic,
signals the pallbearers out of their cars:
and my grandfather is bumped
more carefully than possible
to that place where rock and gumbo
have been, for the moment,
worried aside.

In this land of small lots and persimmon
there is no such thing as looking back:
the preacher, from Ecclesiastes,
settles my grandfather into its wry, inclusive scheme,
and before the last fine grain of Scripture
scours the coffin,
several of the stoutest mourners' eyes
already are at the axles of their Fords and Chevys,
wanting out.

Benediction

Somewhere deep in the grove of cottonwoods
an owl with its dark split tongue
pronounces an end to day,
and the river,
that great brown hussy, that gadabout,
moves on,
its motion its wisdom,
its wayward parts at last becoming one,
its crooked path as seen from the proper height
the soft deflections of a tireless line.

If you love me,
stand with me
here behind the locust
to watch the rising of a full marriage moon.
See? There it is, just over there,
ascending that leaf, just over there,
ascending that limb,
in silhouette ascending the very tip of that perfect thorn.

Can the sound that the bird makes be our own,
the water in the river
that home that can't stay home?

If you love me,
lie with me
here between the owl and the river,
beneath the awful wheeling of a marriage moon.
Let the sound that the bird makes be our own.
Let the water in the river
be our home that can't stay home.
Let there be no move, not now, not ever,
to put an end to end.
Let the earth, proud woman, old friend, roll over.

Let the dance begin.

My Granddaughter, Age 3, Tells Me
the Story of the Wizard of Oz

There is a brain, she says,
right here, she says,
pointing to the front of her head,
but the Scarecrow
doesn't have one yet,
not until the end of the story.

And there is a heart, she says,
right here, she says,
pushing an index finger
hard against her chest,
but the Tin Man
will not have it
until the end of the story.

And there is courage, she says,
right here, she says,
pushing a fist against her stomach,
but the Lion will not have it
unless I tell the story.
Shall I tell the story?

Yes, I say, tell the story,
all of it, from beginning to end.

And I am swept with Dorothy and Toto
up and away to a place
far removed from myself,
to the truth all over again
that nothing is true until told,
not the brain, not the heart, not courage,
not even the witch, who is the last to go,
the teller now in absolute control,
her eye the eye of all storms set straight

at the end of the story.

For My Brother, Who Has New False Teeth

My compliments to the butcher, I tell him,
and he grins widely,
showing a scallop of pink perfect gum,
saying before saying it
that the teeth not only are present, but accounted for,
making them
utterly his own,

whereupon we order
prime rib with everything
but neglect and Coke and rum,
those three devoted whores
who over that long stretch of years
did it to him, he says,
in more ways than one.

Say, I say, do you remember the time
I bit you on the arm
all the way to the bone?
He remembers: crackers and gall
in bed until midnight,
scars no more discernible now
than the heft of crumbs—

and I love my brother so much
I no longer care where the leaf
joins the branch, raw root ends.
The waitress, aware of herself,
meanwhile delivers,
and my brother, passing the compliment on,
chews deep and grins.

This morning I can see more clearly
the shape of the first child,
its head now a shadowed indentation on the pillow.
It is a boy—no, a girl.
I am at the bedside.
It's a girl, Doris says.
With one finger she nudges gently
at the indentation.
I see my own life in the eyes of the child.
I am growing up all over again,
the ages a heavy door, revolving.
There are too many things
yet to be done, to have changed, to be changing.
Doris, I say, wake up!
It is time for the honeymoon to begin.

‖‖

We buy souvenirs for everyone we know,
including those of ours
as yet unborn. (Embroidered pillows,
equal and unblemished before both God and the law,
all the way around.)
I tell Doris that Annie will misplace hers
at the age of four. When she is sixteen
it will be found.

Doris, smiling, nods.
We cannot decide upon a wedding gift—
the old gilded clock or the new Dalmatian.
The dog will bite Robert rather savagely
on the right forearm, I say:
our first grandchild to suffer
a consequential wound.

Consider the alternative, Doris says.

So she romps with the dog
all the way home,
we unaware of time's monotonous showcase
winding down.

|||||||||||||||||||||||||||||||||||||||||||||||||||||||||||||||||||||||||||||||||||||

Early Sunday morning I inform Doris
that I believe she believes too stoutly in God.

And how much, pray tell, is too stoutly?

It happens, I tell her, when
in deference to something unknown and unseen
you depart from this bed prematurely.

A time to lie down, Doris says,
and a time to rise up.

That's what I'm trying to tell you, I say.
Hurry up, please. It is time.

She is at the mirror, adjusting her face.
It is the same skin, the same eyes
she blinked not long ago among the milkcows.
When she returns to the bed
it is as if at the turn of another season.
Yet now there is something almost sacred about her,
more sacred even than before,
coming together as they do,
the will and the word and the deed,
and the smell of calf and breath and milk,
to inform the believer.

Doris parts the curtains
to show me how perfectly half
the moon is.
In the half light
the leaves on the mountain ash
are half conceivable.
In the children's bedroom
I divide the total number
of cribs by two.
Half hard, I return to Doris.
Her face, her shoulders,
her belly, her thighs
have assumed strong half stains
from the personality of the moon.
That half each chooses to love,
as it happens, is a wise choice,
our barkings during half the time
half silent, half in tune.
Until the curtains without moving
close themselves,
and we sleep a deep half sleep
in an otherwise empty room.

Doris walks barefooted down to the river,
there to wash the loincloths and the shirts.
She will be gone all day, growing darker in the sun,
speaking her small songs to the curlews and the salmon.

I'll meanwhile empty the dishwasher, prepare the ice,
watch television, doze and dream of that initial martini.

After which we will catch the first rocket up.
Venus this week, I believe, something routine and casual,
a game of cosmos on the way back, a carafe or two
of unmolested light.

She comes up the path, as always, carrying clean clothes
and two tadpoles in a jelly jar.
As always, she wants to take them with us to Venus.
You just never know what might happen while we're gone,
she says, and, as always, unwilling to disagree,
I grunt just three times, slowly.

||||||||||||||||||||||||||||||||||||||||||||||||||||||||||||||||||||||||||||||||||||||||||

Topeks Red finishes the sixth race
dead last,
and having torn our ticket
very, very carefully
down its middle,
I give Doris the two parts
to dispose of as she might wish.
She tucks them into her upper
cleavage (as I should have guessed)
with our other losses:
an armchair, a Persian rug, a wall clock,
an amulet, a small child,
the differential off a newly-disembodied Ford.

You are beginning to look like something
the cat dragged in, I say,
the cat itself arrested,
a further warp now on the Persian rug.

Doris says that, yes, sure enough, you bet,
losers do indeed have a tendency
to go their own way:
and what do I think about
Amadevil in the seventh?

Well, monkey nipples, I say,
I think he's just about the sorriest
piece of horsemeat
this side of Tucson,

the sweat on his sorrel rump
(down the stretch, dead last)
a muscle-bound delusion.

Doris, old filly, old photo-finish,
is it any wonder that I love you?
When we at last let loose,
the waste from both our lives
is flicked away like something less
than divots.
So name me another name:
Torch's Mountain, Skinflint, Bell's Boy,
Brass Arrow, Li'l Armageddon,
Woe Be Gone.

Until there is nothing left to hock
but these mutual bones.

||||||||||||||||||||||||||||||||||||||||||||||||||||||||||||||||||||||||||||||||||||||||

I go into the haymow with Doris,
into sunslants festive with dust.

Doris fills all those gaps between her teeth
with splinters of hay.

We lie long and warm on our backs,
haybales for pillows.

Doris reaches back to pluck a wire:
music swells the head, a cacophony.

Doris is so godawful beautiful
I want to touch her.

She takes my hand and guides it
along the softness of her sweater.

The splinters of hay taste sweet almost
as sorghum.

As if wingshot,
a swallow dips from a rafter.

We are dying in the haymow year after year,
unable to control the bleeding.

||||||||||||||||||||||||||||||||||||||||||||||||||||||||||||||||||||||||||||||||||||||||||||||||||||||||||||||||

Under a full moon Doris plants potatoes.
When the sign is right, she says,
even the wariest of the catfish bite.

She is barefooted, wearing only a feedsack,
the moon through the cotton
describing her legs precisely,
making them lean and dark and mysterious,
her thighs and buttocks
highlands to be guessed at.

She will not permit me to help her
because, she says, I am
not a believer.

So I open a cold beer and sit on the back porch,
watching.

Doris, now on her haunches,
moves like something prediluvian between the rows.
And I believe that I have never truly seen her
anywhere but there,
gathering and sifting the earth,
patting it smartly into place.
When she rises,
the moon does its work all over again.

I go into the kitchen for another beer.
That sound from within the freezer
is my own muted voice, weeping.
Here lately, I tell Doris,
even the smallest thing can set me off.

She understands.
Wetting her right forefinger
she raises it high above the quilts.
Wind's in the east, she says,
fish bite the least.

I sleep like a small anointed animal
no longer consumed by fire.

〰〰〰〰〰〰〰〰〰〰〰〰〰〰〰〰〰〰〰〰〰〰〰〰〰〰〰〰〰〰〰

At the county fair I buy Doris and me
cotton candy and macaroon slingshots.
Make that four cheeseburgers, son,
with everything.

Doris bets me a silver dollar
that I can't outlast her
on the Tilt-A-Whirl.

Everything goes belly-heavy and pale
and weak at the knees,
including those three star-spangled teasers
at the girlie show.

Doris tests the silver dollar with her teeth.
It'll play well enough, she says,
even in Peoria.

And would I mind awfully much buying her
another cheeseburger?

We admire the Kewpies and the geek,
and especially the Poland-China
with a swab of manure the color of broccoli
on its bristled cheek.

Doris' hair, in a long single pigtail,
tastes like salt-water taffy.

When she looks at me I can feel my fists

exploding with cash.
I want to play roulette with the Ferris wheel.

Shortly after eleven I sneak off
to piss on a tent stake.

At midnight Doris snaps her fingers
and the music stops.
As the lights go out
I think of kissing her eyes.

So we call in the dogs.
High time, she says, that we take our
crusty dusty spat upon barked at taken in
beautiful sawdust bodies
back to home.

\|\|\|\|\|\|\|\|\|\|\|\|\|\|\|\|\|\|\|\|\|\|\|\|\|\|\|\|\|\|\|\|\|\|\|\|\|\|\|\|\|\|\|\|\|\|\|\|\|\|\|\|\|\|\|\|\|\|\|\|\|\|\|\|\|\|\|\|\|\|\|\|\|\|\|\|\|\|\|\|\|\|\|\|

On our half-section of bed
Doris stretches out
squarely in the center

of the west forty.
She is very tired tonight,
she says, and for the moment

wants to initiate no more
babies. And long into an early morning
I think of all those count-

less towheads that got away.
My favorite I think is Ruthie,
big-boned but handsome,

who, after her maternal
grandmother, used to catch
rainwater with which to wash

her hair. She wore braids
until she married,
until she had children,

until one late October evening
she grew suddenly quite frail
and disappeared. I send my

left hand, old dog, good dog,
out to find her,
whereupon Doris sits up and whoops

as if betrayed. Now now, I say.
I say quietly, Sleep on, and
take your rest. *In pace*

requiescat. When Doris mumbling
rolls over and away
I hear the forfeiture of bones

like cribslats being gnawed at
in the bell jar
of a grave.

||||||||||||||||||||||||||||||||||||||||||||||||||||||||||||||||||||||||||||||||||||||||||

In the process of painting the house
Doris and I paint each other.
After five years, sure enough, the paint
begins to peel. We must hurry
to scrape and paint ourselves again,
Doris says. What if my friends
should see all of me?

We are at each other with putty knives
and wire brushes, at the eyes, the lips,
the cheeks, the necks, the bellies, the
navels, at those little trouble spots
beside the nose, those pesky hairlines
at the bending of the knees.

Even so, we have worked too slowly.
One of Doris' friends sees her,
screams, drops her flowers, and
holding her skirt halfway to her throat
disappears over the horizon.

And so it goes, friend after friend
after friend. By the time we are ready
to apply the paint, we are alone, no one
within a hundred thousand miles.

We paint slowly and carefully.
The radio at first will bring us nothing
but static. Later, then, an occasional
hum. By the time we finish we can hear
Texas Jim Robertson singing Land, Sky,
and Water. The weather report comes
through loud and crisp and clear.

All of our friends return. They do not
realize, perhaps, that they had ever
gone away. We have cold beer and cheese.
In the kitchen the women come and go,
castrating Michelangelo. The men sit
in a circle around the bonfire,
practicing dichotomies. Fuck this,
bless that. The moon rises over the
walnut tree, full and alone and cold
and from all outward appearances lovely.

‖‖‖

When Doris at last sins,
I take a reasonably tough line.
You have made your own bed, I say,
and now you must lie in it.

Doris looks at me with eyes
the texture of Circle Nine
in Dante's Inferno.
Not only are you a turd and an infidel,
she says, but you are also trite.
And, what is worse, grammatical.

I plead no contest,
though I remind her that it was I,
this consortium of feces and disbelief,
this sackful of subjunctives and worn-out words,
who challenged the Falls with nothing more
than raw courage and a home-grown barrel.

That does it.
We are in the car, driving
hellbent for Niagara.

Remember that little man
who stood just outside the motel
selling undersized dildos? asks Doris.

That man was Pedro from Mexico, I say,
and those undersized dildos, thank you, ma'am,
were maracas.

And you never actually went over the Falls
in your barrel, either, Doris says.

It is a warm spring evening.
All the farmers in Nebraska
have been cutting and windrowing
the alfalfa. The smell is so
thick and so sweet I inhale deeply
again and again, hoping to get it straight,
once and for all, to be able to keep it.
When the rain begins to fall
we roll up the windows.
Inside the car
distance is an oddity of the past.

The tree toads, as always, Doris says,
knew what they were talking about.
The wipers move back and forth
precisely, and together, threatening
at every swipe to touch.
Forgiveforgive, Forgiveforgive.

||||||||||||||||||||||||||||||||||||||||||||||||||||||||||||||||||||||||||||||||||||

Doris is sometimes wheat in the wind,
the vast shimmering center of Kansas
under a low slow late-June sun.

I stand buried in the bin of the combine,
my father with his left arm
signaling the hired hand.

The chute open,
I spill into the truckbed
to be smothered in grain.

I cannot die often enough.
Doris says that the harvest is great.
But there are no laborers, she says,

no lovers,
only the old soft afterthoughts
of man.

||||||||||||||||||||||||||||||||||||||||||||||||||||||||||||||||||||||||||||||||||||

Doris comes from the milkhouse
walking more upright than the gods,
carrying two small buckets of cream,
and the smell of cream is on her
yet late at night as we lie talking
under a windowslant of quarter moon.

She does not understand why I do not
want to go with her tomorrow to the
family reunion. She does not under-
stand why I do not want to laugh
again at Uncle Elmer's story about the
bald-headed virgin and her capillary

son. She thinks I should be more
charitable, more understanding. And
no, she does not want to throw the
sheet back and move closer. She has
had a long day breathing the dust of
clover and keeping the kickers on

those two young milkcows. If there
were just an ounce or so more of moon-
light, she could show me the bruises.
Just tell me about them, I say, and
she does, each dark and tender ache
enough almost to move the lips to

pity. Well, Uncle Elmer is both
a card and a caution. I laugh
until I cry, and before the night
ends I find myself embracing
even Aunt Ruby, her mustache like a
quaint inclusive broom against the

ancient and petty dryrot of another season.

I advise Doris never to wake me
from my afternoon nap.
I am preparing myself
for the big sleep, I tell her,
and I need all the practice I can get.

I lie at the edge of chill,

the rain outside becoming sleet.
When Doris covers me with yet another quilt
I am torn between her steady arm
and the coming and the going
of my own close breath.

I drift away moving my lips
before an image of empty hands.
Old hands, dear hands, hear me:
I do not want to be remembered
as having been small or mean
or threatening. I want to be known
by the joy I felt but could neither
speak nor write that evening
Doris and I and the children
filled the back yard, the notes
from the younger son's harmonica
folding themselves like the wings of wrens
into the cottonwood and the linden.

The older son meanwhile stood beside me,
his hands deep in his pockets,
from between his teeth
his own tune delicate and indecipherable.
The daughters' words as if small laughter
tempered the ears.
There was no wind.
The new-mown grass was thick with the sweet decline
of vinegar and spite and power.
When suddenly I yodeled
the third echo hung in the air like a large hawk
perfect and immobile above an ash of mountain.

With these stakes of shaved-down cottonwood
I'll describe the boundaries of this acreage,
and, somewhere near the center,
a cabin of ash and oak and hackberry.
Much of the timber has yet to be planted,
to be thinned, cut down,
cured out, fitted and smoothed and primed.
Meanwhile, Anna mixes the drinks,
in her eyes the glint of a full moon
overlooking row on row of maize
and of lespedeza,
the hands of children.

We sit on the front porch, rocking,
reading the river. So many
tiny islands, so many channels.
We are going to where all tributaries
are going—Anna, in her apron
of sweet cinnamon and sweat,
I, with my chest of hopes
all lashed and battened, rowing.

During the summer of the empty haymow,
I sleep one stifling night with Anna
where the straw should be.
A strong hot wind from the south
seems to sway the old barn
from the rafters in the loft
to the deepest cut of stone
at the foundation.

We lie at the center of the mow,
and except for pine board and blanket
there is nothing but moon-speckled space
to turn to.
Anna, who said she could never sleep here,
sleeps first, her stomach in a patch of moonlight
like down on the late summer milkweed.
And I think of Ruthie and George
lying cramped in a corner of the hayfield,
their concern for the failure of crops
no longer, if ever, an issue.

The swallows seem to know
what the wind through the door of the loft knows:
thus the rafters are vacant.
From the center of space in the loft
I can see through a window
more space, not so much as a small child's fist
between me and the bold eye of Sirius.

Anna talks in her sleep—
or is it the wind I hear talking?
Time and again the loft shudders.
There is nothing but space in the haymow,
nothing but space beyond.
And space in the rise and the fall of kingdoms,
where I place my hand.

꠫꠫

When Anna tells me
what the doctor told her
about Ruthie, I cannot curse
near hard enough
to stanch the tears.
So what can a body do
but carry on?

The earth above and below is heavy
with what in its prime
is too gracious almost to bear:
Dear Ruthie, in your box
in the rain and the snow,
stay near! The sloth and the mammoth
are gone, little cricket,
but your mother and I,
and yourself yet a seed
in this thicket of hope,
are still here.

||||||||||||||||||||||||||||||||||||||||||||||||||||||||||||||||||||||||||||||||||||

The face of a deer
appears suddenly at the bedroom window,
its eye at dusk
large and limpid,
its breath against the pane
an early autumn frosting.
In moments then, and suddenly,
it is gone.

Katherine is born at 11:05 p.m.
I do not remember the doctor's
name, or the time that he arrived,
or the number of the flight
he rode away on. There is the smell
of white towels boiling in the kitchen,
the sense of long umbilicals disconnecting.
On a large white pillow facing Anna
the child indulges
the first of her truly
three-dimensional dreams.
And what I guess she sees there
is the eye of the deer
at the window,

good tidings, Kate, long life, sweetheart,
from the window,
tonight and tomorrow and tomorrow.

||||||||||||||||||||||||||||||||||||||||||||||||||||||||||||||||||||||||||||||||||||||||||

When at last the clouds gather,
and the rain begins to fall,
I undress to the waist
and go outside to a spot
between the workshed and the barn,
a clearing at the top of a gentle slope
where at the center
a rock the size of a flywheel
rises from the ground
as if something alive
and on the verge of blooming.

Anna is not far behind me,
her dark hair flat with rain,
rain like beautiful drool
against the white teeth
of her smile. The nipples on her breasts,
chilled by the water, rise and swell.
Seed we are, and have always been.
We stand on the flywheel rock,
hugging and laughing, our wet lips touching.
With the tips of my fingers,
wrinkled with rain,
I can read each of the vertebrae
that linked by fibrous pads
shape Anna's spine.
Seed we are, and will always be.
The rock is cleaner now,
and higher than ever before,
the rain forcing each thing to be itself,
to stir, to crack its shell,

beneath a full sturgeon moon
to dive to the very bottom of the sea
to breathe again.

‖‖

A strong wind from the south
blows through the orchard,
and suddenly the world is apricot:
apricot in a downpour on the ground,
at the ears, apricot,
at the nose, apricot,
the air as far as the eye can see
a shimmer, a haze, of apricot,
apricot in bushel baskets on the porch,
the tart steam of apricot
rising from kettles in the kitchen,
apricot jelling within the gloss
of scalded jars,
each shelf in the cave, the pantry,
swaybacked beneath an orange heft of apricot,
and in bed Anna's face
like a harvest moon
between the pillow
and the cool white sheet
now rising.
The tip of her tongue
ever so unbegrudgingly
against the tip of mine.

‖‖

During the autumn of the bursting mow
I sleep one night with Anna
where another bale or two of clover
should be. A breeze from the south
blows in through the open loft door,
stirring as if down on milkweed
Anna's hair.

Anna, who laughing called me crazy,
who said that though she loves
the smell of cut alfalfa
she could never sleep here,
sleeps first,
her stomach tight as a drum
with that swell incorrigible halfwit, William.

Anna, shifting, says something in her sleep.
She lies curled on her side,
inching her way toward me, into me,
no line at last between my backbone
and the small liquid motion of her skin.

Lord, how sweet to be so close to birth,
watched over by the huge bold eye of Sirius!
How fine to have the harvest in,
the age complete, another age beginning!

ıı

Katherine spends most of the morning
washing seven small stones,
which in the afternoon
she throws
into the river.

That evening she wants to know
if they are still there,
if in the morning
we might be able
to find them.

We wade to each precise spot
where she knows she remembers
she threw them.
The water, I tell her,
has moved them downstream,

and she begins to walk
in the direction
I am pointing.
I follow.
She stops from time to time

to bend over
to bring up a rock, a leaf,
a twig, a grain of sand,
until at last her
fists are thick

with seven small stones.
We take them home and dry them off,
feed them, give them names,
show them to all our friends.
When they are fully grown

we carry them back
to the ongoing lotus
of the river,
where one by one,
in mutual joy and pain,

we throw them in.

⁣||||||||||||||||||||||||||||||||||||||||||||||||||||||||||||||||||||||||||||||||||||||

When Anna prophesies a storm,
clouds or no clouds
we ready the cellar,
pickaxe and lamp, breadbasket and blanket,
and I remember how once
she lied deliberately
to get me with her
alone
beneath the ground, she said,
with nothing but the glass-glossy eyes
of beets and peaches, tomatoes and apricots and corn
to watch us.

Time and again,
to see the gathering clouds,
the flash of lightning,
I cracked the door,
until at last
as if a child
no longer numb of skull
I joined the full sweet intention of her guile.
How clean the world then,
how circumscribed
the field we lay on:
there and over there
the green, the golden harvest,
here and over here
headlands furrowed damply with a broom,
with space enough for constants such as we
to turn upon.

iiiiiiiiiiiiiiiiiiiiiiiiiiiiiiiiiiiiiiiiiiiiiiiiiiiiiiiiiiiiiiiiiiiiiiiiiiiiiiiiiiiiiiiiiiiiiiiiiiiiiiiiiii

At times the brown earth calls me
with a voice just slightly smaller

than the one I use
to turn it down with.

Yes, I am tired of going
up one row and down another,

myself a sorry compromise
between the rumps of horses

and the new-dug furrow.
Yes, I would lie forever

in the field that irks me, and repents.
So deep the plow could never reach me,

shallow enough that I might watch it
passing over.

Under a square of flannel soaked in milk
Anna's face becomes soft
as the underbelly of a dove—
the one, that is, who sits each evening
on the only bare limb on the linden,
calling over and over Love, Love, Love.

The secret, I know, is at the core,
that good great fortune of having, at the core,
something soft to begin with,
something at the core to urge to light,
something to work one's long and brittle passage
back to.

Anna's face unveiled
glows soft as the wood-bound image
behind an oval of glass
at the center of the south wall
in the living room,
my own the face of a small boy
sad and grateful
deep in the sugar and the dough-dust
of a woman's apron.

In the fog you give the horse the reins,
believing that below you, below the wagon,
the center of the road moves by,
slowly, steadily,
believing that now, your reckoning
more absolute than dead,
you are about to find the lane
to turn the corner to pass the mailbox,
that then the dark solid earth
will rise beneath you gently,
will level at last to bend you to the right,

to bring you to a stop half in, half out
of the lean-to, the sign of home
the damp heavy smell of mash and clover.

How old were you, anyway, when you first
were brave enough to drop the reins?
You watch the right front wheel
on the wagon, turning,
and because you know a thing or two
of axle and hub and dumb dependency
you know that the other wheels are turning, too.
Tell me, old man, how many autumns will it be
do you suppose
before you no longer have the nerve
to pick them up again?

<hr />

I want to wash myself in the water
as if to say, Let this be the end of everything
sordid and uncalled for.
Clinging to this body is the dross
of spite and rumor,
from upstream the aftermath of blade
and of sudden storm.
I want to walk unmasked, unshod,
into the river, there in the water to wash myself
until the skin gives way to something solid,
something at last, though burnished,
undulent and warm.
Anna, come with me.
It is night, cold to the bone,
and beneath the feet
the sand that today was so tough with light
is shifting.

From within the First House

From within the first house
I looked out one early morning
to see the milkcow
looking back at me,
her eyes huge and clear,
a tuft of green dung
clinging to her udder.
She stood wide and solid,
the veins in her neck
explosive—
yet something in the chewing
of her cud suggested mystery.
So out of myself
I found myself uncurling:
into the window's glass,
into the dawn of air and eye
beyond the glass repairing.
And here is what the cow
was wondering:
why her milker
had left her standing there
unstripped
that pale, peculiar evening:
had dragged the bucket of milk,
aslosh and bottom-heavy,
across the lot
and over the yard
and up the steps
and out of everything
except for hearing.
And then the silence.
And then the night.
And then the early morning.

And then the screaming.

And then the hands forever
of someone else,
the forehead at the flank
less warm, less reassuring.
And I said to the cow:
I was born that morning.
I arrived trailing the seventh scream.
And the one who left you standing
is my mother.
She is asleep now,
and I am beside her,   ,
at her breast, beholding.
And listen:
this is the first time in all my days
that I have seen things clearly.
And O how fresh, how sweet the world is!
It is a house of milk and tongue
and eye and skin
and breath and breast and quilt
and fingertips and dung,
and that is all it is.

And that is everything!

‖‖‖

Each Board that Formed the Next House

Each board that formed the next house
had been sawed too short:
the same mistake
again and again and again,
until what remained,
as father used to say,
were two rooms
no bigger than the nuts
on a very small gnat.

So we hunched ourselves
and pleased ourselves
with hope for the new baby—
who, upon arrival,
reached for the ceiling
and found it.
And mother said
that such a child
must surely be an omen:
and she named it Franklin,
which she said meant *free man*.

———————————————————————————————————

I Had Been Chained and Padlocked

I had been chained and padlocked
and snapped to the clothesline
because I called my brother
a son of a bitch.
Then let's see how much you enjoy
being one of my puppies,
mother said,
and by evening,
when father came home from work,
I was barking almost deliciously
through the savage salt in my tears.
Beneath the clothesline
I had worn a path,
having been tempted at either end
by cars and cats and other dogs
and curious children,
one of whom I had bitten.
Father tossed me a bone,
said he'd see by Christ
how long I could live in a doghouse
before I changed my little tune.

I hung on,
and then some,
inhaling the hair and the clusters
and the bad breath of the dog
that had sacrificed his home:
until in the middle
of the third night
I called out to return.
In front of Franklin's crib
I swallowed a growl
to say I'd never say it again.
And I curled my fists that night
like Franklin's,
asleep in the bother
and the wonder
of a small skin.

ııı

Franklin Walked Off the Deep End

Franklin walked off the deep end
of the front porch
and rearranged his head,
and the swelling was like a disease,
the neighbor kid said,
and contagious:
and sure enough,
it was mother who caught it,
her stomach becoming so round
that, sitting,
she used it as a table
to snap the beans on.
Then one evening she hurried away,
returning several days later,
and very strangely cured.

What she had with her
she called *Janet,*
and I looked at it
and touched it,
and that night
I tried to tell my brother
either to watch his step
or to stay away
from the front porch
altogether.

||||||||||||||||||||||||||||||||||||||||||||||||||||||||||||||||||||||||||||||||||||||||||||

On a Hot Day after Rain

On a hot day after rain
our cowlot fairly simmers.
Franklin and I, in high-top rubber boots,
each with a length of sumac,

prod the Jersey this way and that,
up and down, back and forth,
mud and manure those staples
kneaded by split steps into gumbo.

The fence around the cowlot
is made of thick planks, creosoted—
father says no doubt to keep some former owner's
blue-blooded big-balled bull in.

We do not have one. Only the Jersey,
and a mulberry tree twenty feet I'd say
from the fence. The lot,
each square inch pocked and thus

with the mark of our own beast
branded, is where my brother and I
first learn the thrill of smell,
we jumping in tandem from the fencetop

to meet a grain-sack swing on its
backswing rising swiftly
toward us, our weight
at the instant of impact

bending as if to break that largest limb
on the mulberry. Eventually, of course,
one knot or the other gives way,
and with Franklin I roll in the swamp,

with Franklin, my brother, in the swamp,
both holding as if for dear sweet life
that other betrayed life between us.
Hello stench of burlap,

effluvium of grain.
Hello mud and manure, hello dollops of water that
purpled in season with berries
out-blind the sun.

Hello first hour of those first ten million years
of skull becoming man,
the brain in the nose
the only brain that matters now,

that space between our snout
and the scent of the gar
more joined than cloven,
less deep than richly layered over.

||||||||||||||||||||||||||||||||||||||||||||||||||||||||||||||||||||||||||||||||||||

Janet Moved Away

Janet moved away
when she was six years old:
to her grandmother's,
where the mouthpiece on the telephone
smelled like cheese.

She came to visit in the summer,
lying with me and Franklin
late into the night
on the sun-porch.
And each time,
until the new wore off,
we spoke of people
and of places and of things
as if we were not really
very closely related,
not really family at all,
but just old friends.

Standing on the Back Porch

Standing on the back porch
of yet another house,
I hit Franklin over the head
with an orange-crate.
It made a funny, purple sound,
and there was mother, materialized,
screaming that I'd
spilled out Franklin's brains.
Like dead weight then
I joined my brother,
searching.
But I found nothing—
because Franklin,
both hands flared like a cradlecap,
was holding himself in.

That night in bed
I showed Franklin
that spot just behind the hip
where I myself had been hit, I said,
but by a German tank.

He felt it with the same fingers
that he had used to hold his brains in,
and that particular time,
because of something moving
deep inside the marrow,
I charged him nothing.

||||||||||||||||||||||||||||||||||||||||||||||||||||||||||||||||||||||||||||||||||||||||||||||

Mother Said She Was Glad Now

Mother said she was glad now
that we hadn't bought that new rug
for the living-room,
because father would have worn
a path there
with his infernal pacing—
back and forth all night all week,
holding the bad hand in the good,
staring down and through the place
where two of his fingers used to be.
They had been sheared off in a pulley,
had dropped then into a bucket
of 10-weight motoroil.

Father put them into a mayonnaise jar
filled with formaldehyde.
He said, *And that's just the beginning.*
Work for the county long enough, he said,
and sooner or later
it'll have you
strung out on a shelf
like a classroom:
from elbow to bunghole,
father said,
from here all the way to there,
he said,
and then some.

Taking the Milk to Grandmother

Not the milk, but the color of milk:
first snow unblemished in a bottle.
Not the bottle, but the feel of bottle
hard and cool against the curling
of a small boy's hand.

On the way, the bottle cradled
in my left arm,
I stop to watch old man Thornton's minks
rising on their hind legs in their cages
watching me.

Not the mink, but the smell of mink,
small manure that trails me down the alley
until, dissembled and sweet,
it becomes the girl the big boys in the bathroom
unzip themselves and over arcs of urine

talk about: Virginia Mae, downright pretty
if she'd lose a little weight,
who eats like a horse and screws like a mink—
not sex, but the heft of sex,
the motion and the smell of sex,

old man Thornton's minks in darkness
repeating themselves, the draw I descend
to begin that final leg to grandmother's house
downhill repeating itself, to the tracks and beyond,
footsteps, my own, repeating and repeating themselves,

until they carry me onto the back porch
where the screendoor opens
and grandmother wide as a monument
fills the space and in both hands takes the milk
and invites me in for an oatmeal cookie

and the last of the milk from yesterday's bottle,
which rinsing and drying (her apron as towel,
the bluebells on her apron as towel:
not the bluebell, but the damp of bluebell
in the gnarl of hand that is grandmother)

she gives to me, bending gives to me,
with it a kiss that is the breath
of milk and cheese, the ancient aftermath of sex.
Kiss. Kiss. Kiss is the sound the act makes,
sex the mink that with its small manure

defines Virginia Mae. Halfway home
I toss the bottle into the air end over end.
At the end of the alley the milkcow grazes:
not the cow, but the ripening of cow,
day into day the ripening of udder

into the ripening of tit,
milk then into the pail and into the bottle
that hard and cool against the curling
of a small boy's hand
finds its way into the hands of grandmother.

Tit. Not tit, but the sound of tit,
an empty bottle that having descended
end over end
from the height of its grand ascension
strikes the hand.

ıılıılıılıılıılıılıılıılıılıılıılıılıılıılıılıılıılıılıılıılıılıılıılıılıılıılıılıılıılıılıılıılıılıılıı

Killing the Swallows

Dusk.
I sit with my brother
on a chair of baled straw
at the center of the haymow,
counting rocks.

We will divide the total
as carefully as if candling eggs,
then decide from whom, and from how many,
to draw the blood.

The rocks have come from the pasture,
from small knobs of ungrassed earth
washed clean by rain.
The swallows do not know this:
that with each rain
a fresh span of death
surfaces, then in the sunlight
fairly gleams.

Nor do they know that darkness
means more, perhaps, than a brief sleep.
Thus they dip their narrow wings,
as if layers of innocence,
into the haymow and
onto the topmost beam.

We sense more than see them,
my brother like a small towheaded priest
over his pyramid of stones,
I thumbing the switch
on the flashlight, waiting.
The birds, ignorant of rain and darkness,
know little more of light:
they disappear soft as down
into the struts and the rafters.

We will kill as many of them
as we have stomachs for,
and call it, if anything, man's need.
We will trust then to the cats
to do what remains
of the honors.

Thus we wait.
And the ritual occurs,
no more untoward than breathing.
The rock from the slingshot
follows its bright light upward,
finds its mark in the seed-heavy belly
of the bird.
Again and again the ritual occurs:
occurs the ritual, again and again and again,
sun rising, sun delivering,
sun going down.

In the gathering shadows
tribesmen touch their fingers
to spears honed bright
with spittle and flint.
They will depend upon
an ageless cluster of daughters,
the Pleiades, to cap their day.
They believe that man, more fortunate,
had been born in wraps of fur or feathers,
and they are far too lean,
and far too proud in blood,
ever to turn away.

||||||||||||||||||||||||||||||||||||||||||||||||||||||||||||||||||||||||||||||||

Rushing the Season

Early March. Grandmother,
rushing the season,
wants to see for herself again
her burial plot (did its boundaries
come through the winter intact? are the names
on the gray-to-white granite missing?)
and one more time again
in my green Ford coupe
I take her.

I don't want to. Jesus,
grandmother, what's the point?
I think, Thank God there's nobody here
to watch us: me beside my green Ford coupe,
one hand smooth
against a swell protective layer
of liquid wax,
grandmother in her wide rosy-beige coat
placing a potted geranium
just this side of the headstone.
When she bends over
I can see where her brown cotton hose end
and the flesh of her white heavy German thighs
begins. Christ, if there was anybody here
wouldn't it be embarrassing.
But it's too early for the buffalo grass,
too early for the new lime growth
that will mark another milestone
on the limbs of the younger cedars,
too soon even for a fresh start of leaves
on the Chinese elms.
Just me and grandmother, Anna,
rushing the season,
placing a geranium above where grandfather
already is, where grandmother
is, she'll tell me later,
about to be.

There is as always, in spite of the sunshine,
a bone-chilling wind bearing down
from the north, and as always
I am freezing my ass to death
in my shirtsleeves. Grandmother,
satisfied at last with the tilt of the geranium,
straightens herself,
stands then with her short arms folded
as if to memorize again the underside
as well as the top
of the scene.

You ever been in a small-town cemetery
like that, with an old woman, alone?
One thing you can count on:
there will be a couple of kingbirds
close by, screaming up a storm.
And though it is never very long
before grandmother returns to the car,
already beside her I am another full head taller.
It is my opinion, for whatever it's worth,
that my grandmother in some strange old-woman way
loves me. I tell her to take her time.
Why not? By now my ass is solid ice.
I am opening the door.

||||||||||||||||||||||||||||||||||||||||||||||||||||||||||||||||||||||||||||||||||||||||||||

In the Treehouse with Franklin

In the treehouse with Franklin
I listen to the pulse of the wood,
song of the hard rock maple,
Franklin beside me mashing an ear
against the largest of the limbs
we hammered all day
blue thumbs into.

At what age was it precisely
that Franklin came at last
to believe in the music of wood?
After the storm, after the flash
that will send this tree,
this treehouse of unpainted pine,
to oblivion,
it is Franklin who with a handsaw
will preserve a length of the limb
that at dusk that day, that hour, that instant,
he grew into.

Whittle and sand, sand and polish,
the hand that holds the wood
an almighty extension,
grain of the hard rock maple
rising to a hard rock sheen.

It is dusk of a long day in August.
In this house of pine and of hot collapse
the will of the hand that held the wood
holds on:
brother, in this gathering darkness,
leaves unmoving,
wing of a dove slanted white
in the shaft of a sturgeon moon,
you are rising to join me,
rung by rung
by rung by rung
to join me,
to sit with me here in this gathering darkness
together
to hear the song.

|||||||||||||||||||||||||||||||||||||||||||||||||||||||||||||||||||||||||||||||||||||||||||||

Whatever Is Elevated and Pure, Precisely on Key

In that house we called the R & M Cafe
I awoke each morning to the sound of Frankie Laine,
the bedroom where I slept curled beside my brother
a thin wall's distance from the nickelodeon.
And my own heart began to know ever so gently
what the wild goose knows, the double edge of its truth
a sanctum of sound, long and sweet and liquid and always tenor.

In the mixed chorus at the high school Glen J. Biberstein
sang with his eyes closed, his chin high,
the tip of his nose pointed at a warp of ceiling
above the transom. *Tenebrae factae sunt,*

the words lofty and mysterious among the mouths
of so many Baptists and Pentecosts and United Brethren.
Whatever is elevated and pure, precisely on key,
Mr. LaVoie, the music teacher, said, is somehow holy,
is enough almost sometimes to see us through.

So do we sell the cafe and move to the promise
of higher ground? Mother, beside a vat of French fries
not yet accounted for, shifts the weight of her sweet
heavy heart from one foot to another. Father
with his floating kidney floats from counter
to booth to table, the padding of his footsteps
yes to no to yes with indecision.

At the controls of the pinball machine the paper-boy
is taking a break. Pete Catlin like a virtuoso
begins to play the keyboard of the nickelodeon.
Omar Boland, retired from the hatchery, explains
the ins and the outs of coccidiosis. And
the sound of Frankie Laine rises high and clean
to a layer of ten-year grease against the ceiling.
Glen J. meanwhile is somewhere distant and probably
alone, rehearsing. Wild goose, brother goose, which
is best: the foot, wandering? the heart, at rest?

||||||||||||||||||||||||||||||||||||||||||||||||||||||||||||||||||||||||||||||||||||||||

On the Road: Sunday, March 6, 1977

Supper at Marlo's Cafe
in Watertown, South Dakota:
two strips of bacon
on a hamburger patty
rife with cheese,
all welded snug as rivets
to an unburned bun.

For two bits the jukebox
will do its best
to keep your mind
off your French fries:

O dropkick me, Jesus,
through the goalposts of life!

A hundred miles, more or less,
to Aberdeen,
where from an unscreened window
near the top of the Ward Hotel
the points of a deserted Spur Lounge
look like the Seven Heavenly Sisters
dressed fit to kill.

In front of the OK Tire Store
a trucker pullchains his air horn
until all of the geese
this side of the Badlands
take up the song.

Inside Room 500 the radiator
does a small unobtrusive dance,
melting the last of the snow on Channel 3.

The bedsheets smell of starch.
There is nothing any longer left to do
or undo.

So I think of my family,
of my wife,
of the four children, one by one,
of the first grandchild,
now 3.5 days old,
out of the hospital and at home now,
and at the edge of sleep
I see her guileless breath usurp the cracks
of her white thin-slatted crib,
shaping then its charge
to outfox the keyhole:

on then beyond the melodic heft
of Marlo's Cafe
in Watertown, South Dakota,
to the Ward Hotel in Aberdeen,
to Room 500,
to the bed where at the edge of sleep
I welcome it to breathe it in
to breathe it out again,
and on and on.

O Michelle!
O infant far from everything but home!
On our long descent to sleep
we are all of us one family, after all,
and all alone.

Collecting for the Wichita Beacon

The first house I step into
has this picture of a Marine corporal
atop the radio,
dungaree jacket pressed to a fare-you-well,
cap tilted back cockeyed
confident.

Tossing aside the paper,
the young woman, eyes so very dark, so
large, so downright beautiful,
says we are winning,
says that in spite of Wake Island and Guadalcanal
it is only a matter of time.
She tells me this again as, fumbling in her purse,
she comes up with three quarters and a forerunner
to the Franklin D. Roosevelt memorial dime.

Before releasing the coins into my hand
she moves the tip of an index finger
ever so lightly
against my palm. O
she has seldom been quite this frightened, never
this lonely. She thinks maybe, honestly,
this time she is going all the way
crazy. Against my face
her kiss is how much more
than a mother's.

I am not there to do any type of singing
when the telegram comes.
Sixty-seven customers, sixty-seven screen-
doors under relentless siege
hanging on.
And time to collect again.
And John Wayne shot again by a slant-eyed sniper.

And my face, where the kiss was, napalm burning.
And I cannot so much as give you the time of day,
and I cannot tell you, not even
to the nearest war,
how old I am.

‖‖

Sowing the Whirlwind

Grandmother Moulton heavy against a crutch
receives her copy of the paper
as if a blessing, her lips
thanking God incessantly
for most everything—for
her grandson John's diving, not jumping,
into that crater at Omaha Beach,
burst of bullets shattering
only the right ankle,
for the end of the war by whatever means,
and I am not halfway around the route
before Hiroshima becomes a word
I was born with never to understand.

❖ ❖ ❖

Each customer is a study in ice,
though early August in my town in Kansas
swelters the white cotton shirt
that swelters the skin.
Each customer stands on bare feet
on the unpainted pine
of that porch most accessible,
one arm extended, across the mouth
the wary suggestion of a grin.
I am for this one early evening
important beyond even the flaming lipstick
of Ruby Shoemaker's dissension. O receive
from the hand of the older son

of Ralph and of Katie Marie
both the lines and what lies between:
that something larger than mere imagination
has taken place, that the heat this day,
this hour, this moment, though insufferable,
is but a beginning.

Each customer thaws enough to work the fingers
to accept what moves in the shimmering heat
like a minnow
mushroomed at the edge
of a lessening pond.

Elwood Anderson, who is queer in the head,
hammers ten-penny nails into an old crosstie
whenever he has more words
than his thick queer tongue can say.
Just how windless is this windless day?
By the time I give old man Fenton the news
already I can hear the ping
carrying clearly over cowlot, over lawn, over alley.
One ping to one nail, one ping
driving one nail so precisely, so deeply home.
How many nails can one tie comprehend?
Elwood Anderson, so sure of himself
he uses a ballpeen,
has eyes the sheen of nailheads
returning the sun,
but as far as I know
he has never seen his way to subscribing
to the Wichita Beacon.

Bless O Lord these gifts
which we are about to receive
through thy merciful bounty. Amen.
This is one of so many cadences
I pump my purple Monarch bike to.

O Jesus is the rock
in a weary land, a weary land, a weary land,
O Jesus is the rock
in a weary land,
a shelter in the time of storm.
That's another.

Inside the Champlin Station
I folded sixty-seven papers to a different,
far more convoluted rhythm.
Scanned each headline sixty-seven times
to hear it
scan. Atomic bomb
dropped on Japan; President warns
of a rain of ruin.
At each downward thrust of my right foot
something in the ankle pops,
and with Johnny Moulton I dive, not jump,
into the crater. Shattered the anklebone,
spared to fight another day
the brain. Scientific landmark of the century
realized. And I remember that movie
about the Sullivans,
all of them going down with their ship,
brother upon brother, the language
of starboard and port and the steady
deep-green gurgle
of death. Why,
when my friend Bullard said Sharkbait,
didn't I slug him?

Though almost dusk
the day sits
hot as the sun, rising,
hot as the rising sun. We have spent
two billion dollars on the greatest

scientific gamble in history—
and won.

I do not stop for a game of one-on-one
with Bullard. I think instead of the cool breeze
blowing down from the ceiling fan
in the pool-hall, the clean click
of ball against ball. Our town is a dry town.
I was a snooker shark I swear at eleven.
Did I mention that Grandmother Moulton's lips
never stop moving? Johnny came limping home again,
died of cancer around nineteen sixty-seven.
When Mr. Truman announced the bomb aboard the Augusta,
one of the crewmen said
I guess I'll be home sooner now.
Ah, home, where are you?

In five days I'll be thirteen,
in thirty-seven years
fifty,
by which date I shall have learned
the following: the code name
for the experimental explosion
in New Mexico (July one six)
was Trinity.

Starboard. Port.
And the Sullivan boys
sharkbait going under,
so steady their deep-green death-green
gurgling.

❖ ❖ ❖

I cannot speak for tomorrow.
An impenetrable cloud of dust today
hides practically everything. Have we in fact
sowed the whirlwind? O Mrs. Sullivan, O babies
still in the bellies of the Honshu women,

take solace in the smaller print.
Shaving Lotion Shortage
Expected to End
Soon.

Mabel Cleveland takes her paper
with something more than ice
at the edge of her grin.
Bless you, anyway, Mabel Cleveland,
and your husband, Shorty,
and your twin snooty daughters Anna and Alma,
who even today are more or less
somewhere, more or less
fully grown. Speaking of which:
I love all of you more than I ever can.

Here's another.
There's a German in the grass
with a bullet up his ass.
Push it in, pull it out,
Uncle Sam Uncle Sam.

Home is where Elwood Anderson sends each ten-penny nail,
ping the sound I go to sleep by,
wild in my little wreckage
to understand.

|||||||||||||||||||||||||||||||||||||||||||||||||||||||||||||||||||||||||||||||||||||||||

Waiting to Jell

We are waiting to jell.
Woods, with his easy, high-hanging hookshot,
is somewhere south of the Mason-Dixon line,
waiting to jell.
In the heart of southcentral Kansas

Bullard speaks gently to his bulldozer,
coaxing it deeper and deeper into the earth:
he is waiting to jell.
Anspaugh, waiting to jell,
is bottle-feeding a naked caveman
with Paul's first letter to the Corinthians.
Skeeter, an instrument in one eye
like a telescoped lens,
is putting together a necklace
made of dimestores.
He, too, is waiting to jell.
And Kloefkorn, having slopped the hogs,
turns up the wick on the lamp
and, with a fresh quill
plucked from the nether eye
of a noncommittal goose,
writes on and on about waiting to jell,
he himself waiting to jell
while recalling Bo Spoon, the coach,
who filled every halftime
with the same incredible prediction:
one of these times, boys, we are going to jell.

We won three and lost seventeen.
But the diamonds in Bo Spoon's eyes
cut through and halved our doubts,
left us reaching for season upon season,
for times and places and turnabouts
then, as today, unborn.

Thus we move and breathe
and pivot our understandings,
waiting to jell.
Woods, at center. Bullard and Anspaugh, forwards.
Skeeter and Kloefkorn at the guards.
The Bulldogs, the starting five, waiting to jell.

Dust meanwhile swirls at the feet.
Coins, like rain, reverse a trend,

roll as if players to stage center,
wobble slowly down, evaporate.
Spoon, having snapped his fingers
and popped his left palm,
smacks the inside of one Oxford heel
against the inside of the other.
It is halftime.
We are far, far behind.
The thick, steamy smell of socks
leaks from consumed rubber shoes.
Yet one of these times, boys, we are going to jell.
And when we do. . . .

And the fine long fingers on Woods' right hand
release the ball:
it rises slowly to the peak of its arc,
and by the time it reaches southcentral Kansas
Bullard already is on his way home,
the snort in the nose of his bulldozer
quiet as grass.
Anspaugh, pointing to an orange omen in the sky,
shifts his text to Ecclesiastes,
and Skeeter, returning from one more meeting of the board,
thanks his lucky stars that what goes down
sometimes comes up.

And the ball by now
is so near the front lip of the basket
that the multitude hushes.
With a quill freshly dipped
Kloefkorn writes the ball
over the lip and into the stale,
magic center of the hoop.
Slowly then it descends, seams turning slowly,
and slowly the net fluffs and rises and falls,
and the home portion of the gathering slowly
erupts, comes slowly to its feet,
its arms slowly outstretched,

its mouths bursting slowly with tongues,
all of them shouting slowly Blood! Blood! Blood!
But Bullard, bone-weary and smelling of lysol,
is curled into sleep at midcourt.
Anspaugh walks off with a cheerleader
in the direction of Reno.
Skeeter, having removed his tennis shoes,
has marked them down to half price.
And Woods, as if witching for water,
extends his long hairless arms
to follow his fingers
out of the auditorium
and along the white broken stripes
on the south-bound pavement.

Alone, Kloefkorn signals the crowd
to remain calm.
With the aid of a bullhorn
he announces that he has sent out
for a new lampwick and a goose unmarked.
Already he can see the fresh ink
forming thin, sharp lines
at the base of the busy quill.

The face of Bo Spoon emerges, focuses,
enters the dressing room.
It is halftime.
We are far, far behind.
The thick, steamy smell of socks
leaks from consumed rubber shoes.
Yet one of these times, boys, we are going to jell.
And when we do. . . .

Dust meanwhile swirls at the feet.
Coins, like rain, reverse a trend,
roll as if players to stage center,
wobble slowly down, evaporate.

Breathing, I must believe.
Believing, I wait.

One of Those

FOR RALPH, MY FATHER

1

In his best monotone
my father sings the Great Speckled Bird,
humming those lines he doesn't remember,
or, what is more likely, never knew,
then for a change of pace
breaks into the Wabash Cannonball.

He is lost in whatever it is
he is doing: patching a screendoor,
affixing a plugin, rearranging the junk
in the cellar. He takes a break
to roll a cigarette from a can of Raleigh.
He licks the tissue firmly into place,
strikes a kitchen match
against a latch on his overalls,
with a deep inhalation
turns the coarse tobacco
into a delicate rod of ash.
I'm saving up coupons, he sings,
to buy one of those; a coupon redeemer,
I'll die, I suppose.

I suppose. Yet in my longest night
I work to believe what lies
beyond the fine print
on the depleting can:
Hang on! The best surprise of them all
is yet to come!

2

I enter my father's house
to gather the coupons
to redeem them. I am, quite suddenly,

fifty. Yet I must believe that
had my father mailed the coupons
all awkward corners would have been
set straight: severed fingers,
floating kidney, double hernia,
the quarrel with my mother
that night in the bedroom,
its first word a wedge
that the weight of time, near
penniless and obtuse,
could not stop driving.

3

Somewhere in some grandiose warehouse
must surely wait the gift to restoration.
With a flashlight I find bundle on bundle
of coupons, each tied with white thread
taken (O how dream links guess to memory!)
from the old black Singer's bobbin.

The beam of light is alive with dust.
It guides me, begins to control me. It is
my first large dog returned
whose leash I stranglehold
to be led by,
uncanny eye disclosing coupons and
coupons, until, quite suddenly,
through a butterfly snag in a windowblind,
the first sharp sign of morning. And its light
strikes the face of my father. He watches me
watching him. He is almost smiling.
What he will say when he speaks
is that dusty text so long sealed shut
at the base of the brain: son,
it has been such a long long time.

4

Meanwhile, there is the silence, meanwhile
then the start of the monotone. Thin old man
with green eyes sharp as spoons
singing, almost smiling, bulge
at the crotch of his blue washpants
that truss that forever
has held him in. Tell me:
what can an old man possibly know
that a younger man however old
doesn't? Until, quite suddenly, the room
brightens to a halo. I blink
to see the coupons gone. Father,
I understand. Father,
with three short steps
I could touch your hand. Christ,
I cannot help myself. I am singing it
truly to know it with him.

‖‖

Cornsilk

FOR ALVA FOIL BAKER

My wife's father is about to be buried.
The minister is saying something
rapidly becoming final.
Under the edge of the canopy,
canopy bluer far than any Kansas sky's blue,
I hold my grandson of almost sixteen months.
A steady southern breeze upblows his hair,
cornsilk of the very highest order

suspended, and I turn us slowly clockwise
because I am playing the game called
viewing the world through the upblown suspended
cornsilk hair of my grandson: O
cornsilk the Chinese elm and the wide green catalpa,
cornsilk the red earth fresh from plowing,
cornsilk the high August sun, the western horizon,
cornsilk the buffalo grass and the near nervous

cornsilk sweep of the kingbird,
and under the spray of red carnations
cornsilk the mind's last memory of my wife's father,
all the days of his life recounted
as if strands of cornsilk
moving light and eternal
in a warm fixed partial
hour of wind.

||||||||||||||||||||||||||||||||||||||||||||||||||||||||||||||||||||||||||||||||||||||

Solitude

In the absolute calm
of an early evening
I leave the house
to be alone,
to know that final word
on the blue lips
of a long day
winding down.

The hour is sweet
with the threat of woodsap,
rising. Cottonwood. Ash.
Redbud. Linden.
The last of the swallows
dips its wings into the loft's
darkening door.

From eight counties away
a tractor sends its steady pulse
to join the beat of the heart
that beats in me.

What I want to say is that
of all the ways to love you
I count this way
among the most
endearing:
to be alone at the edge
of something vast,
letting the bad air out,
taking the good air in.

Onion Syrup

When the dark liquid
begins to bubble,
Mother with twin bricks
elevates the skillet:
from the blade of a paring-knife
severed layers of onion
drop as if quaint catalysts
into the syrup. Heated to mush
they will fill to overflowing
this bronchial house.

Satan that wily serpent
assumes many guises,
croup the name tonight
my mother calls him.
In my throat he reaches
far down to turn me
wrong side out. I cannot endure
the snakebite, cannot swallow
the cure. I pray: dear God
take this cup from me.

After a long spasm
I push back the last
quilt. In the silence
I can almost hear my body
cooling, losing its weight,
detaching itself from the drag
of rock-heavy bones. Mother
with the flat of one hand
holds me down. By and by, she
sings, when the morning comes.

The Great Depression

The phrase is a small snake
transecting dry grass:
my sister sent across town
to live with Grandmother.
Each morning before school
I deliver a quart of unskimmed
Jersey milk into the square
brown hand of an old
German woman. My sister
stands tall and peculiar
in the kitchen, her eyes
saying Nothing lasts forever.
Besides, she is going to learn
to knit and to crochet.
At night I try to imagine
my bedspread assembled
by the thin fingers
of my sister. Beside the bed,
under a glass emptied of milk,
some kind of delicate doily.

Christmas 1939

The car sits
burdened in the
driveway: when
the last bundled
body settles onto
the back seat the
back axle snaps.

Such is Christ-
mas, such the
beginning of each

mysterious trip to
grandfather's dis-
tant farm. Father
circles the low-
slung vehicle,
kicking each tire.
What he is saying
darkens the air,
accelerates a
gathering of clouds.

We have a cousin
who drives fast
and who knows the
Ford dealer in
Argonia. And the
miracle is not
that someone came
along to give us
life beyond the
life we never asked
for, but that
cousin in little
under an hour
returns. A miracle
too that nut and
bolt and black
grease at the elbow
come at last together.

Three miles north
of the Barber County
line the snow
thickens. Christ,
if it isn't one damn
thing it's a dozen.
Father's breath
brings the cloud
all the way inside

and onto the wind-
shield.

The humming of the
heater begins to
turn me to slush.
The miracle is that
there is no end
to miracles. My
little brother in
his sleep grins
like a perfect
moron. I am not
far behind. What
we yield to is the
insolence of faith:
when we waken we
will be there.

||||||||||||||||||||||||||||||||||||||||||||||||||||||||||||||||||||||||||||||||||||||||

Sunday Morning

This morning I am trotting the route,
my father not far away in the old Ford coupe,
its heater humming all the hymns
I ever knew the tunes to,
Sunday papers on the seat at his right
like a massive passenger,
and the pace from beginning to end
doesn't vary, I at a slow heavy trot,
the old Ford in low gear
growling in the clear bright icy
January air like a good large watchdog
creeping on the rollers of its haunches,
always about to lurch, yet never lurching,
my breath meanwhile in measured bursts
preceding me, fogging the eyes,

chilling the face, all things
in the early aftermath of sunrise
a most delicate syncopation, the smoke
from my father's cigarette (I'm
trotting now beside the car,
reaching for papers to fill again
that hollow in my arm) sweet
as the tune being hummed by the heater,
sweet and as warm as the tune
being hummed by the heater,
I trotting beside the open window
catching both the warmth and the song,
and my father, silent behind the wheel,
helping me this morning with the route,
giving me a hand to relieve this
impossible Sunday morning
weight, laying that hand on my shoulder
to wake me, to tell me that the bitter
cold is here, to say, without
my asking, I'll take you.

||||||||||||||||||||||||||||||||||||||||||||||||||||||||||||||||||||||||||||||||||||||||

Prove It

I see Bubba Barnes
sneak a comic book
from the rack in
the Rexall drug-
store, and the next
day at recess
I tell him. He
says Prove it.

I even saw the
name of the comic,
I tell him. Sub-
mariner. Isn't

that right? He
says Prove it.

I don't have to
prove it, I say.
I know you did it
and you know you
did it. So, he
says, prove it, ass-
eyes. Just prove it.

You can go to
hell for swearing,
I say. Bubba says
Prove it. And for
stealing, I say,
and for not tell-
ing the truth. Bub-
ba says Prove it.
Prove it, you
little peckerhead,
he says. Prove it
prove it prove
it prove it
prove it.

|||||||||||||||||||||||||||||||||||||||||||||||||||||||||||||||||||||||||||||||||

Black Cat

To know exactly
how long I can
hold it
I must hold it
until it explodes,
the skin splitting
from the meat
of the thumb

to the base
of the lifeline.

Mother says
I hope you're
satisfied. She
has such good warm
hands, flesh enough
to last a lifetime.
Even so, the iodine
stings: I bite my
lower lip to blood
to keep from crying.

So this is the summer
of my long suffering,
peroxide in the morning,
sulfur and potassium
nitrate in the afternoon.
Carlos meanwhile flushes
a hot M-80 down the stool
at the Baptist Church,
God clearing his throat,
Carlos says,

and they're still
talking about the
flood, still bowing
their heads and
closing their eyes
and raising their
hands, still wanting
mercy, many of them
I think without ever
having been there.

Walking the Tracks

It's the shortest
route to the sand-
pit, the perfect
chance to fill my
pockets with rocks
for the bullfrogs.
I have one hook,
one bobber, one
length of grocery
twine, one sinker,
one dozen night-
crawlers secure in
a Prince Albert can.

And the sun strik-
ing the iron, strik-
ing and striking:
half blinded I miss
my cutoff, keep
right on toward
Kiowa County
walking.

The long ride home
on the slow freight
isn't long enough.
I dangle lost legs
as if sashweights
over the edge of
the flatcar. Smell
of cut alfalfa,
slant of bird-
wing, dusk.

The freight with
its flat wheels
limps into town. O
mother I have been
everywhere. Listen,
listen to me now. I
know everything.

|||||||||||||||||||||||||||||||||||||||||||||||||||||||||||||||||||||||||||||||

Kicking Leaves

All day I have been walking
and kicking leaves,
not paying any attention
to time or direction,
so that when the sun
becomes an orange wafer
at the edge of my left shoulder,
and I cross over the line
into that other land,
I have to smile,
the leaves there as if
the leaves from home,
embarrassed, brisk, compatible.
And I turn to watch you
kicking leaves behind me,
you crossing over
without touching the line,
you kicking the same leaves
I kicked, you behind me
kicking and catching up,
catching up, kicking
so many of those lovely leaves
I can't get enough of
you behind me.

My Daughter Pregnant

FOR TERRY AND DAVE

My daughter pregnant
tells me. When I
hug her I cannot
hug her enough. I
tell you, some things
are still happening out
there, out there
some things are
yet going on.

Mama beaming breaks
out the goblets.
David, you rascal,
see if you have
enough juice left
to pop this plastic
cork from this
vessel of pink
champagne.

We clink glasses.
At the ends of un-
ending arms:
bubbles roseate
as my daughter
pregnant
rising as fast
as they are
bursting.

Creation

When she looked at me and said
Say something from the Bible
I suddenly didn't know
anything to say,
all that multitude of verses I memorized
In Mrs. Heath's class at Sunday-school
gone like the certificates I kept pinned
to my bedroom wall for proof.
It was her eyes that made me go blank,
those night-dark eyes you'd love
to park the cars of your dreams in,
and the midnight hair curled under just so
against the moonlight lobes you'd swap your place
in that front-row pew in Paradise
to nibble on, then all at once
one came to mind,
and I said Turn away from man
in whose nostrils is breath
for of what account is he? That's
not in the Bible, dummy, she said,
and even if it is I don't believe it,
and she took me in her milk-soft arms
and kissed me with her wine-sweet lips
and when she finished I said Isaiah 2:22
and she kissed me again
and that evening
and that early morning
were the first day.

Fixing Flats

Father leans
what little weight
he has into the
wrench and keeps
it there, his will
locked against the
will of the lug-
nut, until finally
something pops,
and sometimes it
is the iron that
gives, and some-
times it is father,
his double hernia
and his floating
kidney as if urchins
combing the gravel
streets for company.

I hold my breath
watching father
pump air until,
the tube
so close to the
bursting point, he
stops. The sound
the bubbles make
when the air hits
the water is my
third-grade teacher
looking at me with
her little lips
puckered behind an
index finger.

Father pushes the
small end of a new
kitchen match
against that pin-
point where the
upward string of
bubbles begins. He
takes the tube from
the water to wipe
it dry with a feedsack.
The match is an arrow
deep into the soft
dark belly of an
unending animal.

Father jacks down
the car, lowering
evening.
For as long as I
can remember two
fingers from his
right hand have
been missing.
When I show him
my bicycle with its
soft rear tire he
says If you think
I'm going to fix that
sonofabitch before
supper you have
another think
coming.

After supper we do
the work enclosed
on the back porch.
Father hums the
Great Speckled
Bird, at the pauses
spitting on the tube
until it bubbles. I
cannot watch him
closely enough,
on my tongue
the grease of supper
lingering. Beyond
the glow of the bulb
directly overhead,
bugs are wanting to
have what we have,
their little bodies
so wonderfully
futile against
the screen.

||||||||||||||||||||||||||||||||||||||||||||||||||||||||||||||||||||||||||||||||||||||||||||||||||||||||

Christmas 1940

In the basement
of the church
our teacher shows
us how to manage
flannel, and soon
enough the pieces
come together:
camel and bright
star, wise man
and shepherd and
Mary beside a
slatted manger.

My part in the play
is to stand still,
my right hand steady-
ing a fresh-cut
length of catalpa.
Baby Jesus is a
large-faced doll
belonging to Velma
Jean's mother. It
was bought, Velma
Jean says her mother
said, at a great
price. Break it or
lose it, you don't
need to bother to
come home. I am
Joseph, but some-
how I am not
the father.

Santa Claus comes in
through a high win-
dow, bells jingling,
over his shoulder a
bedsheet filled to
overflowing. When
he falls we laugh,
and when we learn
next day that he had
cracked his collar-
bone, we laugh
even harder.

I hide my sack of
candy at a place
inside the barn
from which it van-
ishes overnight,
making its
goodness last
forever.

||||||||||||||||||||||||||||||||||||||||||||||||||||||||||||||||||||||||||||||||||||||||||||

The Louvre

FOR GLADYS LUX

Today it's the Louvre. Yesterday
it was Chartres,
where the guide, having said
that the blues in the windows
could not be explained,
tried to explain them. And I remember
how blue was the bottle of Evening in Paris
I spent my last dime on,
how night after Saturday night
the lobes on my girlfriend's ears

drove me crazy. But that was yesterday,
at Chartres. Today it's the Louvre,
where Mona Lisa behind a doubled wall of glass
hangs motionless, defying gravity,
where the backs of the gleaners
bend forever into their harvest,
where man and woman recline together
as if unashamed,
their bodies so immediate
I touch mine. Yesterday, at Chartres,

after the tour and the Gothic singing,
I bought a pocket knife
with Chartres in gold on the handle,
one bright blade and a corkscrew. All
up and down my left index finger
I have scars to prove my love
of pocket knives,
how the dullest among them
can go in a blink to the bone, how
my girlfriend held the bloody bandage

near her lips as if to kiss it. But
that was yesterday, at Chartres. Today
it's the Louvre,
where I stand with so many others, my wife
beside me, all of us wild to create ourselves
with the stroke of whatever brush
so that, created, we might begin
the formulation of another work,
all of us wild to deny
what cannot be denied,

our ashes given to ashes,
our dust to dust.

‖‖

For Proof

I give her my
Barlow. She gasps,
covering her mouth with one
hand, holding the knife
in the other. The handle is so
worn you wouldn't know
it's a Barlow
if you didn't know it. She has
eyes that water at the smallest

kindness. Hers is the first body
I have ever tried to be a cloud
above, hers the first wet face
I have ever kissed. All
the way home I lick and
lick my lips, mining
salt. Under a streetlight
I pause to look down
to see my hands searching
for something to hold and
for something to use to
cut with. Under her pillow
night after night the knife
lies unopened, and she tells me
how touching it she goes to sleep
more easily now, I lying awake
ecstatic and bewildered
at our mutual loss.

|||||||||||||||||||||||||||||||||||||||||||||||||||||||||||||||||||||||||||||||||||||||||

An Interlude for Morning

FOR PHYLLIS ERNST

> If I had a thing to give you,
> I would tell you one more time
> that the world is always turning
> toward the morning.
> —*Gordon Bok*

And I would give you
that morning,
would have you rise
determinate
with the sun's
slow rising. Would
in the high sweet glow of morning

approach to catch from you
a portion of the morning's
overflowing.

Warm is the good earth struck
point-blank by the sun,
warm the good word
turning.

Grass newly-clipped
launches the back yard
into a slow roll of emerald
pasture, a robin
the size of a milkcow
grazing the blades. Lime
from the leaves on the cottonwood
heightens the lips. Now we
understand, don't we, our glasses
raised in a toast to the moment,
what ice is?

With these words,
and the breath of these words,
I give you that morning,
its heat within your body
brightening the beholder's eye.
With these words,
and the breath of these words,
I give you that morning,
and with it all those mornings
toward which evening cannot choose
but move, now
and for as long as
breath and word shall last,
and ever after.

The Day I Pedaled My Girlfriend Betty Lou
All the Way Around the Paper Route

was a warm day in August of forty-five,
her name warm as the day,
her eyes no less dark than her hair,
her skin unblemished ivory. How

with one swipe of her own deft tongue
her red lips reddened. Shall I mention
the following, that her teeth were white
and immeasurably straight? They were.

From where she stood on the cracked sidewalk
in front of the drugstore
she called me, her words,
whatever they might have been,

wonderfully urgent.
I was pumping a purple Hawthorne bike,
its purple faded to a most delicate pastel.
Was it the color, or my motion astride it,

that commanded Betty Lou's dark eye?
In less time than it takes to remember
she was sitting sidesaddle
on the crossbar,

her ivory fingers clutching below the handles
as if they meant to stay there
for the duration. Clockwise
around the fringes of my small hometown

we circled, twin sacks
on either side of the Hawthorne
filled to overflowing
with the high black headlines of war.

And a week from now
the message of victory

with its sickening undertones
will start its murmur: A-bomb,

fallout, halflife, Hiroshima,
radiation, ground zero,
Nagasaki,
vocabulary sufficient

to stun the most highly fortified
of lexicons. Betty Lou meanwhile
wore a pleated skirt
green as those leaves on the catalpas,

and her tan blouse for all its cotton
could not entirely flatten
the points of her breasts. Clockwise
around the fringes of my small hometown

we circled, Betty Lou's thin legs
hanging lovely and lofty from the crossbar,
my pumping of the purple Hawthorne bike
stirring a breeze to send dark hair

flowing into my face, my mouth,
the mix of hair and of breath
that union that maybe believers mean
when they sing of how beautiful

heaven must be. So what do I remember?
That the movement clockwise
did not indefinitely
last. That

when I passed the back yard at Bullard's,
and my buddies at basketball
looked up and started to wave but didn't,
I did. That trying not to sweat

I felt the moisture coursing the spine
like a rivulet. That
when I crashed a paper through
Ruby Nelson's screendoor

Betty Lou's laughter,
out from the ivory palace of her mouth,
gave me the strength of more
than a hundred. That

I can hear the sound of that laughter yet,
eons beyond the lexicon embodying
A-bomb, fallout, halflife, Hiroshima,
radiation, ground zero,

Nagasaki. That the circle we finally finished
is never finished. That
the burned and wasted bodies of children,
though gone, are never gone.

\|

You Have Lived Long Enough

You have lived long enough,
my mother tells me, when
wandering the halls of the
hospital you recognize each
face, each bone beyond each
face, and you have lived
long enough when you enter
each room to talk with each
face, your remembrances
cracking the mouths into
smiles that having lived long
enough you can trace to the
very roots—Aunt Vivian turn-
ing in triumph from her last
canned jar of plums, Uncle
Elmer pounding his cap against
the quaint immobile flywheel
of the tractor, another season
of planting thank god history.

And you have lived long enough
when the clean hard hallway
opens into that room where the
figure atop the whiteness is
yourself, and you do not
hesitate, you instead move
swiftly to your side and taking
your hand you start the story
that you have heard so many
many times yet cannot bring
yourself to tire of again.

||||||||||||||||||||||||||||||||||||||||||||||||||||||||||||||||||||||||||||||||||||||||||||

Undressing by Lamplight

It's the uneven wick that does it,
a flickering that motions the body

already in motion—that,
and the slight sensation of kerosene

sending me to that spot behind the ear
I cannot easily come away from.

Look, monkeynuts, this is the tailend
of the twentieth century, you say,

megawatts enough to outdo the sun,
and I say Hush, I say

This was my grandparents' lamp,
how at the stroke of nightfall

grandfather took the fresh-toweled globe
from the hand of grandmother

to fit it then to the lampbase,
how in lamplight the kitchen

mellowed, flickered and jumped,
this lamp is holy, I say, I say

Help me work the combination
on this infernal bra,

and we are undressing by lamplight,
undressing each other by lamplight,

and she is quiet now,
her eyes in the mirror

when she looks at me
like the eyes you sometimes come across

in the album you seldom open,
large and sepia and

dark with the lovely pain
of human understanding.

|||||||||||||||||||||||||||||||||||||||||||||||||||||||||||||||||||||||||||||||||||||||||||||||

Easter Sunday

At the upright piano
Ernestine Trotter
sits in close and
heavy combat
with the choir: she
will play louder
than the choir
can sing, or
die trying.

The minister speaks
of that force
strong enough
to overcome the
immovable object.

He leans into the
pulpit, tipping it
forward until
somebody ohs.
When the juice is
passed I help my-
self to a double
portion.

Mother says that
for every container
there is the right
lid out there
somewhere. Yet
Ernestine I am told
will never know a
man. I watch her
pound the upright
in the general
direction of
oblivion, with each
stroke watch its
keyboard rise
as if the savior
we are singing about
again.

When I shake the
minister's hand
I shake limp
skin, take the
long steps down-
ward three at a
time. In my father's

house are only four
small rooms. I can-
not wait to shed
these unnatural
clothes, cannot wait
to go outside to
breathe where the
visible sun is.

Last Summer and the One Before

Father holds the melon
out from his buckle
as if a green container
about to christen the bow
of a new world. When the fruit
strikes the ground
I hear the meaning of broken.
With our hands
we scoop the heart crimson and sweet
into our mouths.
I spit a black seed
into a yellowing of yardlight,
turn to see a full moon
rising above the wheatfield
like the start of a new life.

Who knows why the tractor
slipped out of gear,
why its owner didn't look up
from his work at the sicklebar
sooner. I go to the funeral in a shirt
so stiff at the neck I am lost to say
who sat behind me.
Not even the fan overhead
can whirl away the heat
previewing hades, and Rock of Ages
drags like a four-bottom plow
choked time and again
with stubble. Heavens to Betsy, uncle says,
don't you know hardly
anything at all? Life is the learning of
which is which, the fixed law
or the sliding rule,

meaning, I guess, that because
I drink the last full dipper
I must take the bucket alone to be replenished
back to the deepening well.

||||||||||||||||||||||||||||||||||||||||||||||||||||||||||||||||||||||||||||||||||||||||||||||

A Red Ryder BB-Gun for Christmas

It's what I want more than anything,
more almost than love,
which is what I must never forget
for a single instant
God is. Which is why, remembering,
I feel bad about the dream
I can't control,
blood on the wing of the nest-bound dove.

My covenant is never to aim at anything
more human than an empty can. Pow. Besides,
good things come from practice and discipline,
a sharper eye, a steadier hand,
not to mention the nerves. Besides,
who knows what type of prowler
might at any time
break into the family?

Last Christmas the passion was a Barlow,
the most recent scar on my left index finger
now almost healed. When I flick open the blade
and tilt it into the sun I think
bayonet. Last night I prayed myself to sleep,
rain on the roof like small golden pellets
filling again the barrel of my
bottomless dream.

George Eat Old Gray Rat at Pappy's House Yesterday

FOR DAVID LEE

It's the crutch I lean upon
to spell geography,
but I lose the spelldown anyway,
going under on occurrence.
Donna Grace Davis, only daughter
of the superintendent,
wins.

❖ ❖ ❖

Grandmother used her arthritic cane to show me
what to pick up and where to place it,
garden hose, rake, hoe, flowerpot,
the rocker with its cushions
dank from the wind that rising and rising
will slap the rain like buckshot
against the windows. It is not the storm
she fears, it is the threat of dying
out of place. Who was it that said
Be in advance of all parting?

Now the garden hose
hangs in its perfect loops
from a spike in the carless garage,
the rake just here, the hoe there,
the petunias in their delicate bodies
high and dry in the kitchen. Grandmother
could not be happier, more at ease.
We will pop a tub of corn and play Parcheesi
until, sure enough, not long after
I know the storm will never end
the storm will end, and grandmother's arm
like a length of weathered wood
will steady me out of my clothes

and into the bedroom, where into a featherbed
I'll fall like heaviness
dropped from a great height, memory
undermining that moment between the flicker
and the dream, how back at my desk
I held a new yellow pencil in both hands,
how when I determined
what I thought to be its exact center
I pressed it between my thumbs,
snapping forever until the next occurrence
the proud Ticonderoga
of its spine.

\|\|\|\|\|\|\|\|\|\|\|\|\|\|\|\|\|\|\|\|\|\|\|\|\|\|\|\|\|\|\|\|\|\|\|\|\|\|\|\|\|\|\|\|\|\|\|\|\|\|\|\|\|\|\|\|\|\|\|\|\|\|\|\|\|\|\|\|\|\|\|\|\|\|\|\|\|\|\|\|\|\|\|\|\|\|

At Shannon's Creek, Early August

This is the baptism I am not prepared for,
the one that in a moment of no reflection
I agreed to,
and now it is almost time.

We are in Shannon's pasture,
Shannon's herefords nearby, their bellies
heavy with Shannon's buffalo grass,
water from Shannon's creek cooling their cuds,
and we are naked.

And where our clothes were
we are white, amazingly so,
the obese minister with his round face
and his testicles too small to matter,
and Oscar Koeppen out of his wheelchair
moving under his own steam
like a crooked crab
toward the water.

And I am white, too, that fishbelly white
I wouldn't want my date for the life of me to see,
me here because I agreed to be,
because Oscar in a note said he would do it
if I would, that he hoped I would.
He is an old man of no age,
his mouth no less twisted than his limbs,
his larynx unable to turn sound
into what we others know as sense.

They say it was God who made the heavens and the earth,
pasture and water
and the herefords that standing nearby
watch us.
And made the preacher, too,
with me his nearest child, and Oscar,
who accepting the awful wrath of crookedness
asked that this ceremony not be done
in church, where those who do not understand
might smile their perfect lips,
but here in Shannon's creek,
and what I believe is this, that Oscar Koeppen
in his own distended way
believes.

And what I believe is that the preacher,
reciting the word, handling first Oscar, then me,
affirms for himself—as if a sanctification—
what is and what might have been.

And what I believe is that the waterhole we find
to be immersed in
filled before the first agreement,
and that after Oscar's bones are straightened
to fit his box of undetermined pine,
and the preacher with his folded hands
has lost that lust to touch his pitiful sac
to some consenter's skin,

and after age on age the boy
accepts the date who age on age
accepted him—

the waterhole will yet be filling.

‖‖

Drinking with My Father

We begin shortly after the burial
of his second wife,
that woman born to illness,
and my father, released now,
talks with high authority
about those subjects
we know least about,
the inevitabilities of power,
the politics of death.

His eyes are greener
than I remember them,
brighter now than I thought
possible. He uses a
thin white strip of tape
secure on a fruit jar
to measure the bourbon.
If he had his way
we'd draw straws
to select a president,
our current leader meanwhile
an object lesson
unable daily to distinguish
shit from shinola.

Eventually we see through our glasses
clearly, and what we reckon
is that living is its own

excuse for knowing—we mortals
frequently wrong,
never in doubt.

My own eyes owe their greenness
to his. The more we talk,
the further we move from the earth
where his wife lies—
and the more we exist.
What it amounts to
is that in the maelstrom of death
we are risen alive to tell it,
to breathe the cool autumn air
of survival, of worldly fortunes,
of the arrogance that comes from claiming
that misery so interminable
of having been there.

||||||||||||||||||||||||||||||||||||||||||||||||||||||||||||||||||||||||||||||||||||||||||||||||

Firstborn

FOR TERRY LYNN

Remembering you as the beginning
I am not at all surprised
that the earth
took a morning turn:
beasts of the field
stretched their slumbering legs,
birds of the air
their uncontested wings.

Lying in your crib
you breathed for all of us
who had lost for a time
the simple art of breathing.
And the lungs of the universe
swelled then to an immense proportion,

each planet with its orb
equal and opposite,
each star with its sometimes rising,
sometimes falling, moon.

Daughter,
you are the first force
pulling the water
to its habitual shore.
Finding legs at an early age
you rose completely
only to keep on rising,
and we sensed how our world
with you at its summit turned,
and we looked and we saw
that it was good,

and we wanted more.

||||||||||||||||||||||||||||||||||||||||||||||||||||||||||||||||||||||||||||||||||

Walking to the Hinky Dinky with my Grandson, Almost 4

Because I don't really need it I take along
the newest stick, my lumbago yet dormant,
the local dog so warmed by the early March sun
he has lost that lowest animal inclination:
the urge to feed upon the flesh
of the strolling poet.

Now I can carry wood for the simple joy
of touching it, my legs meanwhile declaring
their own post-winter independence.
Is this what it means to be alive?
I want to stop at my neighbor's
to gather in the answer, that neighbor

who for the past three months
has been rising from the bottom of a pool

that has no bottom. I want to ask her
all of those intractable questions
that fill our minds when the lights are out
and it's impossible to imagine morning.

But I walk on by, my grandson at my hip
with a walking-stick of his own
measuring distance, poking holes in the theory
of what grows up grows down.
Our hope is to last long enough
to buy juice and doughnuts, to return home,

to sit together under the same sun that
intensifies my neighbor, all of us
tasting the moment
as if the heart of a melon
cool as the body out at last
from the water, and its taste as sweet.

‖‖

Looking for Halley's Comet

FOR NICOLE ANN,
ONE DAY OLD

All evening I have been looking
for Halley's comet,
my binoculars familiar now
as a loose necktie,
yet I see nothing
but the same old stars,
the same old weary constellations,
none of whom I can name.

So I do what I can,
focus the glasses three clicks
to the right of a partial moon,

jiggle the lenses
until each star
becomes the marvel
I've been told to search for.
Now I have something expansive
to tell my newest granddaughter,
how standing midway
between the maple and the mountain ash
I saw the inexhaustible comet
a dozen times over,
how the night swallowed its breath
as if with silence
to urge me on,
how I came to the ancient conclusion
that the universe is too deep
for one landlubber
alone to sound,
though you, Nicole,
in the length of a single day
disturbed it.

And how the moment
in its arrested clarity
defined all landscapes far and near,
where only yesterday,
standing before a separation
of flawless glass,
I looked far down, amazed
beyond the outstretched hands of height
to find you here.

||||||||||||||||||||||||||||||||||||||||||||||||||||||||||||||||||||||||||||||||||

Taking the Test

Taking the test
she bubbles her gum
without one time bursting the bubble,

each time retrieving the pink glistening sphere
as if a delicate flycatcher.
Her nails are the color of the gum,

her dark hair
windblown.
She is telling me

more than I'll ever care to know
of Neoclassicism,
Moliere you farce, Swift you

Dean with the excremental
brain. Voltaire, Voltaire,
au contraire,

how does your garden grow?
Beyond a window I imagine Spring,
trumpets blaring, the euonymous burning,

the sycamore
like a story from Sunday school
fulfilled. Now she is

biting her lower lip,
time running out, biting the lip
all the way to a tiny

bubble of blood.
With her tongue
she licks and licks

the bright lip clean,
her pen in lovely loops
of constant motion,

with crimson bells and citron shells
and monarchs
dead all in a row.

Watercolor: The Door

Its charm is a low whisper
somewhere between a man's sound
and a woman's,
and you move toward it
with all the caution of age,
knowing how edges sometimes
shift their sudden perspectives
to disengage you.

The amazing thing
is that this old thing
is indeed so old,
done by one of the children,
mounted and framed then
by a pride too inclusive for borders.
The amazing thing
is that the colors—pastels,
except for the whorl of red,
as if a bloodprint, on the
knob—remain as they were
the hour, the moment
you first set eyes upon them.
On the overhead a small surplus
of aqua, yet running.
And in a lower corner, blocked,
almost as if a welcome,
WATERCOLOR:
  THE DOOR.

You cannot open it
to move on to another life
until it dries,
and it never dries.

Driving Back to Kansas to Watch a Wedding

In the back seat
my granddaughter, almost two,
would learn the vocabulary of Kansas,

rock and chalk and Jayhawk,
high sky, I tell her,
for losing your deepest thought in,

and space enough for
barley and wheat
and burial,

not to mention breathing.
East of Salina,
crossing the Smoky Hill,

we speak of salt and of cottonwood,
my granddaughter saying
again and again

more than she knows. Later,
in the park, watching the wedding,
I will hear her voice

so beautifully out of sync
rehearsing the marriage
of sound to sense

and to nonsense,
her mother my daughter
standing to one side holding her,

sunflowers
catching the best
the full sun has to offer.

And what before us is being said
is what so many of us,
in the face of whatever death

would part us, say.
Hold hands. Rock and chalk and
Jayhawk,

high sky and space,
salt and cottonwood:
repeat after me.

‖‖

Independent

FOR GARY GILDNER

I

A recent issue of the hometown paper
turns bloodhound to sniff me out,
and I read that the church
where I learned to have no other gods
before it
has merged with a larger denomination,
the stuccoed building, big as a poor boy's
castle, sold then to the Baptists,
and quick as a miracle I mix myself a drink.

2

Jesus. The world *is* a quaint and ornery place,
isn't it? In the basement during prayer meeting
I used my Scofield Bible to cover my hand
holding hers. Later, in the haymow,
we tied forebearance to necessity
with a length of grocery twine
born to break. Surely you know what I mean.
This must have been what Adam and Eve did,
having blown a kiss goodbye to Eden.

But Baptists. Holy smoke. They too
fornicate, I know, but always after the act
it shows, too much grease on an axle
turning nowhere. Now they move and breathe
and have their being in that place
where I learned never to judge

unless the moment demands it,
and sitting a polished pew as if a pony
I find myself beside her,
reading between the lines of the hymnal
the message of multiplication
ever after. O
life *is* a quaint and ornery movement,
isn't it?

3

The football team meanwhile has beat the daylight
out of the Sharon Bobcats—Sharon, for the Lord's sake,
that hotbed of Catholics where one Saturday night
I saw a perfectly swell fistfight,
the principals equally naked to the waist,
equally stout, equally hungry,
equally drunk,
the sound their fists made
against their equally beautiful bodies
reaching all the way to the lowest bolgia
of the stomach.
But Baptists? I am surprised at my own
astonishment,
I who have not subscribed to the *Independent*
for thirty years, I who haven't
darkened a churchdoor in a month of Sundays,
but apparently I have not yet given up
all the ghosts, and I mix another drink
at the thought of Baptists twitching and jerking
in the church where I learned to endure my neighbor,
and I swear I can't help it, I feel betrayed,
what little hair I have to run a hand through
clipped close by someone else's hand
while I lay sleeping.

4

And there were bums in those days, tramps,
and while the churchfolk extemporized
and worked at finding God
with wet fingers

against the gossamer leaves of Holy Scripture
my mother took them in and gave them
mush and Ovaltine
and wrapped the little wool we had to spare
around their necks and sent them off with words
that must have returned to them a hundredfold
as they sat near the Santa Fe tracks
hunched over a dirtbowl of cinders, Lord,
can you hear what I'm saying? The church
where I learned that the meek shall inherit
what's left of the earth has
been sold like something tangible
to the Baptists,

and I would therefore have another drink,
during which I'll trust my fingers
to find hers somewhere
under Ecclesiastes, that thrill meanwhile
of those beautiful bodies
clashing,
the flattened nose, the blood, the white eye
wild in the hold of its socket,
the bad to the good news being delivered
forever and a day somehow
by whatever institutional animal
slouching home.

||||||||||||||||||||||||||||||||||||||||||||||||||||||||||||||||||||||||||||||||||||||||||||||||||

Cave

Not the one in the southwest corner of the backyard
under the stunted elm,
whose roots my brother and I chopped away at
hour after hour into the dusks
of interminable days,
not the hole in the dark earth
that evolved in spite of our mother's dark
predictions, the hole whose sides

we smoothed with a borrowed spade
until the soil shone bright
and as hard as porcelain,
and not the cover of lath and cardboard
and gunnysack and new-turned earth,
swaybacked and finally tight enough
to deny most light,
but the bedroom where all of us slept
through the long nights of August
while a Kansas moon took its shape
through a butterfly snag in the windowblind.

❖ ❖ ❖

These hands that helped to dig the backyard cave
are yet my hands, this drink in them
cool to the touch, cool and as damp
as the backyard cave my brother and I,
with candle and matches,
first crawled into, lowering carefully
the lid to the secret entrance, on our bellies
following the beam of the flashlight
down the short slope of tunnel
into the cool damp hole. And the candle,
placed into a recess in the south wall,
how it caught with the third kitchen match,
flickering then, then gasping,
and my brother and I settling our backs
against the cool damp earth and sighing,
as if to say This is it. This is the place
where not even Sunday school can reach us.

❖ ❖ ❖

I would have another drink, the effluvium
of whiskey distinct as my mother's breath,
her face near mine,
her heavy form bending over me to tell me
Drink: your croup is loosening, but
it's keeping your father awake. And

what of your own voice earlier that night, mother,
and of father's responding,
shouting in whispers that money is the god
we live to believe in but cannot lay our
hands on, the whispering
intense to the point of knives,
made more intense by my brother's easy breathing,
my sister's face in the snag of moonlight
no more disturbed than a saucer
of untouched cream.

Ancient history is what you can choose
not to remember. All else is a gathering
into the present, and that in turn a gathering.
Time to get ready for Sunday school, mother says,
her body bent, her face close to mine.
It is the kind of face that at night, lying
beside my father, wants to know
just where in the name of Jesus Christ
the money for the children's winter clothes
is supposed to come from. Faith
is the victory, the minister says, and
when we pray I don't, nor does Eileen,
our eyes meeting deeply and squarely
until the praying says Amen.

In the damp of the backyard cave,
the candle gasping,
I tell my little brother something
about her. On his tongue the word Tit
is the pearl of redemption. I tell him
more than I know. His face in the
flicker of candlelight is the face of an angel.
This is not the true cave, understand,
this is the hole in the southwest corner
of the backyard,
the jut of an elmroot the nail I hang my hat on.

He wants to know if what I have learned
will ever happen to him. Faith
is the victory, I say. I say Amen.

In the true cave the August nights
do not relent, snag of moonlight
on my sister's face, my brother so evenly
breathing. I would have another drink.
When the candle goes out, and the last match
fails to flame, my brother and I
talk softly in the darkness,
threats of God and of money
as if the trailing edges of a vast
but dissipating dream. Between her legs,
I tell him, already are traces of hair.
And I remember the sense of awe
that rode on his intake of air,
the palpable sound of his laughter. While
in the bedroom the whispering
slowed time's motion. The bedroom,
the true cave, not the backyard hole
with its spent candle, its silence,
the words from my brother and me
suspended, but the room where all of us sleep
through the long nights of August
while a Kansas moon takes its shape
through a butterfly snag in the windowblind.

⁣|||||||||||||||||||||||||||||||||||||||||||||||||||||||||||||||||||||||||||||||||||||||||||||

Drinking the Tin Cup Dry

Tin against the boy's lip,
cool water slaking the tongue,
and my father, the hired hand,
hip-deep in wheat in the bed
of the unpainted wagon,
shoveling.

Father,
I cannot drink deeply enough
to drink this tin cup dry.
With each effort the stubble
rotates to become the darkened soil
that having housed the seed
gives rise to another windless day,
and you are at it again,
sickle and chaff and the women
in their blue bandanas (I among them,
the incorrigible, the tagalong,
wanting to inhale the world)
bringing bread and purple grapes
and lunchmeat. And you, father,
the hired hand, stopping for nothing,
not for sympathy, least of all for hunger,
until the last of the kernels from the combine
lies dutifully spread.

Father,
all of this aches to be ancient history.
But the tin cup
finds its way into my hand
at the oddest hour, the party
rampant with the thighs of city girls
and the tinkling of ice in bourbon,
and there is nothing for it
but to lift and drink:

my face
in the cool water, beyond it
you in the wagonbed
up to that place that did its work
to place me here
breathing the death of us all
in the midst of such plentiful grain.

Last of the Mohicans

FOR ROBERT HEPBURN

Each morning to start things off
Miss Yoder read to us
from a book so thick
I could not stop watching it,
read to us a story of capture,
and of flight and then of capture,
each morning her voice
going suddenly silent
at a moment when something awful
or maybe something terribly sweet
was about to happen,

and that's the way I have come
to live the other parts of my life,
my eyes on a book whose thickness
almost imperceptibly lessens,
she had read the story *praise be!* and *alas!*
so many times before,

and when one morning she wasn't there,
and thereafter never was,
how I expected her substitute to carry on,
though she never did,
that unfinished book
gone forever with Miss Yoder, herself a mystery
unfinished,
though day by day I have come
to realize the romantic extremities
of capture and of flight and then of capture,
of taking up what someone else

began, however incidental or deliberate,
however thick the volume we must alone conclude,
however thin.

||||||||||||||||||||||||||||||||||||||||||||||||||||||||||||||||||||||||||||||||||||||||||||||||||||

Running Home

You leave the pool hall
        walking
                but because it's a brisk evening

and you have energy enough
        to last a lifetime
                you begin to run—

slowly, at first,
        because you have plenty of time,
                and because there is yet light enough

for you to notice that
        not only are there trees,
                but also limbs and leaves

with their shapes described
        more sharply than imaginable
                against a darkening sky. Until

suddenly that darkening sky
        fulfills itself, and
                you increase the pace,

as if the darkness were itself
        a subtle premonition,
                until the pace becomes a sprint

you can't sustain,
        though you sustain it,
                the premonition now reality,

someone or something
        not far behind you, closing in,
                until the rattle of your feet

against the pine boards of the bridge
        just south of Mabel Cleveland's shanty
            seems palpable,

but looking right and left
        for the long arm of truth and mercy
            you see only the eyes of maybe animals,

beneath you the flat gravel road
        assuming a sudden curvature
            to send you laboring uphill—

O kiss my dead ass, Marvin,
        this must be a movie,
            this must be the awful climax,

over the crest if not in the ditches
        let there be cavalry—
            until fear is the taste

of your own fear
        strong as alum on the tongue
            and the last thing you hear is

the cue-ball going so smartly
        click! against the 8-ball,
            the 8-ball heavy

as any young boy's flesh, here
        or in the sweet hereafter
            going down.

Jumping Rope

> Down by the ocean, down by the sea,
> Johnny broke a bottle and blamed it on me.

O it's the rhythm we jump to, the rhythm,
our long braided rope
nibbling at the blue-green blades
of Daddy's ryegrass,

though Johnny of course must be tattled on,
I told Ma and Ma told Pa,
and Johnny of course must be punished,
but it's the rhythm of the punishment

that matters, not the deed that
warrants punishment,
Johnny taking his sad licks
one-two-three, ha-ha-ha,

until the rhythm of the punishment ends
and we switch to the utter nonsense of
fudge, fudge, fetch the judge,
Mommy just had a newborn baby—

and it's the rhythm we jump to,
not the miracle of birth,
not even the notice that
it wasn't a boy, it wasn't a girl,

it was just a plain old baby: and
rhythm it is that takes us
through the dense abrogation of duty,
wrap it up in tissue paper,

put it on the elevator,
and rhythm it is that lifts us
into theoretical oblivion—
how many floors did it go up?—

my girlfriend jumping her
plaid pleated skirt into numbers
too high to be challenged,
into pepper too hot to be consumed,

but it's the rhythm, not the lofty numbers,
not the intensive heat,
we jump to,
each heart the standard pulse by which—

regardless of all the anomalies around us—
we measure the everlasting beat,
rich man, poor man, beggar man, thief,
doctor, lawyer, Indian chief.

||||||||||||||||||||||||||||||||||||||||||||||||||||||||||||||||||||||||||||||||||||||||

Driving Back Home in My Wife's Father's Old Chevrolet

It's a gunboat, sure enough,
long as a pickpocket's hands,
heavy as the guilt I shouldered
after that first time I did it
in the back seat of a different
Chevrolet.

He bought it brand new, Caprice Classic,
his small frame behind the wheel
all smile and elbow,
washed and waxed it every Saturday,
come hell or high water,
with a soft cloth rubbing its massive metal
to a high crimson sheen.

Now a dozen years after his death
I'm driving back home in my wife's father's old Chevrolet,
windows down, half of Lancaster County
posing as dust on the dashboard—
at my right the Little Blue meandering,

at my left a sweet laborious wheeling
of purebred Angus,
all around me not so much
as a single peckertrack
on her dad's upholstery. O
I'm sober as the judge who helped to make me
sober, clean as the underbelly
of a river catfish—

and I'm driving back home in my wife's father's old Chevrolet,
back to where I think I see his daughter
at the front door waiting,
all smile and elbow,
eager as that first encounter
whose name I can't recall
to take me in.

||||||||||||||||||||||||||||||||||||||||||||||||||||||||||||||||||||||||||||||||||

Wildwood, Early Autumn

FOR ROBERT AND KATE

This night above stars
sparkling the water
I sit alone at the pond's grassy edge
waiting for the line suddenly
to lose its slack,
channel catfish sleek as love
in a slant of mid-September moon.

And don't breathe a word of this
to anyone,
but what I'm hearing
is the music that came to me
so many nights ago
as I sat with the children's mother
on the front porch,

banjo and guitar and mandolin
taking turns in the hands
of the younger son, each chord
sweet as the amber wine
we sipped on,

and don't breathe a word of this
to anyone,
but the liquid in those tunes
must have found its way
to where the desert wants more
than anything else to bloom—Peaceful
Easy Feeling, Blackberry Blossom,
Autumn Leaves, Devil's Dream,
Comes a Time, Red-Haired Boy, Steam-
Powered Aeroplane—refreshing
each rib on each
up-and-coming spine,

and don't breathe a word of this
to anyone,
but the catch is this:
the melodies of earth
are never done: bullfrog,
thunderbird, a west wind
soughing through the saguaro—
and the fish I'll hook
but not possess,
its body, sleek as love,
this night forever at home
wherever home is.

Write a Blank-Verse Poem Using Someone Else's Voice, Someone Dead, Someone Who You Believe Was Not Treated Fairly While Alive

I'm Lot's Wife, maybe you know me: I'm that
Woman in the Bible who was turned
Into a pillar of salt for disobedience.
Well, kiddo, I'm not looking for sympathy.
In the first place, I'm a *pillar*—not a *block,*
Not a *chunk,* but a *pillar.* Second, I'm the queen
Of the pasture, the salt of this bovine earth. Lot,
On the other hand, that picture of obedience,
Escaped from Sodom, where to save his skin
He tried to sell his own daughters into
The hands of disease and slobber, that liver of his
Like the rest of him, yellow with wine.
And sure enough, he backslid into corruption
Darker than the inside of an Angus.
I wouldn't trade places with him right now
On anybody's bet. Let the bootlicker burn.
And call my own change of form whatever you like,
I call it Jehovah's body-slam that backfired.
You see, not bowing slavishly down can be
A form of prayer. So I'm no longer merely
Lot's Wife, no longer a servile sop,
But a pillar feeding the cattle to become
One of them, their calves in turn wobbling
To find their legs, against me rich as any
Lover's kiss their non-judgmental tongues.

Achilles' Heel

The student who asks for an explanation
has blue eyes and an oval face
and a voice that implies—

in addition to what it requests—
I just can't understand anything
unless   someone   alive   explains   it.

Because I want to believe myself alive
I recount the ancient story—
Thetis gripping her young son's heel
to dip his body head-first into the river Styx,
goddess neglecting then to dip the heel,
so that eventually he'll die
from a wound in that only vulnerable spot,
arrow released from the bow of Paris,
that other heel.

But she doesn't smile,
probably doesn't yet quite get it,
so I tell her how human fallibility
must somehow be accounted for,
how when my brother lay groaning
after a hemorrhoidectomy,
his dark eyes asking the ceiling *Why?*
I told him that our mother
dipped him newborn
into a Kansas equivalent of the river Styx,
then like Thetis neglected to make immune
that portion of the anatomy she suspended
him from.

And he didn't smile,
so while I had him captive and inert
I explained the ins and the outs
of classical irony,
how a woman though a goddess
had a faulty memory,
how Achilles though clad in first-rate armor
died dead as a stone at the hand
of a third-rate warrior.

The student with the blue eyes and oval face
closes the blue eyes, nods the oval face.
Is she asleep or thinking deeply? No matter:
when she returns already I have moved
to the death of Hector, his body
dragging an oval
outside the beleagured walls of Troy,

Achilles riding high and for the moment
invincible in the saddle of his chariot,
sword raised and silver
against a slant of blinding
but universal sun.

〰〰〰〰〰〰〰〰〰〰〰〰〰〰〰〰〰〰〰〰〰〰〰〰〰〰〰〰〰〰〰〰

At Maggie's Pond

Both the near and the far
                banks have been grubbed
                                and leveled,

so that now no longer is that
                good green illusion, sanctuary,
                                intact.

Even so,
                I cast a surface lure
                                with practiced nonchalance,

as if nobody in the nearby farmhouse
                sits watching. When the truly big one
                                strikes, I'll bring it slowly

to its liquid knees
                to hold it up in sunlight
                                to marvel at the soundless sound

of two gills breathing.
    Later, in a deep iron skillet,
        the many portions of the fish

will sizzle to an almost
    weightless brown. Or would,
        had I not released it

back to its world of dart
    and of slow-motion moss—so thus and
        therefore, all my children,

find your places near the fire
    and for the frail duration of a fresh log
        hear the lexicon of sanctum:

root and limb and leaf and canopy,
    shadow of night's lone hawk
        descending to its nest—

that lofty cradle
    rocked by moon and flame
        upon the water.

||||||||||||||||||||||||||||||||||||||||||||||||||||||||||||||||||||||||||||||||||||||||||||

Burning the House Down

Because the house we live in
must surely be made of boards
from all those other previous houses,
I choose just now
to think of that place
I very nearly burned to the ground
that afternoon in early August,
my buddy beside me watching,
his box of matches limp at his side,
open and spilling.

We played the game called Firefly,
each with a box of kitchen matches,

and running and striking and throwing
we swirled the dirt on the gravel road
that ran from my house to his,
we turned the buffalo grass
from green to dust, our pathways
taking us on routes
we hadn't mutually agreed to,
one of them from the living-room

to the kitchen, where suddenly I
stopped to turn to strike a match
to toss to start my buddy burning,
that being the object of Firefly,
to keep oneself intact
while burning down the other,
but my buddy swerved,
the matchflame in its flight
barely missing the fine hair on his neck,
and later I'll learn that the flame

stayed alive just long enough
to ignite the kindling in the box
beside the range,
igniting then the box itself, next
the petals of pink and of purple
blooming the wallpaper,
next the linoleum, next
the slats of tongue and of groove
describing the floor, next the table and the chairs
sitting like wooden soldiers awaiting supper.

I am too big to be forced
belly-down on my mother's lap
to be spanked, but my mother
with her left hand forces me down,
with her right hand blisters me until the weeping
I hear is not my own, but my mother's,

weeping that heightens into sobbing
sufficient to shake my mother's body
as if the frame of something impossible
ever to disassemble coming down.

I ran from the kitchen, heard the screendoor
slam, heard my buddy behind me, and having
circled the small stuccoed church across the alley
heard the clangclangclang of the fire engine,
Harold Simpson in the house beside the church
having seen the smoke, then the flames,
Harold Simpson who with his
hurried call to the station
saved the house from burning
entirely down, Mr. Simpson risking his life

to drag the flaming wooden table
with its four flaming soldiers
outside, the firemen
for some unaccountable reason
neglecting the house to train the hose on
first the table, then the chairs, with a mighty
rope of water knocking them sizzling end over end
across the dry August lawn, my buddy beside me
watching, his box of matches limp at his side,
open and spilling.

I am too big to be spanked this way
because, very simply, I am too big—
but also because I am old enough to know
of passion, old enough to see the spark
in my girlfriend's eye when I invite her
into the hand-dug cave to sit beside me
to smell the damp earth yielding
something more than earth,
the candle in its recess
flickering—

knowing somehow even then
that every passion
must surely be made of moments
from all those other previous passions,
my girl in the candle's shifting shadows
too immediate for words,
so in silence we sit on the damp
earthen floor of the hand-dug cave,
our grotto, our hideaway,
our cool hands finally touching.

When father home from work
saw the smoldering kitchen
he cursed not me,
not the loss of something solid
he could, with sufficient sweat,
eventually replace,
but cursed instead the widening distance
between himself and mother
that each misfortune led to, God-
damn and Christ Almighty

hanging like belly-heavy smoke
in the hot sparse windless August air,
me not long before
lying belly-down on my mother's lap,
her right hand punishing itself
as it punished me,
passion in each measured blow,
passion in the sound of her sobbing,
passion tangible almost
as the boards before their burning,

as the burning itself,
as the heat from the orange flames,
as the flickering of those flames
flickering in turn the faces
of the congregation,

among it the face of Mr. Simpson
praying, that face
in regular attendance at the stuccoed church,
Mr. Simpson believing not only that God exists,
but that he likewise hears and answers prayer,

yet the kitchen is destroyed,
yet the house otherwise is saved,
and I am too big to be spanked this way
but too small to say what
I feel to be happening,
my girl beside me in the hand-dug cave
warming my hand with the touch of hers,
our house from its ashes
board by improbable board
to this day rising.

Dress

Once again my sister loses the battle,
meaning no store-bought dress,
meaning that again the old woman

here across the alley is sewing another outfit,
something not much fancier than a feedsack,
my sister standing on a wooden stepstool

while Mrs. Linshied kneels to adjust the hem,
my sister standing as tall as she can,
embarrassed and angry,

her green eyes looking straight ahead so hard
I look there, too,
but there isn't anything to see

except a purple flowing of pink wallpaper
until finally Mrs. Linshied finishes
and rises slowly to find her purse

to pay me, a few unused pins
sprouting from between her lips, old lips,
old porcupine, old hand

dipping into the purse for eighty cents,
three quarters and a nickel,
and taking the coins

I drop her paper on the seat of a rocking chair
which I kick when I turn to leave,
bad news all over the front page,

we're losing,
more Japs than bullets to kill them,
and that dumb old rocker

squeaking like something
small and cornered as
I shut the door.

‖‖‖

Swallowing the Soap

Near the sink,
in our kitchen with its gaudy wallpaper,
its curled linoleum,
mother with a used bar of Lava
stands ready to cleanse my mouth,
mouth that learned
its better share of expletives
from its father,
mouth that opens wide
to receive the soap,
and when mother loses her grip
I swallow the bar on purpose,
hoping to teach her a lesson.

Because I pretend to be choking
mother slaps my back
as if pounding stakes,
then shortly, tears down her face,
she turns to prayer.
When I am convinced that
she has suffered enough
I make a sound like *Gulp*
and resume my breathing.

Next time the punishment
is a length of tamarack
fine as a quirt
across the forearm. It didn't
hurt, I tell my small brother later.

When he says *Horseshit it didn't*
I chase him to the far corner of the cowlot,
where I wrestle him to the ground
to punch both of his
skinny shoulders
silly.

|||||||||||||||||||||||||||||||||||||||||||||||||||||||||||||||||||||||||||||||||||||||||||

Dancing in the Cornfield

FOR MARGARET

Blame it on Porky Holland,
that obese rulebreaker who got caught
smoking in the cloakroom,
so for a month of Saturday nights
there'll be no dancing in the Center,
meaning that each couple
will have to find its own private place.

Mavis and I choose Clarence Bonham's cornfield.
We go there at dusk,
giving ourselves plenty of time
to inhale the impending harvest,
plenty of time to touch the silk on the tassels
and to ooh and aah at the height of the stalks
and the ears the size of a grown boy's forearm.

And before the first cloud
begins to obscure the moon
already Mavis is barefooted and dancing,
so I play something snappy on the jukebox
that isn't there and join her,
and you should be here to see us, see us
dancing in the cornfield,

dancing in old Clarence Bonham's cornfield,
and when the rain moves in
I change the record to something slow,
and we are dancing slowly in the cornfield,
slowly together dancing in the cornfield,
our bodies like the tallest cornstalks
swaying,

and when we kiss, wet lip to lip,
our love and all our secrets
as if kernels of golden corn
spill over and down,
kernels too many for mortals like us to count
on the dark and ever-
softening ground.

||||||||||||||||||||||||||||||||||||||||||||||||||||||||||||||||||||||||||||||||||||||||||||

Epiphany

It happens not so much on schedule
as at those moments when
something with something else
beautifully collides,

Nelson taking the ball from Mitchell
on a fast break, for example,
then stopping suddenly short
to break the school record from twenty feet,
the ball at the height of its high soft arc
like a full moon fully risen,

or the student in Composition
reading aloud the surprising words
of her essay,
weeping at the new loss
of something lost a long time ago,
the eyes of the boy on the back row
saying I must have been blind—
she's wonderful,

the ball descending then
to flounce the net
like a rayon skirt,

the young man on the back row
studying his hands
as if learning
for the first time ever
what they might be holding.

||||||||||||||||||||||||||||||||||||||||||||||||||||||||||||||||||||||||||||||||||||||||||||||||

Odyssey

Today under a steady sun
        this garden hose is the only
                active downspout,

water gushing
        into a long trough of bricks
              laid yesterday

by the hands of my grandson and me,
        Will at four too busy almost
            to stop for lemonade,

his spirit infectious:
        time and again I stay away
            much longer than reasonable

from my beaded beer.
        Now the water over the bricks
           is a channel to float a ship on,

call it, for lack of something nobler,
        The Cottonwood. The four giant sails
           it doesn't have

catch the August breeze that
        if Aeolus were just
           would be blowing. Always

there is a country to be away from,
      always a bed with one of its headposts
            olive, its roots too deep to be sounded,

to return to, always
      because of this one time
            my grandson on bare feet

motionless, watching The Cottonwood
      sailing and sailing
          sideways

over the edge of the earth.

||||||||||||||||||||||||||||||||||||||||||||||||||||||||||||||||||||||||||||||||||||||

Last Day of School

Boys in the nearby alley
are lighting crackers
and sending rockets
high into a late-afternoon sun.
A circle of girls meanwhile
wants to know if they might

load their balloons with water
from the backyard hose.
I watch them fill and
knot the balloons,
lie back and close my eyes,
wanting to hear but not observe

the onslaught. Mostly
it is the rapid fire of laughter
until suddenly it seems
darkness in its silence
wakens me. With a flashlight
I move slowly into that field

of delicate strife,
where once-bloated bombs
lie incredibly spent on the gravel,
fragments of red and yellow,
white and purple and green. When
a voice calls me to come inside

I answer with an echo
that loses itself
in the highest branches of the linden.
I switch off the light then
to see more clearly the stars,
the waning moon. I am

trying to remember that
class in science with its mockup
of the order of the universe,
what rotates this way or that,
who in this relentless scheme
is circling whom.

||||||||||||||||||||||||||||||||||||||||||||||||||||||||||||||||||||||||||||||||||||||||

Jacks

Some things don't come back to you, after all,
though yesterday on a bicycle
I lifted my hands from the handlebars
and sped a good fifty feet
before smacking into a curb,
my first full airborne somersault in thirty years,
a real beauty, I'd love
to have it on film,

but today, sitting here
on the cool cement of the front porch,
I cannot bring back my skill at jacks,
this hand like a workglove
encircling the rubber ball,

these fingers like so many stubs
reaching for fallen stars.

I'm losing,
but what the child doesn't realize is that
I'm not. I'm watching her
closely, watching her small fingers
pick the jacks like berries
from a silver tree, ones, twos, threes, fours,
eggs-in-the-basket, pigs-in-the-pen, her eyes
quick like the fish you throw the food to
in bubbling water,

and the game is over
almost before it began,
my granddaughter laughing her perfect teeth
against my chest which she says
though I'm worse at jacks
than anyone she knows
she loves.

||||||||||||||||||||||||||||||||||||||||||||||||||||||||||||||||||||||||||||||||||||||||

Fishing with My Two Boys at a Spring-Fed Pond in Kansas

Truth
like those sunfish
swimming under that overhang of willows
darts in and out among the shadows:
my boys are no longer
boys.

I sit on a campstool
trying my hand with a surface lure.
My sons meanwhile
circle the pond slowly,
looking for that perfect spot.

In their belief that such a place exists
they yet are boys, after all.
And with the luck that goes
with keeping the faith
they find it,
each landing a bass
sufficient for what lies ahead,
the multitude.

At dusk the girls, who are women,
arrive,
and by the time the first bullfrog
clears its ancient throat
we are eating the hot white flesh of the fish,
prepared and cooked by the boys
on the coals of a bonfire
tended by them,
and soon the lights in the tents
go on, then off,
and the men lie down with the women,
and their babes, who are children,
giggle until the moon drops into a cloud

❖ ❖ ❖

and by feel I work a nightcrawler
onto a treble hook,
then spit in the general direction
of that wiggling bait,
hoping to hit it,
wanting what every lucky father wants,
more luck.

Outage

We sit suddenly in darkness
        unable to believe that
                what we cannot see

is what we're seeing, clatter
        from the television likewise
                stilled

as if a clean and consummate
        assassination. When
                I suggest The Hangout

for a cheeseburger
        and a pitcher of beer
                I am roundly applauded.

At eleven we return
        to find the outage holding.
                With a flashlight we scavenge

basement and drawer,
        one lamp and three yellow candles
                our reward. Now

in the flickering of lamp-
        light and candleflame
                we talk and talk,

measuring syllables,
        trilling phonemes. O
                how reasonable the human voice

given half a chance
        can be. And the
                aroma that rises from

wax and lampwick,
        how it brings to life those moments
                we thought so blindly

buried. When the power
in a blink returns
we sit silent and stunned,

seeing each other again
in such a quaint and altogether
different light.

The Color of Dusk

Morning

He thought, *By dusk I'll know for sure.*
By dusk, by all my reckonings,
She'll not be here.

He had finished the morning chores.
An early sunslant caught one corner
Of the table's oilcloth,
So bright the old man felt a moment's ache
Behind the eyes. November now
Seemed little more than one more spot of time.
Yet Alvin Turner couldn't see himself as wasting.
Too much remained to touch, to do.
Not that he meant a grain of disrespect:
The woman lying in the other room
Was Martha yet, and would be until—
Until death, he thought.
Until today, at dusk.

He gathered up the breakfast dishes then
And in a pan of water
Drawn at sunup from the cistern
Set them soaking. This delay
Had come to be
A part of his routine:
At ten o'clock or so he'd drop
Whatever he was doing,
Check Martha, bank the fire,
And, lingering,
Wash and rinse and put away the dishes.

Until that time today he tended to the granary,
Thinking: something more than fieldmice
Seemed muleheaded about entering.

Some of the mash, he knew,
Was missing, and some milo.
The wind? He tightened every hinge,
Gauged every crack along the door and wall,
Along the rock foundation.
At last then with a scoop
He rearranged the grain,
Discovering, in the farthest corner,
The hole that let the varmints in.
The shed, worn back to pine by wind and rain,
Was fast becoming tin:
Bits and pieces splotched the floor
Like sharded, gaunt linoleum.
Alvin Turner flattened one more coffee can,
With roofnails pounded it in place.
He had come to the task at a single pace,
And through it all that pace remained:
Thinking, as he slid the heavy boltlock home,
For now, that ought to do it.

Outside, the sun seemed hurrying.
Alvin Turner touched his hatbrim,
His hand then at his watchfob, tugging.
Pshaw! he said aloud, amazed.

It was already twenty minutes after ten.

Afternoon

The house that early afternoon was warm,
A taste of coffee clinging dryly
To the tip of Alvin Turner's tongue.
Martha lay asleep,
An untouched bowl of broth half lost
Among the medication.
Alvin had eaten again alone,
And for some time now stood beside his pallet
There in Martha's room.

He thought that he had seen,
Beyond the shim-thin eyelids,
Some new omen:
A settling of the features,
A bland surrender into gelatin,
The quiver of a single sign
No harsher than the touch of leaf to water.
But Alvin Turner sensed he saw it there,
Thinking again: *By dusk I'll know for sure.*
By dusk, by all my reckonings,
She'll not be here.

And if she was a fencepost,
He thought later, filling the pockets of a mackinaw
With staples, and lifting a clawhammer
From its wire-hooked holder,
Even the milkcows would have an easy time of it,
Grazing the fence down.
He paced the acreage slowly,
Following the fenceline southward down the driveway,
Then turning east, keeping himself
Between the fence and a persistent maze
Of hedge that lined a rocky road.
By now the sun had started downward
Toward the hill that served as
Alvin Turner's pasture.
The old man felt it warmly on his back.
Not even where it crossed a deepening gulley
Did the fence today show any sign of yielding.
Alvin walked it, even so, methodically,
East, then north along the road,
Then west toward the hill and pasture.
The wheatground at his left, a furrowed gumbo,
Sloped slowly upward to the hill-backed house,
And by the time he reached the northbound shelterbelt
Alvin Turner knew that he was breathing.

He stopped to level out his wind,
The sun now out of sight behind the hill.
And with its dropping Alvin Turner,
Standing not much wider than catalpa,
Briefly chilled. Thinking,
As he later moved uphill
To flank the pasture,
The days are short this time of year,
And growing shorter.

Dusk

Cracked corn to the chickens:
And in the distant east a trace of shadow.
Alvin Turner, from a window, watched it,
Saw it receding, fading, disappearing.
Dusk.
Not light, he thought, *not dark,*
And now not even shadow.
Dusk.

He turned and stepped around his pallet
Toward the sickbed. Martha, on her back,
No thicker than a comforter,
Sidelonged her eyes to see him.

Alvin?

The voice came from far behind the lips.

I'm here, he said.

Alvin?

He found her hand then,
Bones like catgut strung through crepe.
I'm here.

He knew.
He had waited a long time.
First, for everything he joined to live forever,

Then for the next best thing:
A quick and easy parting.

I patched the granary, he said.
I walked the fence. Tomorrow—

And suddenly the fibers in her hand
Contracted, taking Alvin Turner with them.

Martha!

He said it half in anger,
Then reacting to his own reaction

Martha! he said again.

She was dead, her grip gone loose.
As though for one brief, willful moment
She had dozed off-guard—
And in that moment Alvin Turner
Heard the snapping of a fenceline,
Saw rodents big as baby buildings
Grinning, gnawing pine.

That was something he had not foreseen,
Could never—not so long as he drew breath—
Abide.

He had to think, *Betrayed?*
Then searched the face.
The eyes had widened upward,
No more luminous now than eggshell.
And the mouth, the chin: so fine,
So lost inside a waste of hair
That Alvin Turner shuddered in his anger.

Betrayed?

He found himself beside the woodstove then,
A stick of aged persimmon in his hand.
And like a club he raised it,

With one primeval grunt
Released it end to end,
The crash of windowpane a threat
To lure the answer in.

Betrayed?

But there was nothing.
Inside the room, and out:
Only the silent blend of early evening,
The texture, the color of dusk.

Night

To yield the land that no man finally owns,
Then call it loss:
Is this the height of arrogance,
The turtle's puny voice?

Alvin Turner, musing, trimmed a lampwick,
Centered the light then on the kitchen table.
He had swept and thrown away the shattered glass,
Had boarded tongue-in-groove the opening—
Rolling then his pallet to a bundle,
And holding it before him,
like a plump outdated gift,
Had said to Martha, *Please—excuse the fit.*
It wasn't you. It wasn't you at all.
And saying it he felt the anger in his eyes
Go cool, then coolly linger.

The lamp burned even.
He took a jar of green beans from the cupboard,
Some peaches and some bread.
His twisting of the lid, it seemed,
Let loose a screaming in the henhouse,
And in a single movement
Alvin Turner flicked his shotgun from the corner,
A fist of shells.

The shadow near the brooder paused, point blank,
As if to listen,
And in that instant Alvin Turner, loading,
Broke one stride to fire.
Against the low-slung shed

The shot like thunder
Splayed the hound-sized figure,
Alvin Turner on it then
More heavy than a sashweight,
Working his heel against a tube
Of thick coyote throat.

And that was it.
The predator went airless, limp,
And Alvin Turner,
Settled later in the kitchen,
Could visualize the crows at dawn assembling.

All that, and how much more,
As he unlaced his boots to finish supper.

||||||||||||||||||||||||||||||||||||||||||||||||||||||||||||||||||||||||||||||||||||||||||

Threnody

> Whatever you lose
> will come back to you
> if it belonged to you.
>
> *from Finnish folklore*

I

And so it is that the wallet
with the secret compartments
arrives in the morning mail,
and I can tell by the heft, and
by the sound the crease makes
folded back, that nothing
has been touched much less

taken, the lone bill and
the cream-colored condom each in
its darkly-appointed place.

2

I try to remember for whom the
condom, paid for by a boy with
a small king's ransom, had been
at last intended. The names
can be bought at no great price,
yet each name wears only its sound,
no teeth to spit a word through,
no bones to carry forth that con-
summation so devoutly to be reached
for, call it flesh.

3

Jack, will it be like that when
you are gone? What can I
fairly expect the morning mail to
bring? Neighbor and friend, do
you belong as much to the fire
as to the wind? And what can I
do beyond letting go but hold
on and on, and how can I know what
is truly mine before I am pushed to
ask if not satisfy the question?

||||||||||||||||||||||||||||||||||||||||||||||||||||||||||||||||||||||||||||||||||||||||||||||||||||

This Is the Photograph Not Taken

This is the photograph not taken,
the one of the young man
standing in a field of bluestem
grinning to show a fine white stand of teeth,
teeth clamping tightly
what looks to be a grassblade.

What the photograph not taken
does not tell us
is that the seasons
winter us all,
that the young man drew his last breath
harvesting that same brown field,
that the grassblade rises
from the overwhelming dust that
in the photograph not taken
stops his lungs.

|||||||||||||||||||||||||||||||||||||||||||||||||||||||||||||||||||||||||||||||||||||

Back to Kansas

Yet the journey is one
back to more than Kansas,
back to that hideaway
so secret it exists
abundantly in every state—

and the eyes of the girl
who says she long ago outgrew
the borders of Kansas,
how they dilate
to a greenness so sparse
it can only be Kansas,

so there you have it:
the woman as place,
the place as the secret
that every love
exults to share,

and driving back to Kansas
you know that all of this is
hyperbole, the lofty bullshit
of poetry,
that all you want to do
is to park once more

in that Kansas grove where
as youngsters
you screwed your mutual socks off,
purgatory that vague grayness
the chaste and the nutless

settle for,
affection what you feel
when heaven parts its cover

to show you what the eyes
at the moment of wonder are
made of,

the stars!
the stars!

||||||||||||||||||||||||||||||||||||||||||||||||||||||||||||||||||||||||||||||||||||

Going There Sometime

And the water there
will be cleaner sometime
than at this time
and the fine sand
finer

and the shadows cast
by the leaves on the cotton-
wood less elusive then
at the base of a dog-day sun
more sharply defined

and the wild grapes having held their breaths
these many seasons
will explode their ripeness
into the throat of our
impending evening

and what I say here
I will say there

and your answer with
your lips precisely
parted
will be the second half
of all things nurtured

back to living.

||||||||||||||||||||||||||||||||||||||||||||||||||||||||||||||||||||||||||||||||||||||

Legend

> If rain is falling while the sun
> is shining, you know that somewhere
> the Devil is beating his wife.
>
> *Southcentral Kansas saying*

And you can imagine the wife
early in the morning
watching the weather report
and biting her tail
and saying Oh, Hell, not again,
can imagine her wondering
what the deuce such

an odd circumstance of cloud and of sun
has to do with a whipping. Each time
she searches her memory for a clue:
surely, she thinks, way back
in those halcyon days
of wine and of thornless roses
I must have done something

strictly and femininely wrong. But
though nothing of the sort
registers on her mind,

she accepts nonetheless as gospel
that she did it,
and when her beloved
tosses the stub of his Roi-Tan

into a cauldron and
takes her by the wrist
to bend her wings so impossibly high
behind her back
to strike her with the strop
he'll use tomorrow morning
to put a keen edge on his razor

she'll take her solace
in knowing how much a fiction
all this hullabaloo of Hades really is,
herself especially,
because the Devil never took a wife
and never will, she the victim
of a Jayhawk imagination,

sunflower boys with peewee peckers for brains,
and knowing this she smiles almost
all the way to laughter,
the strop meanwhile
on the verge of drawing blood,
the menfolk meanwhile
vast and alone on the plains,

picking their teeth with slivers of pine
and squinting their ancient eyes
beyond the clouds that are
dropping the rain
into a bright if
not altogether
blinding sun.

Odyssey

I hustle through the biology exam,
my last one of the semester,
the professor behind me
hunched like the ultimate troglodyte,
and in less time than it takes to tell it
I'm on the road, headed for home,
headed into my first substantial break
since matriculation four long months ago,
and my foot can't wait.
I'm poetry in motion
on a blacktop humming in close harmony
with the retreads on my grass-green Chevrolet.

But my girl has the flu,
she's a senior in high school,
and the high school itself sits unadorned,
a chamber of echoes. In the drugstore
I kick the pinball machine until in silence
it hollers **Tilt**. A light snowfall is predicted
for Christmas Day. With my good friend Carlos
I drive from the railroad station
at one end of the main street
to the empty high school at the other end.
Carlos has decided to stay at least another year
with the section crew, Atchison, Topeka, & Santa Fe,
Panhandle Division. He says Hell's bells, buckaroo,
let's drive to Harper for a Dr. Pepper
and some salted peanuts.

The snowfall doesn't happen.
I open my gifts, hoping for that noun
I thought I couldn't wait to be away from: book.

Say, did you know that Homer
wrote two very long poems eight
hundred years before
the birth of Christ?

Say, did you know that the world
was destroyed they say by water
long before it was destroyed
again they say by water? Say . . .
When I kiss everyone goodbye
everyone says Be careful.
Yet I can't help thinking about that guy
who was forced to drink hemlock because
he wouldn't sit still. And sure enough,
this foot of mine misbehaves again,
heavy as the head of a hammer
against the pedal.

Not Dreaming

AT A FOOTBALL GAME, EARLY FALL

Don't tell me that this grandstand
isn't a solid disguise
for the ship that will take me away
from what must surely be illusory.

To see figures in gold and black,
with their bumps and grinds—
they are far too much of what they are
to be believed in. Already

beneath me the hull of this massive bark
heaves heavily to what I'm
told is starboard. And those other
bodies beyond the bumps and grinds—

don't tell me they are anything more than hulks
brilliant and anonymous
adrift on their way to drowning. And
don't tell me that always

there isn't another place arcadian
to be rowed to,
fronds and pistachios
and natives lining the shore,

their faces without speaking
saying Go away, saying
Welcome. Don't tell me
they are figments

of a windjammer's imagination. If so,
why is this grandstand
heaving heavily to starboard? And why am I
here, on this field of green and of fury,

beside you, not dreaming?

Separations

We'll see,
mother says,
meaning probably not,

meaning that the cowboy outfit
will either remain forever
on the catalog's slick page

or maybe what is worse
ride off into the sunset
on the body of the boy

whose mother said yes.
We'll see, mother says,
and I join her at the window

to watch my father
with his pitiful knapsack
become a flyspeck

at the center of the narrow
gravel road. Already
I am a full head taller

than my mother. Before long
I'll have a date, my first
with someone mother

will strongly disapprove of.
We'll see, she says,
her large eyes vacant

in the glass we strain to look
through, but
even as the words are spoken

the diminutive that was
my father
drops out of sight.

The Day the Earthquake Was
Scheduled to Happen but Didn't

I'm out in the back yard
filling the bird feeder,
looking off in the general direction

of the Missouri boondocks, where
the earthquake was scheduled to happen
but didn't,

when all at once a voice like a tremor
unsettles my ear, saying how
if I intend to have the sidewalks

shoveled clean before nightfall
I'd better stop dawdling,
I'd better remove the lead

from wherever I have it stashed
and shift my archaic frame
into a more productive gear,

so insofar as my constitution allows
I do just that,
but scoop as I may

I can't out-scoop the sundown,
meaning that I'm still rearranging snow
when a quarter-moon shows itself

glorious and albino
atop the horizon. So I take a break,
lean on the handle of the shovel

like a common laborer,
watch the moon in its rising
become a portable nest

for all those birds I hope one day
to be a part of
somehow among the branches

of the steadfast linden.

Non-Stop Begonias

Each morning I sit for one hour
in the sanctity of my back yard,
sipping black coffee and

studying the non-stop begonias.
That's what they're called, all right,
their large thin petals of white and pink

blooming non-stop as if the oriental blades
of some fair maidens' fans. It's
not a bad life, this

early-morning hour of concentration,
though yesterday when the clouds rolled in
I almost yielded,

raindrops more plentiful than moments
pelting the skin. But I stayed on. I
could sense a modicum of their secret

escaping into the dense electric air
from them to me,
and when the clouds gave way to blue

I stood full-length
without benefit of crutch or cane,
without crutch or cane I walked then

non-stop into any and everything it took
to bring me back to where
I am this morning.

On a Porch Swing Swinging

On a porch swing swinging
I watch a warm
Indian-summer moon

give way to the long and
sudden shadows of evening.
From atop this well-tended

slope I follow a colt
on its way to horse
cavorting on an inland sea

of pasture. I imagine its
young haunches
bunching,

its young nostrils
flaring.
Between the yearling

and the swing where I am swinging
lies a crossroad,
and I think of the suicide

who might be buried there,
its grave like most of us
at last unmarked. Well,

life goes on and on, doesn't it,
the red on the bloom
of the flower

as if the blood that in
spite of frost
next year cannot be

stanched. The sun meanwhile
yields to the moment,
that temporary power.

On a porch swing swinging
I watch what darkness has
to offer. Inhaling deeply,

I close my eyes. Look:
no matter how fully
all of you disappear,

I see you.

||||||||||||||||||||||||||||||||||||||||||||||||||||||||||||||||||||||||||||||||||||

After the Drunk Crushed My Father

what was left
wasn't much,
certainly not the automobile,

its brown body
inert
in a state of hunkered and

twisted shock, or
later the house, that shoebox,
or its bread and water

furnishings. But
something has to be
taken from death

to keep death
from taking everything,
so I select the rocker

my father upon his father's death
selected, one
half cherry wood, the other half

blood and knuckles and baling
wire, the man
who restores it speaking

with a thick Bavarian accent. Without
so much as the trace
of a boast

he says he knows by Jesus his
onions—which he does,
the rocker emerging too pure

to be altogether feasible. So
I'll have to work at it,
work at believing that

not only does it now exist
pristine and solid,
but that its existence

matters. Who, after all,
cares? Yet I think
I remember grandfather sitting

in this rocker, thick arms
working an accordion
whose bellows leaked considerable

air. Singing, I think it was,
shall we gather
at the river? He too was German

with a Dutchman's accent. And
his son, my father:
dead the officer surmised

before the Dodge came to rest
on its top, how
it lay there

heavy with its heavy internals
exposed, lay there
on the curve of its top

like the cradle in that
dead poet's poem
so endlessly rocking.

Treehouse

Through the kitchen window
I watch two boys
high in a black walnut

complete a treehouse
left to them by other renters
who last week loaded their blue

Apache and were
gone. They had
come to the neighborhood

as newlyweds,
had constructed the platform,
they said, as a high-rise extension

of their honeymoon. And
on more than several nights
I heard their voices

carrying clearly down,
syllables laced with laughter,
with the clinking of glasses. So

much for April into late September.
Now an Indian summer,
like the boys themselves,

has begun to happen,
and through both the window
and a falling of early-evening leaves

I can see their silhouettes at work,
hammers at the ends of anxious arms
tapping a muffled code

I think I'm at the edge of breaking.
Into a goblet I pour myself
the rough equivalent

of a Shirley Temple. O my life
now has an order and a plan:
to stand here sipping and watching

until the full moon rises, until
with its light it opens the door
the boys will have closed and with a cob

secured. But I am neither here nor there,
neither building nor leaving
town. And though already

I am dead on my feet
I have the dead's advantage.
I have all night.

||||||||||||||||||||||||||||||||||||||||||||||||||||||||||||||||||||||||||||||||||||||

Singing Hymns with Unitarians

The Unitarian sings with a mouth
almost closed,
words from Jefferson and Thoreau

streaming in a duality of breath
neither hot nor cold
from the Unitarian's transcendental

nostrils. And it is not possible
to be among the congregation
without loving both the creator

and the creation. In the beginning
didn't all of us begin? And
doesn't that include the hummingbird

feeding at that fleck of purple
flowerhead in the stained-
glass window?

I open my mouth to chew at words
already chewed
by a raft of ancestors.

The hummingbird too grows fat
on its own deception. When all of this
is finished, will anything matter?

The word on the papyrus page?
The note at the wing of the bird
as it lifts away?

|||||||||||||||||||||||||||||||||||||||||||||||||||||||||||||||||||||||||||||||||||||||

A City Waking Up

An early-morning shower
softens the sounds
of a city waking up,

south wind moving the leaves,
moving the raindrops
into the leaves,

and for a long morning
I lie in bed
on a wide white sheet

thinking of rain, thinking
of others and what others
thought of rain,

grandmother washing her hair
in rainwater
caught in a galvanized tub,

Father with a funnel
pouring rainwater
into the cells of the battery

in the Model-T, itinerant preacher
back home on impulse, or perhaps
goaded by some holy tine,

leading his flock outside
and into the eye of a gullywasher,
there to perform a wholesale act

of baptism, all eyes skyward but
closed, sprinkling and immersion
taking each worshipper down

to essential bone. And that legend
of W. C. Fields on his
last boozy legs,

reading the Bible, *looking,* as he
said, *for loopholes,*
praying he'll die to the sound

of rain on the rooftop. And
how the prayer was answered,
thanks to friends

who joined the garden hose
to compassion. And
of Wendell Berry

on his homestead in Kentucky,
writing of rain, writing
especially of rain after drought,

calling his waking late at night
to the pattering of rain
My sweetness. And

it's my sweetness, too, this
early-morning shower
in early September,

a city waking up, school children
dumped from the bus
like so many hilarious crustaceans,

my body adrift on a river of bed
going south to the sea
going nowhere.

Covenant

Here is the story I might have heard,
        more likely dreamed: the woman
                after the first trimester

required by village covenant
        to compose a lullaby,
                to sing it daily then

to the gathering child, only
        from memory and in deliberate
                isolation,

the man not permitted to listen
        until the infant had been delivered
                and pronounced both whole and

welcome. And this is a ritual
        I'd go to church to live with,
                solace in the belief

that not so very far away
        always a woman sits singing her own
                creation

to that small creation breathing
        as if a delicate fish inside her,
                always not so far away

a confluence of word and of music
        flowing somehow into the ear
                of the unborn,

there to do whatever the inexplicable does
        to sustain us,
                my mother meanwhile who couldn't

carry a tune in a washtub
       singing as she carried the washtub
              outside to empty the rinsewater,

that same tub later
       filled with the well-wrung
              family wash, each item on the line

moving in the breeze
       like a quaint crustacean,
              each movement singing.

Learning the Drum

To hit something, almost anything,
       with a stick,
              to tap the stick

against the door of the granary,
       to open the door
              to enter the granary

to tap the stick against a wall
       to hear the sound
              more sharply define itself,

to inhale the yeast of the grain,
       to vary the length
              of the stick, its diameter,

to move from wood to whatever head
       reveals itself, that length
              of corrugated tin

blown last night from the roof
       of the henhouse,
              to tap the tin,

to find a companion stick,
       to try the tapping now
              with a stick in each hand,

to tap wood and tin until
       breathing itself
              becomes a cadence,

until the sticks can scarcely
       be distinguished
              from the fingers,

until the fingers become the sticks,
       fingers tapping skin,
              one's own skin

layered over bone, until this skin
       gives way to skin
              from other animals,

skin and snare beneath the drumhead
       speaking the language
              of fire, of water, of cave,

of whatever in this universe
       of flim and of flam it takes
              to keep us rolling.

⁞⁞

Rainfall

       . . . mercy drops 'round us are falling,
       but for the showers we plead.
       old hymn

When the clouds at last produce something more
than gray gloom

I follow my grandfather outside, and when he stops
between the granary and the henhouse

I stop, too, and when he reaches his speckled hand
to remove his brown felt hat

I reach for my hat, too, though I don't have one,
and gracious how cold the rain is,

how plentiful, my grandfather's face uplifted,
his old mouth in a smile

I do my best to imitate, because I believe I know
deeply what I don't,

how rainfall can relieve if not revive—not rain,
but rainfall, because

water doesn't mean shucks until it descends. So
here we stand, granary

with its coffeecan patches to our right, henhouse
with its damp and gathering congregation

to our left, beneath us dust becoming gumbo,
upon and into us

rainfall arriving at last, though arriving too late,
crops withered beyond redemption,

grandmother likewise, but even so I inhale
with my grandfather

that mix of soil and of moisture akin to something
else I'm ignorant of,

the effluvium of birth, so that for the moment
the scent is simply that

of soil and of moisture, grandmother meanwhile
lying parched on a leather duofold

beside a livingroom window, she perhaps
strong enough to see

beyond the window, perhaps alert enough
to remember the words

to the song I heard her whispering this morning
before the clouds rolled in,

mercy delinquent and insufficient, though just now
you wouldn't know it,

grandfather drenched to the bone, I drenched also
beside him,

holding in my hand the hat I never thought to bring,
neither of us dirty to start with,

both of us coming clean.

|||||||||||||||||||||||||||||||||||||||||||||||||||||||||||||||||||||||||||||||||||||

KTSW, Sunday Morning

After the Bluestem Roundup,
       after little Jimmy Dickens
              has sung the final line
                     of Me and My Teddy Bear,

I insert the jack that
       connects the Catholic Church—
              and don't ask me how it
                   happens,

but somewhere along the line
       I miscue the commercial,
              sending Patty-cake,
                   Patty-cake, Rainbow man

deep into the heart of Father
       Lightbody's homily.
              I write an X then
                   for each angry caller

until the number defies tabulation.
       Faithful listeners
              denounce me with names
                   I can't find even

in the Old Testament. What can
    I say? Time and again
        I turn the other cheek,
            each time remembering

that when push comes to shove
    this earth will belong
        to the meek. But
            I quiet the multitude

only by going off-duty. Because
    it's a warm April afternoon
        I drive to the prairie
            to count all those

lovely cattle that aren't mine.
    Who was it that said
        of Kansas, love a place
        like that, and

you can be content in a garden
    of sand? I am tempted
        to pray this person
            into the lowest corner

of perdition, but this day is much
    too immaculate to be
        wasted consecrating flicker
            at the expense of flame.

I therefore park my sky-blue Chevy
    at the side of an ancient
        rock fence where
            for the longest time

I listen to the theology of space—
    where no words exist
        to nail a message to, and
            where the hem of no garment

calls (as if calling finally matters)
    to be kissed.

Saturday Night

I walk out of Urie's barber shop
smelling like Urie's barber shop:
Sweet-Pea Talcum and Bay Rum.
I don't mention it to anyone,
but down in my heart
I know that tonight
I could have any girl in town.

Even so, I hurry home
where a garden hose hangs
from a limb on the Chinese elm.
Under a cold rope of water
I scrub until Urie's barber shop
soaks into the bunchgrass,
our only drain.

Another thirty minutes
and the orange sun will be long gone.
Windless. Now and again a leaf
the color of embarrassment
falling. Cicadas
high in a grandstand of branches
cheering me on. From
within a beehive of lather
Mind your own business! is what
I tell them.

I just want to be alone,
yet toweled and dressed
I go downtown—
to the corner booth in the drugstore,
where I sit and sit,
smelling of the powerful soap I used
to dispel the power of Urie's.
And though I don't want anything

of consequence to happen,
I watch the door beside
the rack of comics
closely,
waiting for it to happen.

||||||||||||||||||||||||||||||||||||||||||||||||||||||||||||||||||||||||||||||||||||||||

Last Visit

This nursing home stinks. Chicken
feathers. *Wet* chicken feathers.
My grandfather in blue overalls
sitting on the edge of an
unmade bed. My grandfather

looking up from the floor to see me
standing in front of him,
his mouth calling me by my brother's
name. John. My brother. Who
cut an artery many years ago

while swimming in a sandpit two miles
east of town. Red. O
red is the color of my brother's
blood. And spurt. Spurt
is what the blood does as it

leaves the artery. Behind his eyes
my grandfather seems to be thinking.
Spurt. I found the relevant
pressure point and applied
pressure. The spurt became a trickle,

a red thread down the fishbelly white
of my brother's arm. My grandfather
smiles. This nursing home stinks.
This southcentral Kansas nursing home
smells like feathers. Chicken

feathers. *Wet* chicken feathers. Chicken
hanging upside-down on the clothes-
line, chicken decapitated, chicken
soon to be scalded and plucked clean
and disemboweled and dismembered,

each member coated thickly with flour,
then skillet-fried and served
to a family too graciously alive
ever to be otherwise. My brother
white as flour from the loss of

blood. Red. O red is the color. And
my grandfather sitting in blue overalls
on the edge of an unmade bed
in this southcentral Kansas nursing home
that smells like wet feathers, that

stinks. John, he says, Johnny. Is that you?

||||||||||||||||||||||||||||||||||||||||||||||||||||||||||||||||||||||||||||||||||||||||||||||||||

Geese

I hear them honking
            before I see them,
                        a low-flying V

going wherever V's go
            when the sap in the ash
                        gives way to gravity.

And I am tempted to draw
            some natural-world
                        conclusion,

to say that the birds
            know something the rest
                        of us don't, and maybe

they do, though my mother
        at eighty-three
                takes her cue each year

from the first frost, she
        and her boyfriend then
                as if a skein of two

on the wing for Texas. So
        it seems to me that
                the natural world

and the other one
        considerably overlap.
                I hear them honking

before I see them, my mother
        and her boyfriend
                in a blue pickup

lifting off, the motion
        of my mother's out-
                stretched arm

as natural as any natural
        world can be
                in its act of going.

<hr />

Afternoon in October

About the only thing
        that interests me now,
                my father said then,

is the weather. The
        previous year he had
                given up on Scotch,

his nightly shot
        no longer helping him
                into sleep.

Shortly thereafter he took
        an additional pledge:
                no more left

turns. Ironic, isn't it,
        that the driver who
                killed him

was so supremely drunk
        it never occurred to him
                to brake left,

it never having earlier
        occurred to him
                to acknowledge the color

red. On a clear bright
        windless afternoon
                in late October

I sit alone on a pine-slatted
        bench, thinking about
                my father,

about what finally came
        to interest him,
                about those vows

he gave himself so briefly
        before that moment
                of prodigal

impact. And about time, how
        it means everything and
                nothing. At my right

a bur oak cannot contain its
        secret: it wants
                to be climbed into,

it wants me to detach myself
           to do the climbing,
                     it wants to hold me

as if the son that somehow
           slipped away
                     in the arms of its

dark and haunted branches.

|||||||||||||||||||||||||||||||||||||||||||||||||||||||||||||||||||||||||||||||||||||||||||||||||

Counting the Cows

Because earlier in the day I walked the fencelines
I know that none has escaped or wandered off,
and though I realize that should the count fall short

I'd have two options, count again or shrug my shoulders,
I go to the field to count them, anyway, knowing as I do
that counting is itself sufficient cause for counting,

something sweet in the accumulation, you understand,
and if the count should complement the ledger
how much sweeter then the effort. And if the count

falls short, as occasionally it does? Always I choose
to shrug the shoulders, my consolation more than equal
to potential loss, the credit being this: that I have

seen and have inhaled, at dusk, the lovely bulk of cow,
that its path returns no less than takes me away from
home. All of this is what my grandfather in the course

of an autumn morning more or less informs me. We are
in that room where grandmother died, her body at last
a fencepost under a hand-tied quilt. And before the sun

quite drops behind its hill I'll be moving in my father's
familiar Chevrolet, gravel pelting its underside
like the rain that so far not even prayer has been able

to induce. Dusk. At my left I see the darkening silhouettes
of grandfather's cows, their heads lowered as if ritual
into the occasional nourishment

of bunchgrass. One. Two. Three. All there, each cud
in a land of milk and of honey, you understand,
and accounted for.

||||||||||||||||||||||||||||||||||||||||||||||||||||||||||||||||||||||||||||||||||||||||||||

Church

My girlfriend scolds me
        because I lifted an offering plate
                from the Baptist church.

Tonight, the plate overflowing
        with fresh-buttered popcorn,
                we sit listening to the radio,

waiting for Joe Louis to say something
        before he climbs into the ring
                to throttle Tami Mauriello.

She asks, Why did you? She says,
        I don't want to have children
                with a common thief. How

can I explain to her my affinity
        for such well-turned mahogany?
                Not to mention

the sense of balance derived from
        taking out instead of
                putting in. When the popcorn

is almost gone I can see what I knew
        already, that the bottom
                of the plate is lined

with magenta felt. Two-thirds
    into the opening round
        Louis leaves Mauriello

senseless against the ropes. My girl
    sits straight-backed
        on the sofa, licking butter

from her salty lips. I pull a crumbled
    one-dollar bill from my pocket,
        drop it softly

into the plate. Eldonna, whose breasts
    are identical twins, shakes
        her head: she shall

not be purchased at any price. What
    I want to whisper into her
        delicate ear is what

I cannot muster the courage to whisper:
    Because I do not deserve to be
        forgiven, I ask only this:

forgiveness.

|||||||||||||||||||||||||||||||||||||||||||||||||||||||||||||||||||||||||||||||||||||||||||||||||

Sustaining the Curse

> Rona, a woman who may have lived
> on the shore of the Kaipara Harbor,
> went to get water because her children
> were crying at night. The moon
> disappeared behind a cloud and Rona
> cursed it because she stumbled in the
> darkness—so the moon came down
> and took her up into the sky, where
> she is still to be seen on its face.
>
> *Maori legend*

And still to be heard are those cries
from so many bewildered children,

many of them nonetheless destined to
survive. Rona, you were right to have cursed

but wrong to have cursed the moon.
Did the moon obscure itself? No,

it was the cloud that provided the
obfuscation—or, if not the cloud,

the breeze from the west that
moved the cloud, or the low-pressure

belt just off the shoreline that
shaped the breeze that blew the cloud

that obscured the moon. Even so, moon
in its loftiness should have seen

what you were about, what you intended,
in turn should have done whatever

moon might do to enlighten. But no,
moon takes you instead to its face,

giving you life everlasting while
so many bewildered children lie

crying for water. Well, let them
cry. Let many of them survive. And let

some of these in their own eventual
darknesses sustain the curse.

Welcome to Carlos

Don't blame Carlos for having been raised
          south of the tracks. South
          or north, he is his

mother's son, and his father's, his mother a
          hanger-up-of-clothes, his father a
          gandy-dancer on the

Panhandle Division of the Atchison, Topeka
          & Santa Fe. From the beginning
          Carlos knew more than

he knew. Knew how to sing before the advent
          of song, how to read before
          movable type. Carlos

could rhyme anything from hell to breakfast,
          from Kansas to Timbuktu.
          Knew the power that

derives from position. Shit, cried the King,
          Carlos said, and 80,000 subjects
          lowered their trousers and

squatted abjectly above the burning sand.
          Knew how to talk out of only
          one side of his mouth.

Knew how to spell Deuteronomy. Knew how to
          whistle long, long before his
          vermilion lips

had come of age.

Stuka

The word for the long long moment is Stuka.
 When Carlos says it,
 Germans drop like fallen angels
 from a blue sky made cumulus with flak.

He makes a song of it: Stuka, Stuka,
 hallelujah! Stuka, Stuka,
 hallelujah! Stuka, Stuka,
 hallelujah! The Krauts are coming in!

Because I am my German grandmother's German
 grandson, I don't know
 whether to attack or surrender,
 defecate or go blind.

But there is something undeniably mysterious
 in Stuka that not even
 bloodline can deny, so I
 acknowledge it for what it is: language,

with its mix of melody and of connotation.
 Stuka. Carlos says it,
 and together we watch the Germans
 fill the sky as if an ostentation

of poppies. Stuka. Carlos says it. On
 the screen it moves
 like a bad lovely bird
 into the maw of a Flying Tiger.

Stuka. Carlos says it. Language. Union
 of melody and of connotation.
 Like Lucifer. Like
 Mephisto. Like Tubert Cook,

who sits on the bench in front of the pool hall
 singing the song
 of his own demise, song
 of the black-pigmented tumor, melanoma.

Home

When Carlos and I on impulse run away from home
        we spend the first few days
        of the rest of our days
        rejoicing. Over and over
        I hum the chorus of Just a Closer Walk with Thee.
        Carlos clicks the heels of his cordovans
        until their spit-shines ripple
        like the surfaces of wind-blown ponds.

Carlos says, We must walk in the direction
of timber and moving water.

Rejoicing gives way to thanks, thanks to silence,
        silence to doubt, doubt to action,
        action to affirmation.
        We grow fat in the larders
        of others' abundance, redundant
        among the sudden walls of canyons,
        humble in a lost and relentless
        minimum of shade.

Bare feet hanging cool in the Lake of Forgetfulness
        we forget. On the Primrose Path
        we stop to smell the roses. When
        we hear the Sirens singing
        we sing, guarding our distance.

Carlos says, We must walk in the direction
of timber and moving water.

We arrive in time to build with sun-bleached branches
        the raft of our dreams, poling it then
        upstream
        on the River of No Return.

Gypsy Rose

Drunk Carlos is, am I, on Gypsy Rose,
       it having arrived as if the sweetest manna when
       just west of town the freight derailed—
       Carlos on the scene, as he himself confessed,
       as if spontaneous combustion in reverse, Carlos
       with bottles of Gypsy Rose
       fulfilling his arms, Carlos stashing the honeydew
       in moonshadow behind Urie Detweiler's tombstone—

ah, drunk Carlos is, am I, Carlos having
       become his brother's keeper keeping me, leading
       me to the cemetery, to the manna
       cached in moonshadow behind a tombstone, Urie's,
       Urie the barber who in his other life
       had steadied his razor-hand with bourbon—

ah, drunk Carlos is, am I, time depleted,
       the moon in stasis, eternity here
       in a nutshell, and more where this
       came from, Carlos says, cases of Gypsy Rose
       blooming the weeds on the right-of-way,
       unfortunate, Carlos says, yet fortunate, because,
       Carlos says, for every assertion

there is an equal and opposite retraction, Gypsy
       Rose aromatic as the exploding of sulphur
       and potassium nitrate, as sweet on the tongue
       as the kiss that has yet to happen. Ah,
       this is my maiden trek into the limberlost,
       meaning that my inebriation is the novelty
       I enjoy but don't precisely know yet

how to handle, ingest, manipulate, Carlos
       with his back against the tombstone
       reciting a litany of grape—*fill the cup*
       and *be merry with the fruitful grape* and
       fill me with the old familiar juice—until
       our small community of bones

rises to the rare occasion, rises like
> those bones we sing about in church becoming
> connected, ah yes, Urie up from his slumber
> to toast the night, as Carlos says,
> with a shot of rotgut, Carlos
> in moonshadow with his back against the tombstone,

Carlos speaking of his father who soon
> will do his part to return the tracks to what
> they were before the fall occurred,
> will do his best to keep those rails as God
> and the Santa Fe intended them to be, ah yes,
> like all of us, together.

‖‖

Back Roads

In his Church of the International
> I travel the back roads
> with Carlos because, Carlos says,
> if you don't know where you're going,
> any road can take you there.

We arrive sometimes here, sometimes there,
> sometimes some place in between.
> Tonight it's old man Simpson's pond,
> where thanks to an accommodating dusk
> we catch a bullfrog the size of mercy
> to garnish the largemouth bass.

In an iron skillet over an open flame
> we cook the white, white flesh
> of the fish, legs of the bullfrog
> dancing their spastic dance.
> A quarter-moon rocks in the limbs
> of a honey locust, Venus
> on its own long limb
> attending. It is a privilege
> to be here, Carlos says, apropos
> of everything.

He will say it again on our way home.
                He will have slowed his Church
                of the International to a stop
                at the side of the road,
                not only to inhale the night,
                not only to hear the voice of the turtle,
                but to confess that sometimes
                not even a triumvirate of tools is sufficient
                to the closing of a deep-enough fissure.
                Because now both of the pickup's headlights
                will have gone dead, leaving us
                with only the sheen of a quarter-moon.

How wonderfully human the human voice can be
                when nothing more than a natural world
                obtrudes. We will listen to each other,
                and to our silences, until the quarter-moon
                tugs us slowly home, growl in the throat
                of the Church of the International
                akin to prayer.

Balls

The rumor is that Carlos' father
has taught himself to weld,
and with the knowledge
came a swift promotion. Carlos
shrugs. Now his father in overalls
does the family shopping
with a black igniter
swinging from the hammer loop.
He carries the bulging sack
home across the tracks
in silence,
one boot in front of the other,

and except for the igniter
swinging as if keeping time
this universe
unchanged.

And rumor has it that Carlos' father
is thinking of moving the family
to that open acreage just north
of the high school. Balls. You can
charge that one to the dust, Carlos says,
and let the rain settle it.

|||||||||||||||||||||||||||||||||||||||||||||||||||||||||||||||||||||||||||||||||||||||||||||

The Great Depression

In the treehouse at dusk
        I finger the old Barlow that
        earlier in the day
        I swapped with my buddy Carlos
        sight-unseen for.

The blade is dull,
        but you can bet not half as dull
        as the blade on the old Barlow that
        my buddy Carlos
        earlier in the day received
        sight-unseen from me.

When before long total darkness
        settles among the branches
        I'll trade even-up with God:
        my belief in Him
        for grit enough
        to outlast indeterminate sorrow.

Now here's another unlikely deal,
        thanks to this Great Depression:
        my sister sent away to Timbuktu
        to live with Grandma.

Tonight the moon will be a perfect
            half. I know this because
            last night it so nearly was.
            I watched it climb on wavering rungs
            until my neck no less
            than the lower half of me
            could not stop aching.

Eventually a cloud will obscure this moon,
            eventually a west wind (guttural
            against invisible leaves, my suddenly
            lonely mother's lonely voice) will
            insist: One day
            you'll look back at this and wonder
            why in the world you ever created
            such a terrible fuss.

A west wind rises.
            I count by ones
            until all of the numbers are gone,
            then I count again.

‖‖

Revival

At his request I go with Carlos to the tent revival
            to watch him, at his request,
            not being saved.

Sister Hook is a barrel with enormous eyes. Closed,
            they drop tears the size of marbles
            as her gargantuan throat erupts:
            O love of God, how rich, how pure,
            how measureless and strong . . .

Following Carlos' lead, I ease off my shoes, my socks,
            wriggle my bare toes
            in an aromatic heft of sawdust. When
            personal testimonies are invited, Carlos

abstains. Last week, a paucity of onlookers
at the grave, Carlos watched his father
descend into red compacted dirt. High
noon. Glare at the center of a distant
tombstone. Seems strange, doesn't it,
Carlos had whispered, that sun and death
should travel together.

Sister Hook's contralto refuses to take wing. It
hums with the August breeze
against the guylines. *It shall*
forevermore endure the saints' and angels'
songs . . .

A scroll twice the size of my classroom's blackboard
depicts in elemental colors
the past, the present, the future,
Sister Hook with a length of sumac
pinpointing successive disasters—
from The Fall at the far left
to Armageddon at the right. I
wriggle my toes in sawdust. A dam bursts,
and blood flows against our horses' fetlocks,
rises to touch their bellies, rises
to tarnish the silver on the bits of their bridles.

Seven becomes an incremental repetition: seven vials,
seven dooms, seven kings.
It is not easy to detect where the litany
ends and the song begins—visions,
bowls of wrath, fornication, Babylon,
frogs and dragons, Gog and Magog, chariots,
slaves, fire and brimstone, harlots
and abominations, fowls filled with the flesh
of false prophets and their armies—these
without benefit of transition join *My sins*
have been cast in the depths of the sea,
down deep in the sea, marbles again

from the closed eyes of Sister Hook,
until the eyes open and the litany
returns—brass and iron, scarlet and silk,
gold and silver, stones, ointments, flour,
oil, frankincense, wine, beasts, wheat, sheep,
cinnamon—and I can smell it, but it isn't
cinnamon, it is instead a fine mist, prelude
to rain, brought into the tent by a gathering
southern breeze, and I reach down
to secure a handful of sawdust: ashes
to ashes, the preacher at Carlos' father's
grave-side service had said, dust to dust,
and he released whatever it was he
imagines he held in his hand, watched it
fall on the lid of the coffin, Carlos' father
in his earlier life not having looked up
in time to take warning from the green board,
not seeing then the engine until it was too late,
his fellow gandydancers down track with the motorcar,
his body reduced to a rag at the edge
of a stubblefield, his right hand
gripping the torch whose hiss
would have negated any shouting
intended to save him.

When an invitation to come forward to be saved is extended,
    Carlos declines. We wriggle our toes
    in the sawdust. Thunder and lightning and
    rainfall add their drama to a scenario
    of tent-contained mayhem. Carlos grins.

Sister Hook exhorts, weeps, with knuckles on a plump fist
    knocks at the black door
    of her Bible, sings: *so deep*
    they shall never be brought against me,
    down deep in the sea. At the altar
    tongues of fire prevail, glossolalia
    with an occasional interpretation: in my

father's mansion are many rooms. Carlos
in his milk-white shirt, his tan washpants,
perfectly pressed, sits upright on his
wood-slatted chair, feet in sawdust, face
with its light-brown skin at peace, it seems,
with its bones. Thunder and lightning and
rain—these three, but the greatest of these
is rain. When the final invitation
finally is offered, Carlos
declines.

At Simpson's pond we sit by the fire that because we
        don't need it we
        desperately desire. Thunder
and lightning and rain—these three,
but the greatest of these is their
absence. Moon the size, more or less,
of Sister Hook's face. On a field of ebony
stars too numerous to matter.

Carlos breaks out his banjo, tells me that not being saved
        is at last the only salvation.
        In the far, far distance the long, long dissonance
of a train. Carlos says, My father
was more than a decent man. Fire
to a fish, he says. Amigo! How
do you ever explain?

||||||||||||||||||||||||||||||||||||||||||||||||||||||||||||||||||||||||||||||||||||||||||

Reap the Wild Wind

In the drugstore
Josephine mixes, according to Carlos,
the thickest malts
west of the Mississippi, her helpmate
meanwhile in a back room
filling prescriptions,

some of them legal. Because Doc,
according to Carlos,
is the local bootlegger, this town
being drier, Carlos says,
than a popcorn fart.

We take our drinks with us to the movie,
popcorn and Susan Hayward equally
bittersweet. Popcorn. Josephine malt.
Druscilla Alston. Giant squid. Ray
Milland. John Wayne and a bitter-
sweet ending.

Which later somehow compels me to take Carlos
another step into my chamber of haunts:
Yesterday my father laid hands on my mother.
There was, I tell him,
some blood on the dashboard.

And so forth. After which we return
to the drugstore, Josephine gone, Doc
with a glass, his accomplice,
at the Bally.

And so forth. When we leave, Carlos says,
Amigo, if you need anything, just
give me a whistle. If I can't find it,
I'll teach you how to live
without it.

Carlos heads south, I north.

Quixotic

Carlos reads books whose pages come to him, he says,
        on the wings of small birds,
        on the unassuming backs of turtles.

Tonight he sits in a booth in the Tumbleweed Cafe,
        tilting at windmills, Susanne
        by way of absence

having become his lovely Dulcinea. In her honor
        he has ordered that the Tumbleweed—
        den of iniquity—

close its doors until further notice, those days
        between the closing and the notice
        to be devoted to a myriad

of purgings. I meanwhile order a hot-beef sandwich
        and a schooner of cold milk.
        Not far away a Coca-Cola clock

ticks down the seconds. When no one closes the doors
        Carlos turns the page. He looks up
        to tell me this and that

about Susanne, her hopes, her dreams, her potential
        whereabouts, her perfectly questionable
        rationale for being

elsewhere. When no one closes the doors we do so
        ourselves, leaving behind the clock-
        worn faces of regular customers.

Soon we are standing in the drugstore beside the Bally,
        waiting for Doc with his whisky
        to redeem the day. Carlos

touches the machine as if its form were substance
        recently restored, and human. In young man-
        hood, as in knighthood, Carlos says,

there are ways of adjusting everything.

Circus

With a flat-bed truck and a logchain
        Simpson retrieves the black International,
        it having gone to the bottom of the pond
        when an unexpected thermal
        turned deep ice into deeper water.

With Carlos I rub dry cotton towels
        against head and plug, crankshaft
        and sprocket, breather, belt and rim
        until behold! our Church
        of the International shines again.

After which Carlos pumps each zerk to over-
        flowing with blue-black grease
        from a silver gun. And the miracle
        is not that the pickup glistens,
        but that when the key to the kingdom
        is turned by the healing hand of Carlos
        the kingdom runs.

Did I mention that Simpson, they say, is not
        quite all there? Yet
        he seems complete enough
        when we find him
        where we knew he'd be,
        in the pool hall playing
        dominoes—Thanks, oldtimer,
        adios, cruel world, we're off
        to join the circus!—and winning.

Limits

We would indeed join the circus. We
      therefore drive the ledges
      of our universe. But
      there's a limit, Carlos says,
      to the International. Call it
      gas. Call it tiretread. Call it
      the grim infinitudes of carburetion.

Beyond the village limits, and above,
      a canopy of stars
      becomes, in total silence,
      the Main Event. Clowns
      break, in total silence, their
      balloons. Barkers hush. Women
      wearing next to nothing
      disappear with quiet dignity
      into a silver gathering of mist.

Sunrise is what happens when clouds
      permit the sun to rise. Sun
      rising, sun overhead, sun
      going down—

and we have joined the circus, Carlos says,
      by coming back to town.

Giddy

It's the promise of another Spring
      that does it—sap, audacious, rising—
      and I too rise
      to stand with Carlos
      between the depot and the hell-for-breakfast freight,
      each counting the cars, each

becoming giddy on heft and momentum
and the relentless clickety-clack,
each inhaling the hiss
left hanging from a volatile engine,
until drunk on the swift bouquet of power
we sway with the swaying of the platform
until direction is anyone's opinion,
until moments before we free-fall to oblivion
silence mightily descends: Goodbye, caboose,
goodbye man on the receding moon,
goodbye, goodbye, and

hello, skeins of geese, Carlos and I transported
　　　to anybody's pasture, Carlos on his back
on the hood of the International,
its windshield his pillow, I on my back
on dollops of reviving bunchgrass,
overhead a blue sky vast and bottomless,
geese too plentiful to count
in dark cirrus lines
waving in slow motion, and inveterate, one
into and after another, I giddy
on height and perpetual slowness
and the aroma undeniable
of weightlessness, this body
inebriate on promise, on what
must surely lie—as surely as
Carlos and I are lying—somewhere
beyond us.

||||||||||||||||||||||||||||||||||||||||||||||||||||||||||||||||||||||||||||||||||||||||||

Sand Creek

With its name Sand Creek speaks truth:
　　　Creek Made of Sand. Yet when dark clouds
gather, and rain descends, and day
into night into day evolves a pattern,

Sand Creek becomes the river we cannot
stay away from, Carlos with his would-be paddle
in the bow, I with my would-be rudder
in the stern.

In our would-be canoe we read the river,
would-be prow as if a prophet
parting water. Carlos says, No way
that can be charted is the way, and
I catch his drift: Sand Creek, thanks
to a sudden drop and a large prodigal rock,
describes an arc over the flora and the fauna
of the pasture, water swift and clean and cold,
temptation far too great not to be dipped up
to be scoured with.

Sand Creek speaking truth admonishes truth:
Except for the banjo in Carlos' hands,
we are standing naked and ankle-deep in sand
in moving water, ebbing current
bringing forth the knees. Yellow sun
in a blue sky. Meadowlark on a fencepost
surfing its repertoire of five falsettos. And
what we know is what we do not say—that
this brief rush is what we have in lieu of water
ever rushing. And the pure contiguous notes
from Carlos' banjo, how they drift like bodies
weightless over the mows of barns and their sweet
sweet clover. Tell me: How can we tell the shoreline
from the shore?

Now the channel that is the serpent's spine
returns to its bed of shifting sand. Tell me:
Who is the voice behind the voice
I have lived my life thus far to hear? When
anything is added to the cup already full,
the cup runs over.

Dirt

Carlos says, Never pull Superman's cape
       or relieve yourself into the wind.
       Compost, he says, is a rotten idea
       that works. Carlos says—because
       now and again
       he catches a flatcar out of town—
       When you spend a lot of time
       in one place, one place
       spends a lot of time in you.

Believe, Carlos says, what you believe
       late at night when what
       you have been told to believe
       has washed itself from the soft skin
       of your stoutest face. When you
       kill time, turn yourself in. When
       the turnkey turns, escape
       to fight another day. Learn
       to shit fire, then
       share your savings with the poor.

Carlos says, Learn how to make optimum use
       of etcetera. He says, Go forth
       and do likewise,
       stay home and cultivate your garden.
       When a rabid Baptist
       chases you up a tall, tall tree,
       enjoy the view. The dead, Carlos says,
       get by with everything. So
       this is my, Carlos says, goal:
       To be worthy of dirt.

Departures

Under moonglow I have sleepwalked
   to stand on the platform adjoining the depot,
   there to count the cars on the impending freight.
   Soon enough it lumbers into the station,
   squealing like the hog it is and
   needing water.

I stand adrift in a fog of hiss and
   dream. Beyond the tracks, Carlos sleeps, or
   should be sleeping,
   his nomadic mind gathering the silent wool
   he'll fashion into a shroud
   of redemptive sound. Why then
   through that narrow scrim between cars
   do I believe I see him spic and span
   moving toward me? And why, if I am
   seeing him, does he not see me?

Hiss and steam, steam into dream. One.
   Two. Three. Before I went to school I could
   count to ten. AT&SF. Sixseveneight. Slow
   blur. Slim shape. Brief shadow. I lose count
   long before the caboose with its signifying light
   no longer signifies.

I stoop to draw a circle around me
   within which I'll stand until the dense air
   clears, then break the circle
   to dreamwalk back to where
   I'll try to believe, when the dream comes true,
   I came from.

Pennies

It's always the bad penny, Carlos says,
        that returns,
        and what returns as I stand here
        looking down at Carlos
        are Carlos' words, those spoken
        and those left silent to be inferred from,
        meaning that sometimes the good penny, too,
        comes back to disenchant the bad,
        meaning that because Carlos lived to whistle
        I too can whistle,
        that because Carlos knew the value of the word
        I too can hope to overthrow the tyranny of mute.

Carlos is dead. I speak the words as,
        standing here above him,
        I know enough not to believe them.
        Carlos is dead. I see him
        catching that slow freight heading west,
        see him doing whatever the body does
        when it's not deceiving. Somewhere
        someone not visible sings
        A mighty fortress is our God. When
        I touch Carlos' hand it touches mine.
        The moment sits blatant with consolation:
        Those tracks that bright as coins carry out
        carry in.

Song

Bullfrog, bunchgrass, catfish, carp.
Play it with your banjo,
play it on your harp.

If harp means harmonica
the boy will not object
should he be sent
to Heaven. Meanwhile, he
baits a treble hook with liver,
sends the blood-red blob
singing like a sweet soprano
into the water.

Sunset, moonrise, midnight, dawn.
Play it with a grassblade
on your pennywhistle tongue.

Leaving rod and reel to their own devices
the boy, believing
he has music inside him,
positions a grassblade
on his tongue,
spends most of the rest of the day
looking for a possible tune.

And in the tent at night, in the pale moonlight,
you can hear those bullfrogs serenading,
do re mi.

Snagging the bullfrog is not as easy
as some might believe. Dangle
slowly a small feathered lure
in front of the bullfrog's snout.
Shake it. Hope he'll take it
in the blink of an eye
into the cavern of his mouth.

And in the tent at night, in the pale moonlight,
me and my best friend,
Norma Jean.

In back of the tent, behind a cedar,
warm pecker in a cold hand,
the boy would memorize something
to retain the moment: cluster
of stars, nighthawk, shadows
on a three-quarter moon.
Tomorrow, maybe, he'll tell her
one of the many remarkable things
he has learned.

‖‖

Flannel

Are these tall leafless stems
here in a marshy overflow
bulrushes? Moses,
sweet baby, where are you?

In Sunday-school
our teacher depicted Bible stories
on a flannelboard, perhaps
without intending it
suggesting that what cannot
be represented visually and with flannel
does not exist. Moses exists
because in flannel he lies
in a flannel crib that sits
half hidden among
tall leafless stems of flannel
that bespeak existence. Yellow
the flannel face of Moses, white
the flannel crib, brown the many
flannel leafless stems. Blue, then,

the flannel cutout that
makes a reality of sky.

Something about a baby lying in a crib
half sunk in marshwater
squeezed at the heart, squeezing intensified
when the flannel form of Pharaoh
appeared on the board, off to one side
yet walking toward the rushes,
flannel baby and flannel badass
on their way to a deadly
flannel confrontation.

I part the tall stems
not to discover the hidden baby
but instead to select a dozen rushes
to form a bouquet
I'll place in a bottle to place on a stump
to dignify the campsite.

With flannel our teacher
could breathe the breath of life
into almost anything: camel, shepherd,
prodigal, wise man, Mary, sheep,
oxen, Gabriel, Jonah, samaritan, Daniel
and the lion and the lion's den.
There seemed to be no bottom
to her well of flannel. And when
she took away the scene
behold! the scene
somewhere among the bulrushes
somehow remained.

When eventually we circle the fire
to wait for that moment

when the coffee declares itself
finished
I can see through dancing flames
bulrushes dancing. Moses,
sweet baby, where are you? The sky
is a dark flannel sea of bright flannel
stars, beyond them
in flannel not yet cut and placed
the promise of an end to parting.

|||||||||||||||||||||||||||||||||||||||||||||||||||||||||||||||||||||||||||||||||||||||||||||||||||||||

Bushmill

Irish whiskey for the Padre
and by the time guitar and banjo
have been fine-tuned

Padre's feet, with Padre above them,
have begun their dancing,
a jig that Padre calls Irish

improvisation—whiskey meanwhile
finding its way
from one flamelit face to another,

finding its way back then
to the one who offered it,
bottle in one hand, cigar

in the other, feet in rapid
and precise improvisation
around the fire and

around again, guitar and banjo
joined now by harmonica
to augment the fever— *O*

*you don't shake it like you
used to*—Padre quivering
like a Pentecostal dervish,

like a fellow with the heebie-jeebies,
like he has sure enough
ants in his Bushmill pants,

but grinning all the while
like a sophomore, like a gopher,
like if he had a brain

he'd have good sense,
like he'd like to disagree
by way of these contortions

with the words of the tune— *O
you don't shake it like you
used to*

anymore—until the song's sudden
ending seems to startle Padre,
to bring him up short

as if a hidden wire
meant to trip him,
and he falls not into but

over the fire, his body an arch
over the coals,
Bushmill in one hand, cigar

in the other, body a bridge
in stasis absorbing heat,
marking time,

body that when a fresh tune begins
like a Johnny-jump-up
jumps up,

unscathed and free and loose
as Andy the rag doll
out of its cradle,

yet rocking.

Song

Man with the Martin
sings softly to an audience
of warmflesh and firelight:

> *Get back to the well*
> *every now and then,*
> *when your spirit is dry*
> *and your mind is growing dim . . .*

How old was I
when as a boy I
lay on my belly
on cold concrete
drinking water
rising from God
knows where: how
old was I then?

It was a spring house
whose spring-fed water
flowed into a creek
that fed into a pond
that provided water
for cattle and horses,
catfish and carp and
unbelievable turtles,
some of them snappers,
all of them at one
time or another
rising to the surface of my
occasional dream:
how old was I then?

Man with the Martin
sings softly to an audience
of owlcall and starshine:

>*You don't have to run*
>*with the Joneses,*
>*whoever the Joneses*
>*might be . . .*

Who knows or cares
who owned and managed
the spring house,
whose cattle and horses
drank at the spring-fed
pond? Their names
no less than their land
have been sold
to the highest bidder,
and so on.

That long afternoon
when with nightcrawlers
I caught the world's
largest catfish
I couldn't stop
talking, *Jesus Christ*
my only mark
of punctuation. When
later, ready
to call it a day,
I hauled in the stringer
to see only bones
and distended eyes
on a huge head mostly mouth,
I couldn't say anything
more than *turtle.* There
wasn't anything
more to say.

Man with the Martin
sings softly to an audience
of tincup and ashglow:

> *And you begin to think*
> *it's time your time has come.*
> *Get back to the well*
> *from where your spirit has come.*

On the way home
I stopped again
at the spring house
to drink the cold
running water. As
I drank I looked far
down to see the shining
pebbles the water
seemed to be rising
from, looked harder
then to see what might
lie beyond. Source, I
thought. And I thought,
Where does the source
of the first source
come from?

Many times as a boy I kicked
the same rock
all the way
from the spring house
to the back door
of my backwoods home.
And there was magic
in the rock and
in the kicking and
in the clean running

water as I lay on cold
cement in the spring
house drinking, magic
too in warmflesh and
firelight, owlcall and
starshine, tincup and
ashglow: as a boy
how old am I now? Christ
Jesus! How old
was I then?

‖‖

Instrumental

At the moment it's *All in G*
on the banjo, notes
precise, cat-quick and clean
sent out and up
to whatever has ears to listen.

Without words the message
makes consummate sense,
without words no tower
with its forked, dissenting
tongues babbling.

Maybe this is pretty much
the way it was meant to be,
if anything is,
melody the sole arbiter
leveling pride and prejudice,

spite and greed, deceit and
inhibition. O brothers and sisters!
In the beginning was the word
restrained, its deadly decipherings
on hold until the music stops

and the word like the snake it
so often is
returns.

Requiem

The leaves on the fallen cottonwood
are lime,
in my mouth a tartness
like the juice from the
quickened pace of time.

I stand beside the river
on a patch of solid earth
beside a sapling
stout as a farm boy's arm,
above me a gathering of branches
deciphering the wind:

> *from the moment*
> *of our first rising up*
> *we are*
> *falling down.*

Catfishing

Catfishing on the Loup
I land a Gideon Bible
dry and secure
inside the miracle
of a plastic Ziploc bag.

Is my dark-eyed brother the sweet
peckerhead responsible? He says, No.
He says that his innocence, behold,
runs whiter than the driven snow.

One of my sons asks the following:
What did you use for bait? Blood?
Chicken guts? Liver? I tell him:
nightcrawler.

That evening, near a campfire,
we indulge Virgilian lots,
opening the Bible at random
and, with eyes diverted,
pinpointing a verse: *And
Jesus said, leave her alone.
Why troublest thou her? She
hath wrought on me a good thing.*

Around midnight the other son
returns to the fire
holding high a four-pound
channel, its long body
luminous in a glow of cottonwood coals.

It was Mary of Bethany, someone says,
who sacrificed a portion
of costly ointment,
with it anointing the head of Jesus.
And why not? Soon he
would be sacrificed and, unlike the poor,
there would not be another
to replace him. He said so himself.

I open another beer. I ask my son,
What variety of bait
enticed the channel? Liver?
Chicken gut? Nightcrawler? He tells me:
Gideon.

Someone stirs the coals to life
with a short length
of honeylocust. It came
from the same indifferent tree
I'll happen upon

in the morning, brisk hike
in dubious combat with a hangover.
It'll be that branch just over there:
I'll see it as the walking-stick
one day I'll lean on,
thorns on its white wood
sanded smoothly to freckles,
and I'll touch them with the reverence
that comes each night
when the last of the fire is gone.

||||||||||||||||||||||||||||||||||||||||||||||||||||||||||||||||||||||||||||||||||||||||||

Woodshed

Tonight my brother, high
on sobriety,
improvises another verse
to add to those other verses
improvised by others:

> *Now Larry had a sister,*
> *The sister's name was Nan.*
> *When Larry smacked his sister,*
> *He took his whuppin' like a man.*

Tonight my brother sings
like the wolf must have sung
on its way to naming the river,
my brother's voice
like the voice of the wolf
unrepentant because untamed.

> *Take your whuppin' like a man, boy.*
> *Take your whuppin' like a man.*
> *Get your ass on down to the woodshed*
> *And take your whuppin' like a man.*

O how easy it would be tonight
to fall in love with sound,
with the human voice
sending its sweet vibrations
upward to whatever heaven—treetop,
nighthawk, cirrus, moon. All of us
going to or coming back from
the woodshed, all of us
doing so divinely again what
all creatures here before
have divinely done.

||||||||||||||||||||||||||||||||||||||||||||||||||||||||||||||||||||||||||||||||||||||||||

Connections

Sometimes, no matter what
you say or do to the contrary,

every damn thing goes right,
the center holds, the pieces

come together, that pastel pink
at the edges of the clouds

at sunset so precisely the color
of the inside of the shell

Grandmother placed on the linoleum
to keep the front door open,

shell she told me to hold to my
ear if I want to learn the sound

the sea makes, its sound so
nearly that of this evening's

moving water, Loup and sea, cloud
and shell, Grandmother in a big boat

rocking on the high seas from Karlshuld
to Kansas to the living-room

where rocking she put together the
cloud-white spread with its patterns

of stars so intricate I sleep
when the other stars don't show

so warmly under.

||||||||||||||||||||||||||||||||||||||||||||||||||||||||||||||||||||||||||||||||||||||||

Blues

> Music is silence.
> The reason we have the notes
> is to emphasize the silence.
>
> *Dizzy Gillespie*

Our lead guitarist, preacher's boy
out from the wilds of Oklahoma,
fits a capo to the neck of his Martin,

then after some acoustic calisthenics
moves into a litany
of blues—Hesitation Blues, Sweet Baby

Blues, Gambler's Blues—lead guitarist
by himself
on a campstool downstream

singing the blues to anything not
outright opposed to listening. Asks
the bullfrog, How long do I have to

wait? Can I get you now, or mama
do I have to hesitate? Tells the
bunchgrass, She can search

the whole world over, she'll never
find a man like me. To the
catfish: Five long years

with just one woman,
and she had the nerve to kick me
out. To the carp: I love my baby,

love to watch her walk
across the room. Lead guitarist
let loose from Oklahoma

picks and sings as if in concert
at the Met, his audience
of bullfrog, bunchgrass, catfish, carp

quiet as stones with appreciation. And
O how the notes accentuate
the silence! I close my eyes

to hear it more clearly,
make of my hands two vessels devoid
of wrath and spite to take it in.

I tell you, brother, sister, something here
sure as sin is happening, something here
Lordy Lordy is going on!

Before we come to know the true value
of whiskey,
we trade two quarts for several deer,
trade with the Kickapoos, who surely know
already—their being at ease
in familiar country—the value of meat.

Well, we are erring, I'm guessing,
on the wrong side of caution, not saving
as much of our store as possible
for future consumption.

The meat goes down well, encouraged
by a gill or two of that which
we didn't trade.

Saturday last, at St. Charles, some of us
danced with French ladies
who the next day drank and feasted
on the body of Christ. All of us, it seems,
eating and drinking, then eating
and drinking, wild
to keep body and soul somehow
and for whatever reasons
alive.

||||||||||||||||||||||||||||||||||||||||||||||||||||||||||||||||||||||||||||||||||||||||||||

Strop is the sound the leather made
when my father, having decided the time was ripe,
honed his razor.

Now *strop* is the sound each lash makes
as we punish Private Moses Reed.

And I watched in awe and envy as my father,
his square face white with lather,
so delicately leveled the whiskers.

Now *strop* is the sound the lash makes, Reed
running the gauntlet four times.

Whiskers and lather gone, my father stood
smiling,
touching his face with his fingers.

Now *strop* is the sound the lash makes
on its way to one hundred, well laid on.

Strop is the sound the palm of my father's
hand made when with gusto
he slapped his pale cheeks into pinkness.

Now *strop* is the sound the lash makes
as justice, red in color, winds down.

‖‖

When Sergeant Floyd dies
the nearby river goes right on
flowing.

Our Captains nonetheless
give it the name of the one it

ignores: Floyd's River.
When we return, should we
return,
I'll devise a way to honor

my fallen friend. At the least
I'll stand quietly
at the head of his grave.

At the most I'll enter the water
that carries his name,
there to bathe.

||||||||||||||||||||||||||||||||||||||||||||||||||||||||||||||||||||||||||||||||||||||||

Here is the scene I hope always to carry
with me: bottom land covered with timber.

Whatever a man constructs with his hands
is sacred, if its wood comforts and shelters.

I see a grove of cedars and I want to stop
for the rest of my life to inhale it.

Sitting near the waning campfire, I bring
its coals to life with a length of sycamore,

which was the tree, wasn't it, that Zacchaeus
climbed to see Jesus.

Give me time, a river, and a cluster of tools,
and I will build us a house made of driftwood.

In my newest dream I am dovetailing bottom-
land timber for the coffin in my dream one day

I'll lie down in.

||||||||||||||||||||||||||||||||||||||||||||||||||||||||||||||||||||||||||||||||||||||||

Sacagawea's young body refuses
to deliver.

She lies in her lodge, in misery, yet
doing her best not to show it.

But her face is a page that even a
carpenter with a total of nineteen

days of schooling can read,
her dark eyes slitted in pain.

Captain Lewis, at the end of his
makeshift rope, acts on the advice

of Jessaume, mixes the crushed rattle
of a snake with water, offers it then

to Sacagawea, who in her agony
drinks it, who in ten minutes

delivers. The moment brings forth
more than a baby, a boy, Jean Baptiste:

joy unspeakable on the countenance
of the almond mother,

on the face of the Captain belief
doing battle with doubt.

And Charbonneau: so inflated
you'd think he'd done something.

I go to sleep that night with the name
of my firstborn determined: Benjamin,

or maybe William. I'll discuss it
with the woman, Maria, I'll marry.

I go to sleep with Maria and our child,
and the child I hear crying, on my mind.

‖‖‖

Sacagawea. Bird Woman. Janey. A peace medal
for your thoughts.

When Charbonneau slapped her
I wanted to affix the short board to the long
for his crucifixion. Believe me, I have
square nails enough to carry out the ceremony,
and more than enough determination.

But I bite my lower lip almost to blood,
reminding myself that I am a quiet, steady man,
one not given to any form of explosive tantrum. Ah,
but that Charbonneau, that rattlesnake!

She sits feeding little Pomp, saying nothing—but
surely thinking. Sacagawea: a peace medal
for those thoughts.

She is our youngest, our only woman, only
mother, only one who might recognize
her Shoshoni territory, only one then
to help us in our need for horses.

She sits feeding little Pomp, saying nothing—but
surely thinking. Bird Woman: a peace medal
for those thoughts.

Her husband, her master, her unfortunate excuse
for her being here, goes meanwhile free,
serpentines this boundless garden
with what no abuser deserves—impunity.

||||||||||||||||||||||||||||||||||||||||||||||||||||||||||||||||||||||||||||||||||

We bury the *Experiment* with full military honors,
and at the height of the service
I repent somewhat

my having dared to smile at its failure. Truth is,
I wanted it to work, wanted it to float
our necessary burdens

from here all the way to there—wanted to see
the expression of fulfillment
on Captain Lewis's face
join with the others in doing and saying whatever
the success of wild experimentation
leads to. I am a woodworker,

but if iron and skin can be used in lieu of timber
to build a vessel or a house,
so be it. My blessing

upon all works assembled by human hands: Such
works are holy. The Great Mystery
must therefore have human

hands, must therefore both weep and chuckle
with its creation. The grave
for the Captain's boat

is uncommonly long, uncommonly wide,
uncommonly shallow. May
no animal, high or low,

disturb its remains. Or fail to smile when its
story is told, or in silence
remembered.

|||||||||||||||||||||||||||||||||||||||||||||||||||||||||||||||||||||||||||||||||||||||||

O glory be to the water and sunlight
that feed the rapid growth
of the cottonwood,

tree without which all of us would be
lying somewhere in the
mountains, a scattering of bones.

And thanks to the natives, who
teach us how to dig the narrow trench
to contain the flames
to burn the center of the wood
to hasten our proceeding on.

O glory be to the water and sunlight
that feed the rapid growth
of the cottonwood,

tree without which all of us would be
somewhere in the mountains,
a scattering of bones
so long time lying.

Amen.

Ignorant of the sextant, of any instrument
beyond the common compass
and the hammer,

I nonetheless offer my own woodlover's
calculation: We are in the middle
of nowhere.

And this: The middle goes with us
wherever we go.

At the campfire someone whose face is
flicker and shadow tells
of the nomadic nation

that carries with it the bundle of sacred
corn, who believes that the
center of the universe

moves with the corn—meaning, I guess,
that this nation with its
sacred corn

moves always in the middle of everywhere.
Nowhere. Everywhere. I hope
I am yet alive should they

one day meet, should they one day
sit down with corn enough
for all of us to share,

bread enough for all of us to break.

You climb the ladder (whatever its
composition) as you built it, one rung
at a time—and with patience. Patience,

revealed on these growth rings
as we transect the cottonwood's
massive trunk, trunk we'll suspend

above the fire to hurry along the
hollowing-out. Christ! All those years
as an apprentice carpenter, and here I am,

with an axe and less than a gill
of hope, gutting a cottonwood! Up
or down, brother, it's one rung at a time.

And I remember Sergeant Floyd
going down, remember the aroma
of soil and wood up from the grave,

remember his last words fine as
sawdust offered to Captain Clark: *I
am going away. I want you to write me*

a letter. Two days later, the vote
tallied, I assumed the dead man's
rank. Sergeant. Rank and ladder, one

step at a time. Sergeant Patrick
Gass. Whose charge it is to extend
the life we left behind. Sergeant Charles

Floyd, his bones at rest on a high hill
overlooking a river that as we work
to shape cottonwood to canoe

bears his name.

If I could grow a blue spruce
bearing blue beads
I'd be at least a Captain or a Chief—ascending more
than one rung, if I could grow a blue spruce
bearing blue beads,
at a time.

Witness the Chinook
coveting Sacagawea's blue-beaded belt.
Witness Captain Clark
coveting the sea-otter robe
worn by the coveting Chinook, the most
beautiful robe, the Captain said, that
he had ever seen.

I watched the Captain work
to effect a trade, first by offering a flag,
next a medal. But nothing short
of our Bird Woman's belt would answer.

For a long while Sacagawea wavered, and
then, having been offered a coat of azure cloth,
she consented.

It is good at times to be in the company
of those who are feeling good,
for whatever reason. The Chinook chief,
holding the blue-beaded belt like a grail
in the bronze boat of his hands. Sacagawea,
pleased to have been of help, with her coat
of azure cloth. And the Captain in his robe
of many otters looking more stately, surely,
than any other Captain asail
on any other inland sea. Ah,

if I could grow a blue spruce
bearing blue beads
I'd be at least a Captain or a Chief—ascending more
than one rung, if I could grow a blue spruce
bearing blue beads,
at a time.

||||||||||||||||||||||||||||||||||||||||||||||||||||||||||||||||||||||||||||||||||||||||

Elk. Elk. Elk.
Breakfast. Dinner. Supper.
Rain. Rain. Rain.
Morning. Noon. Evening.

Give me a drum and a length of ash
and this tin-eared carpenter
will give you a tin-eared beat
to dance your tin-eared
tedious life to.

Ah, in this world of dried clay and timber
who hid the sun? Rain. Rain. Rain. Who
in this universal restaurant
devised the menu? Elk. Elk. Elk.

And the natives come and the natives go,
and this tin-eared carpenter with his drumstick
strikes his drum, powwow with its circle
that never ends.

And the Clatsops come and the Clatsops go,
bringing with them women for some,
fleas for everyone.

Each endless evening I stand outside
among the raindrops
spanking pillow and blanket with a tin-eared
fist. Each morning pillow and blanket
crawl with multitudinous creatures

who must have spent the bulk of the night
reproducing.

And another day of rainfall and elk
begins. And here is what your tin-eared carpenter
learns: What lasts forever goes on
for a long, long time.

||||||||||||||||||||||||||||||||||||||||||||||||||||||||||||||||||||||||||||||||||||||||||

The Big Lake That Stinks is what
Sacagawea calls the ocean.

She tells me of her hike to the shore,
how she watched little Pomp

frolic in the shallows, how she
forced his nose into the water

to teach him the meaning of stench.
Then, she says, they went to where

the skeleton of a whale
sits giant and funny on the sand,

bones picked clean by the savages,
she says, bones big as war-clubs

already bleaching. Later,
Captain Clark, happy as a schoolboy

to have traded for three hundred
pounds of whale meat and a few

gallons of oil, will say how Providence
this time turned the tables, allowing

us Jonahs to eat the whale instead
of the whale eating us.

It is late evening, between the death
of the campfire and the likely start

of another rain. And unless my eyes
betray me I can see two stars above the tip

of a white pine. Sacagawea, I believe, is
smiling, holding Pomp, who sleeps

silent as a stone, in the cradle
of his young mother's lap.

||||||||||||||||||||||||||||||||||||||||||||||||||||||||||||||||||||||||||||||||||||||

The word is out: Today Sergeant Gass
has reached the halfway mark
of his allotted time.

To celebrate he takes himself alone
to the water where, attired only
in what he was born with,

he bathes—then, removing his razor
from its cedar box, he shaves
his bulldog face

smooth as any rock in the Columbia
River. Shortly before dusk then,
because the word is out,

the celebrants gather—one squirrel, one
woodpecker, one magpie,
two deer (deceased),

and untold swarms of mosquitoes. Gass
welcomes them all with open
arms, with a bulldog face

shaved smooth as any rock in the Columbia
River. The Captains, themselves one
year older, offer handshakes

and apologies for there being no stout
libations. The sergeant smiles,
forgives them, reaches

into a pocket for the empty flask he knows will be
there. The squirrel nearby is
chiefly gray, beautifully

festive with small brown spots. He will excuse
himself from the gala early
to go home to his burrow

somewhere in this sad and lovely ground.

⁣||||||||||||||||||||||||||||||||||||||||||||||||||||||||||||||||||||||||||||||||||||

There must have been a meadow somewhere
where the first bird sang, a meadow somewhere
where the first flower bloomed.

We must have found such a meadow yesterday
where in the midst of emerald splendor
we camped the night.

Almost daily I see flora that I cannot name beyond
description: tiny, tall, blue, yellow,
leaves with edges like sawteeth.

Those few that I know the names of sing on the
tongue: sweet myrrh, angelica, timothy
grass, serviceberry, aster, flax.

Last night we camped in the midst of emerald
aromatic as the dark moist hair
of the woman

I look forward to spending the less feral years
of my life with. I will speak to her
of this meadow where, I will

tell her, the first bird must have sung, where the
first of all the flora on God's green earth
must have bloomed.

When Cruzatte for whatever reason
refuses to break out the fiddle,
we manage with our own lame voices
to fill the unfillable void.

Something in the form of a hum
to begin with, something that eventually
wants words, words that
like the humming are easy

and poorly but devoutly
remembered.

And once upon a time
I tied on my carpenter's apron
to become the waiter to serve them,
pouring from my flask a stream
of unending wine to fill their goblets.

Ah, music. Ah, words. How, singing
softly, the meanest among us
becomes all heartstring and
moonglow.

And the flask I serve them from
is the one I brought from home, from
Catfish Camp to the Ohio to the place
I chanced to be standing on
when I joined the Corps
to be stationed here where at night
what we can't otherwise say in daylight
we can say in song.

If I could write a song
I'd fill its lines
with the names of creeks and rivers—sing
Soldier, sing Onion, sing Milk.

If I could write a song
I'd give its tune
these words to drift along with: Deer-lick,
Blackbird, Porcupine, Plum.

Ah, and these: Little Bow, Moha,
Butterfly, Wash. And these: Round Knob,
Cannonball, Water That Cries.

If I could write a song
I'd sing my song
to the waters I'd write my song for—sing
Hidden, sing Dog, sing Warrior.

Ah, and these: White Clay, White Paint,
White Goat, Rose. And these: Musselshell,
Pania, Little Sioux, Smoke.

If I could write a song
I'd fill its lines
with the names of creeks and rivers—sing
Marrow, sing Charlotte, sing Mud.

If I could write a song—sing
Biscuit, sing Lookout, sing Medicine—by all
that is holy, by the hammer
and the timber I build with, by God—I'd
write one!

⁣iiiiiiiiiiiiiiiiiiiiiiiiiiiiiiiiiiiiiiiiiiiiiiiiiiiiiiiiiiiiiiiiiiiiiiiiiiiiiiiiiiiiiiiiii

When I see the cows
I turn to observe Sergeant Ordway

grinning like a black-
tailed prairie dog.

And I remind him of that party
so many moons ago

we indulged with the Mandans.
He nods, yet grinning,

remembers perhaps
his vow: to frolic until the cows

come home. Sergeant Ordway:
The cows have come home

by way of our returning. Ah,
cows—all of them,

those standing
solid as posts, chewing their

cuds, those stretching
long necks over and beyond

a long low fence of hedge
to reach where the grass is greener.

Learning Chautauqua

On my knees on the tattered seat
of my grandfather's old blue pickup
I work to memorize everything
on both sides of the road

all the way from the lost farm
to the found one, one quarter section
of hill and rock and Kansas gumbo,
faith and hope and charity

made palpable as flesh,
Grandfather in good spirits
coaxing the blue Dodge with its burdens
up one rise and up another,

talking to me as if I know what he's
talking about, debt and depression
and a bumper wheat harvest
lost in a maelstrom of greed

and deceit. Grandfather
nonetheless in good spirits
points to the highest hill, Lookout
Mountain, hill that before long,

Grandfather coaxing the Dodge, I'll
memorize—and the rock and
the gumbo, too, and especially the word
on the sign announcing the name

of the county Grandfather
will work with horses until the horses,
then Grandfather, yield—Chautauqua—and
on my knees on the tattered seat

I am learning Chautauqua, committing
for the rest of my life
Chautauqua to memory,
hill and rock and gumbo and

Chautauqua, my grandfather
with his horses working one quarter section
in Chautauqua County in Kansas,
my grandfather at the wheel now

talking to his grandson about sowing
and reaping, grandson nodding, grandson
without knowing anything,
taking in everything,

in his mammalian brain learning Chautauqua,
learning to spell Chautauqua
to make Chautauqua more than word, more
than sound, more

than the doubt that must be entertained
when hill and rock and gumbo
pose like the scene on a dimestore card
as the promised land.

Countries

My mother's mother, who loves everything
she doesn't hate,
says—shortly before we plow into
another mandatory Thanksgiving
dinner—I don't like green olives,
and I'm glad I don't like them,
because if I liked them
I'd eat them, and I don't like them.

She speaks with an accent,
her early years in Bavaria not willing
entirely to relent. When she returns grace

I study the green olives
mounded near the center of the table,
each with a red eye studying me.

She wants God to split his many mercies
right down the middle, one half going
to her relatives in the Old Country,
the other half going to her family
here in the new one. She tells God that
she hates this war and wants it
over now, if not sooner. Amen.

Later, folding carefully each holiday version
of the *Wichita Beacon,* I'll remember
my grandmother's only daughter's favorite
lament: there is no rest for the wicked.
Later yet, early into another June,
I'll deliver with my wicked German hands
news of Omaha Beach, will not be surprised,
when I hand my grandmother a copy,
to find her weeping.

But at the moment the family sits
intact, in spirit
if not entirely in body, loving the moment
if not the war or these green, red-eyed olives,
my grandmother's daughter calling me, when
occasionally I speak my mind,
another country heard from.

||||||||||||||||||||||||||||||||||||||||||||||||||||||||||||||||||||||||||||||||||||||||

Bushes Burning

Two in particular, the one
Moses confronted, or vice versa, on his way
to the fulfillment of a promise
someone for reasons no doubt
theologically justified
didn't keep, the other

all those others within and on the outskirts
of Hiroshima, little boys, so to speak,
arm in arm with little girls burning.

I was thirteen, young enough to be lucky,
old enough to identify a shiver for what it is
when it moves unilaterally up the spine.
In Mrs. Heath's Sunday-school class
I sat in silence cheering on the underdog,
wanting old Moses to make it.
In the Champlin station, folding the *Beacon*,
I sat victorious and bewildered.
When I delivered the papers
into the hands of others
I discerned each time a brotherhood
blue as ignition.

And the church bells rang and kept on
ringing. It was August, and hot,
and already I had broken
at least two of the ten commandments. But
how could anyone *not* hate my neighbor, *not*
covet the woman in red during the sermon
in front of me?

                              Much later,
I'll learn that the code name
for the testing of the atomic bomb in New Mexico
was not Vengeance but Trinity. Before then,
parked in a blue Chevrolet in a windbreak
lush with tamarack and lilac,
my girlfriend will whisper into the porches
of my ear, I'll tell you a secret
if you promise not to keep it.

And a week later our theater, the Rialto,
will give up its sacramental ghost, will
burn to the ground, it and the *Sands
of Iwo Jima*.

                                        Fevered,
I'll watch both Fact and its half-brother Fiction
go down in flames, Hell right here on earth,
whereupon around midnight I'll drift into sleep
wondering how and why and when,
in the name of all we deem holy, we go wrong.

‖‖

For Some Strange Reason

After losing fourteen straight
for some strange reason
we turn the tables on Medicine Lodge,
final score 49–47.

On the way home, dream-smooth
inside Bo Spoon's reconditioned car,
Bullard breaks a silence to say,
Coach, how does it feel

to win one? Behind the wheel
Bo Spoon, his first season winding
down, seems to be thinking
deeply. At last, quietly basso

profundo, he says, Like a bluebird
just flew out my asshole. And maybe
it's the pure pinpointing of language
that leads to my confession:

we humbled Medicine not for some
strange reason, not something
cosmic or apocalyptic, but because
three of its starting five

had the flu. But a win is a win,
after all, isn't it,
and we float home
adrift in Coach's newly aromatic

2-tone 4-door 8-cylinder
Bel-Air Chevrolet—Bo
at the wheel, Bullard
beside him, Woods at my right

with his last-second tie-breaking
high hook-shot
hanging,
me at his left

with that liberated bird
for some strange reason
palpable
on my shoulder, spilling

its bluebird brains out counter-
tenor
in a pure incessant
gratefulness of song.

〜〜〜

Covenants

> FOR TRACY AND PAT,
>
> NICOLE AND ROBERT,
>
> CAROLINE AND NATE

In darkness
in that space we call the greenhouse room
we sit together to listen to the
silence of growth: sumac,
trumpetvine, raspberry, hosta, rose.
And the lily, tiger lily,
the growl in its orange throat
subdued. And the magnolia
that so soon will spread the soft
soft leather of its leaves

to cool us as we gather
to hear and to speak our
vows. *I do. They do. We do.*

In darkness
in that space we call the greenhouse room
we sit together to watch the rising
of a full blue moon. O mother,
tell me how the moon, how anything,
can move from insufficient to complete, O father,
how those stars beyond the greenhouse glass
seem near enough almost
to greet. *Hello, you Seven Heavenly
Sisters. Hello, Bear.
Haven't I seen your bright
bright eyes
somewhere else before?*

In darkness
in that space we call the greenhouse room
we sit to know the quiet
presence of each other,
to hear in silence the promise
of the song: *This world is always turning
toward the morning.*
O mother, father, how many

moon-blanched creatures might be up there
watching us as we watch them? We
turn. We touch. Because I am
you are. Because you are
I am.

Walking the Grounds at St. Elizabeth Hospital, DC

> For my enemy is dead,
> a man divine as myself is dead.
>
> *Walt Whitman, "Reconciliation"*

On a clear early-September evening
      our guide takes us to see his workplace,
            St. E's overlooking the Potomac,

refuge, he says, for Civil War casualties
      whose next step was the final one,
            a modest cemetery on a wooded hillside

one stone's throw west of the hospital.
      He points to a lighted window on the second
            floor, room that for several years

served as home to Ezra Pound. We stand
      at the sagging fence bordering the cemetery,
            its headstones gray and strangely akimbo

against a low slant of orange sun.
      Rebel and Yankee. Black and White. Young
            and old. Sane and otherwise. Composite

made possible, says our guide, through
      differences in chance and of opinion.
            Nobody comes here, he says—no tourists,

that is—because the hospital accommodates
      only the mentally deficient,
            and the cemetery, as you can see, he says,

is less than spectacular. We watch
      the sun go down as the lights of our
            seat of government go on. Not so many

years ago our guide sat as an under-
        graduate in one of my classes, torn
                between medicine and literature. Tonight

he speaks of both Pound and those whom
        tomorrow he'll so gently cajole,
                mammal in a skirmish with reptile, war

and rumors of war, truce made possible
        only by the darkness
                that falls on both sides of the river.

FOR DR. R. B.

|||||||||||||||||||||||||||||||||||||||||||||||||||||||||||||||||||||||||||||||||||||||||||

Somewhere in the Vicinity of Ecclesiastes

FOR JUDSON MITCHUM

After telling the young woman
        at the front desk
                that, yes,

I'd prefer a smoke-free room,
        I ask her if I
                might also

have a room free of Bibles. She
        looks at me
                as if

I were Judas Iscariot plotting
        a comeback. I'm
                allergic

to Holy Writ, I explain, and I left
        my medication
                in Duluth.

She looks at me with eyes blue
     as the heavens.
          When she

smiles I commit at least three of
     the seven deadly
          sins.

Even so, I sleep that night only
     with the Gideons,
          their effluvia

seeping so selectively into my old
     blue cotton
          sweater

that wearing it how many mornings
     later I cannot
          help but

forgive myself for who I was, for who
     I am, for what
          in the course

of time and of chance I might become.

The Almost Dead

They come in sizes both odd and even,
     many, perhaps most,
          moving as if healthy

among the truly healthy,
     some, maybe many,
          unaware that one of their

multitudinous valves is about to rupture,
     releasing its inoperable hiss.
          Others wear their brevity of days

like the bumper-sticker
	only the short-timer comprehends:
		Mortality—don't leave home without it.

At parties they are the ones who
	smile sideways when the conversation
		turns to apparel, who

place their hands lightly
	on the shoulders of the undeserving.
		At dusk they sit for long moments

rocking the neighbors' most recent twins,
	doubt and premonition.
		When the leaves fall they

nod, knowing in their limb of limbs
	the unbearable weight of all
		alternatives.

‖‖‖

Soul

FOR GLENN BUSH

Each time I look at my friend's
	red sunset maple, in season
		or otherwise,

I think of soul, that butterfly
	as yet not pinned to
		anybody's wall,

how that afternoon it left his
	self-destructed flesh
		to find its way

beyond the sealed garage to greener
	pastures. But what precisely
		it is, or what it

means, eludes me. Metaphor—soul
　　　as butterfly—is the best
　　　　　that I can do,

connection tenuous and trite, yet
　　　(forgive me) nonetheless
　　　　　until this moment

sufficient. As a boy my belief
　　　was this: that with a
　　　　　feedsack net

I'd ensnare every butterfly extant
　　　in Harper County, entrapment
　　　　　being that unassailable

proof in the heart of all puddings.
　　　But with each death each
　　　　　butterfly's soul

escaped in the form of a butterfly,
　　　odorless and very nearly
　　　　　soundless,

not even the occasional *snick* of a
　　　delicate motor,
　　　　　missing.

||||||||||||||||||||||||||||||||||||||||||||||||||||||||||||||||||||||||||||||||||||||||||||||

Remembering Religion

　　　Despite all plumage and posture, I say
　　　Still that God is in mud and corruption.
　　　He made this work and He is of it all.

　　　Paul Zimmer, The Great Bird of Love

Throughout August it was sawdust and tentpole,
canvas and guyline
and a makeshift platform of pine
on which rested the old Baldwin the heavy woman
fussed mightily over, her heavenly breasts

heaving in sync with *Beulah Land* and *Saved*
in the Twinkling of an Eye.

And it was the evangelist
with his delicate Easter-lily skin
backhandling and caressing his King James Bible
as he drooled and proclaimed the births and deaths
of those fierce and non-identical twins,
Desire and Armageddon.

I, too, remember religion, its horrors, its
elusive promises, its utmost threats.
When the invitation to be saved was extended
I was sometimes saved, sometimes,
for reasons I couldn't always understand,
forever doomed.

And always it was heat made possible
by August, temperature augmented with firebrands
spat from the blue blue tongues
of the truly aroused
by way of the Holy Spirit.

And I remember how religion so intensely, so
beautifully excluded those beauties
beyond the pitiful man-pitched sky
we squirmed and huddled under: moon, star,
a quilt of darkness
spun from the altogether curious mind
of whatever maker.

||||||||||||||||||||||||||||||||||||||||||||||||||||||||||||||||||||||||||||||||||||||||||||

Brothers

Through the living room window
I watch a cardinal with its red
whiten the snow on the roof
of the feeder.

It must have been tutored
by a pinioned Houdini, its beak
at a seed in the hull quicker
than my early-morning eye.

Or perhaps I'm half asleep,
milky residue of dream
trailing me
like my little brother used to

all the way sometimes to the floor
of the unfinished treehouse, where
day into dusk into night we'd
talk, first with bravado, then *sotto voce*,

until gravity augmented by the threat
of curfew
brought us down, and raising
outstretched arms into wings

we dipped into the house
like swallows into the loft
and abracadabra
disappeared.

॥॥

Desiring Desire

Now in the early morning I lie awake
with my eyes closed, desiring
desire. In its place
its shirt-tail cousin, looking forward,
carries on. And I do look forward
to finishing the bird house, I do,
something inherent in its wood
wanting first to be noticed, then
touched, then put together
to become something more

than the sum of its parts. And what
to place along the V of roof
to keep that roof from leaking? An
aluminum can, probably beer can
snipped open and folded and hammered
to size and to shape, carefully.

Because when as a boy my brother
cut an artery on a shard of tin
he almost didn't stop bleeding. And
I remember how quickly
my wanting him to survive
became my passion, my desire,
nothing to rival its sweet intensity
until, my brother having survived,
I discovered new blood
in the elongated prelude to fulfillment.

Light through the curtain grows
stronger. Yellow. And feathered. I do
look forward to painting the bird house, I do,

coat over coat until yellow
becomes the object I desire just now
to desire. And the bird I look forward
to watching, its wings taking it—where
else?—where it has to go.

Balsa

How those thin and delicate strips
handled carefully and affixed just so
to other weightless shapes
evolve into Spitfire and Flying Tiger,
balsa on the home front
contributing to the war effort
by giving little pismires like me
something better than disruption
to do,

until balsa like rubber bands
and white-wall tires
march off to join the Army, Navy,
Air Force, Marines,
which is fine, because suddenly
we little pismires aren't altogether
little any more—we need something
heftier than balsa
to hang our apprehensions on,

so we walk the tracks to harvest
scrap iron, gargantuan nuts and bolts,
rods and coils and cast-off pieces
we must resort to thingamajig
to name, pieces from cargo freights
that keep the tracks
shiny as the dimes we sell the iron for,
dimes we spend to watch on the screen
both sacrifice and scavenging at work,

Spitfire and Flyer Tiger at the throats
of Messerschmitt and Zero, balsa
in the form somehow of landing craft
spilling our heroes onto a beach

already further softened by the bodies
of other heroes, so many of them
buoyed by the lapping tide,
so many of them light as cordwood
bobbing.

‖‖‖

Star of the East

I stand with my sister near the altar
at the front of the sanctuary
singing Star of the East, O
Bethlehem's star,
guiding us on to Heaven afar.

It's Christmas Eve. The church
smells like dry fur on the collar
of an old heavy coat. My sister, she's
an angel if there ever was one,
with her right hand
squeezes my left. To reach the high notes
she closes her eyes: O star
that leads to Heaven above . . .

My sister is my mother's daughter, and
I am my mother's son—Mother,
who couldn't carry a tune
in a sack, nonetheless
singing a tune each morning
as she filled the sacks—a sandwich,
an apple, a wedge of cheese the color
of a Kansas sunrise.

It's because my sister is my mother's daughter that
she must close her eyes to reach
the high notes, and it's because
I am my mother's son that
I must return the squeeze of my sister's hand

to reach the low ones. Eventually
this song will end, its sweet discordances
going the way of all that's born
of breath and tongue. Eventually
Santa Claus will burst
like an obese miracle red and white
into the sanctuary, where eventually
he'll remove the burden from his back
to distribute sacks of candy
to the children, I and my sister
among them, we two meanwhile
singing our jittery little hearts out,
Heaven no more above than below,
Heaven in the hands that fill the sacks,
Heaven in the notes both high and low,
Heaven in the act of being here
alive together
singing.

||||||||||||||||||||||||||||||||||||||||||||||||||||||||||||||||||||||||||||||||||||||||

In a Church Basement Damp from Last Night's Rain

I pull strings to give me the light the windows
mud-splattered in their wells
fail to offer,

though I do not expect the jaundiced light,
however comprehensive,
to be sufficient unto the task: to find

Grandmother's leather-bound dog-eared
Bible. Yes, of course—she
had it with her last night

at the mid-week service, she told me,
had it open to Paul's letter to Philemon,
had it lying in her wide German lap

as with a wide German index finger
she followed the words
as the preacher intoned them:

Yea, brother, let me have joy of thee
in the Lord: refresh my bowels
in the Lord. And she asked me,

Would you mind, little Liebchen,
going to the church
to see if you can

find it? Yes, and of course—whereupon
I walk the rows
of worn brown metal chairs, heavy

aromatic aftermath of rain invading,
pervading the cement basement,
bulbs of light as if subalterns

showing the way. But there is no Bible,
nothing but the rows of chairs
and the small wooden pulpit

behind which stood the preacher
reading Paul's letter. So I
return to hear then the joyful news: the lost

has been found. It was just where I left it,
Grandmother says, though she doesn't say
where she left it. And though I am young

I nonetheless see my grandmother
for what she is: clear-eyed and devious,
her misplaced Bible a ruse

to bring her prodigal grandson
home for supper. Even so, her potato soup
alive with onion simmering in the kitchen

is not equal to the quelling of the church's
cool damp basement,
how with its effluvium it conjures up each

sometimes distant, sometimes immediate
apprehension. Even so, yes, and
of course—I'll have another

bowl of soup, please and thank you,
with bread and butter,
another schooner of cold Jersey milk,

another savory wedge of whatever
dessert it takes to refresh the bowels,
to keep us from losing the dear

and desperate company of one another.

||||||||||||||||||||||||||||||||||||||||||||||||||||||||||||||||||||||||||||||||||||||||||||||||||||||

Sawdust

I hang around
until the last customer

with her sack of groceries
waddles out the door. It's the smell

of sawdust I'm wanting, Uncle Charlie
in his blue bib overalls

scattering sawdust on the dark wooden
floor, then with a pushbroom

moving it around the candy counter,
the meat counter, all the other

counters until somehow
it comes to rest in a mound

my uncle uses a black dustpan to deplete,
and certainly I'm sleepy,

it's almost midnight but it's the smell
of sawdust I'm wanting, sawdust

a benediction, sawdust
an aromatic selah to end a psalm, sawdust

going with me like the buddy
who says he'll meet you in the alley

behind the movie house for a secret smoke,
and on time shows up,

tissues and tobacco and kitchen matches,
all the way home.

||||||||||||||||||||||||||||||||||||||||||||||||||||||||||||||||||||||||||||||||||||||||||||||||

Javelin

Not really wanting to throw the javelin
I nonetheless throw it. Look,
it's what I can do to avoid
last-period study hall, Miss
Molly Cloud Houston smiling
as if in her dotage
anarchy were the infant miracle
she alone gave birth to.

So I'm outside reaping the harvest
of not being inside. In lazy increments
I throw the javelin from one end
of the gridiron to the other. Nothing
is expected of me. What hopes
for a championship we harbor
lie with the sprinters and the hurdlers.

Over the course of four uncolored seasons
I'll throw the javelin ten thousand times,
salvage one bronze medal. Before
I decided whether to give it

to the girl in the yellow sweater
I'll tie it to the end of the string
that hangs above the quilt
on my bed of stone. Pull it and the light
goes out. Pull it and the light goes on.

IIIIIIIIIIIIIIIIIIIIIIIIIIIIIIIIIIIIIIIIIIIIIIIIIIIIIIIIIIIIIIIIIIIIIIIIIIIIIIIIIIIIIIIIIIIIII

Moving

This large plane moves, it seems,
without moving,
but I can detect its smooth velocity
by looking down

to see a measured earth moving,
it seems,
beneath me, its distances curious and,
except for those instruments

I couldn't read if I were holding them
in my lap, not
measurable. So
how far away am I, do you suppose,

from the sun
Icarus with his wings of wax flew
too close to?
I see his body by way of Auden's poem,

who had his poem
by way of Brueghel's painting, falling
into the sea,
ploughman on land and ship with its

passengers on water
not apparently noticing, or perhaps not
caring, that
suffering and death are twins about

to be born again,
I drinking hot black coffee
over the lushness
of Nebraska, Iowa, Minnesota, the

woman in front of me
standing to move even as the rest
of us so strictly accounted for
sit moving.

||||||||||||||||||||||||||||||||||||||||||||||||||||||||||||||||||||||||||||||||||||||||||||

Living with Others

It's what we have little choice
but to do,

this living with others, including
of course those

not living. It's easy, most
of the time, except

for the woman in line behind me
whose lips are a megaphone

announcing dissatisfaction
with all things

warm and breathing. And the man
back home at rest

in the boneyard,
his ghost the grim facsimile

of the affluent peckerhead who
wanted his daily news

on time, but begrudged the paperboy
his monthly payment.

But what you can't abide
you can curse and live with,

sweet side abutting the sour,
others around you

doing the same, living with others—
monkey nut, angel tit, goony

bird, god—and the whosoever that
surely meaneth me.

||||||||||||||||||||||||||||||||||||||||||||||||||||||||||||||||||||||||||||||||||||||||||

Library of No Return

Lost in the stacks,
        disbelief having yielded to panic,
                panic to resignation,

I inhale the mustiness
        of obediently upright spines.
                Though I'm a novice, call me

greenhorn, I'm determined
        to stay here looking until
                Hell or its earthly equivalent

freezes over. So this is what
        it means to be navigating
                a library of no return,

to be forever adrift
        in the ebb and flow of ages,
                to choose each landing

with large and equal drams
        of wonder and care.
                Who might have guessed

the universe so ancient, so
        unaccountably vast!
                Before Hell freezes over

I'll learn that in Dante's
    Inferno Hell freezes
        over, in the Greeks that

once upon a time
    the earth's beleaguered
        creatures, excepting

two, were destroyed by water.
    Is there nothing new,
        after all,

under the lights that make
    the night the sky?
        Lost in the stacks

I find my way at last by way
    of words: *No way that
        can be charted is the way.*

In the Black Hills Whistling Dixie

I'm in the Black Hills whistling Dixie, whistling
I'm So Lonesome I Could Die, whistling
Amazing Grace,

though I wasn't raised in the South, though
I'm not lonesome, though
I don't believe

I'm either a wretch or a worm born in sin. I'm
just a pilgrim in the Black Hills, whistling
Dixie, driving along

Black Hawk Road, inhaling an integration
of seasons—autumn's almost gone
and winter's coming on.

Later, in Spearfish, I'll dine on junkyard nachos
and a flat tire sandwich in a well-lighted
expanse named Sanford's,

expanse that in an earlier life was a service station
and a three-door body shop, but now
it's Black Hawk Road

snaking down and up and around, cottonwoods
on fire so near you can reach out and
almost touch them, burn

almost your hands on their hot autumn leaves.
First snow tonight, maybe, the waitress
at the body shop will say,

but not enough probably to stick. Junkyard nachos
and a flat tire sandwich and
while you're at it

toss in some thermostat soup, the waitress's body
when she serves me so perfectly in tune
with what she's doing.

In the Black Hills whistling Dixie I'm lost
in a cosmos of mysteries, whistling
lost, whistling

mysteries, Yankee Doodle and Autumn Leaves and
Holy, Holy, Holy, trees other than
cottonwoods, trees with names

I haven't the words to name throwing themselves
like willing sacrifices into the
gathering fire. And

by the time I see the tower I'll be whistling
Way Down Yonder in the Indian Nation,
not meaning respect or disrespect,

not meaning anything but whistling. And look:
there's a painted pony in the pasture, and
a Harley with a helmet

on its black leather hump scorching the highway. So
I whistle On the Road Again, whistle
Camptown Ladies, whistle

I've Got a Home in Glory Land, Devil's Tower
ahead, Great Spirit above, sun
behind a thin cloud

dancing, windows on the rent-a-car rolled down, wind
blowing white hair unequally in each
of the four great directions.

||||||||||||||||||||||||||||||||||||||||||||||||||||||||||||||||||||||||||||||||||||||||||||||

At Hemlock Hollow near Logan, Ohio

FOR PAUL

With a short length of horsetail
he abrades an old penny
until the face of Lincoln emerges
shiny as an unobstructed sun.

At our feet more plants
than you could shake a length
of white oak at assault the eyes,
the nose, the most primitive layer
of the layered brain.

Over our heads birdsong
erupts from a wild irregularity
of throats. Curlew. Towhee.
Nutcatcher. Wren.

I climb to the top of a tulip tree
to see more clearly the underbelly
of a turkey vulture. Beyond its
fire-and-brimstone head, half hidden
in a fluff of cumulus, grins
the bearded face of everybody's Jesus.

When I die, he says, cover me
with firepink and angelica,
with the blooms of wild geraniums,
with larkspur white and indigo.
Give me time, then, to do what
death makes possible—to grow.

|||||||||||||||||||||||||||||||||||||||||||||||||||||||||||||||||||||||||||||||||||||

Funeral for an Old Woman

FOR TRACY ANN

Today Grandmother smells like the roses
her green thumb tended,
like honeysuckle, like the lilacs
blooming in her yard.

On her left forearm is the bruise
our infant daughter gave her,
less than a week ago,
sucking.

German. From Karlshuld, near
Munich. She came to this country
to visit her brother, Jake. She
didn't return.

She'll not return. She smells like roses,
like honeysuckle, like the lilacs
blooming in her yard, her
thick German accent not returning.

When I point to the bruise
my wife, weeping, smiles. She is standing
beside me at the coffin, holding
our infant daughter in her arms.

For My Wife's Mother

> Consider the lilies of the field, how they grow;
> they toil not, neither do they spin: And yet I say
> unto you, That even Solomon in all his glory was
> not arrayed like one of these.
>
> *Matthew 6: 28–29*

Consider also the branches on the tree,
how apparently not toiling they reach
to know what the trunk can never
know, how, broken, they become the crutches
in the hands of men and women who,
not yet altogether broken,
buy bread and milk for themselves, seeds
for the birds who nest in those branches
not yet altogether broken.

Consider also the quilt that covers
my wife's mother,
how stitches formed by her earlier hands
form a pattern so apparently at odds
with the pattern that lies
fading underneath: sweet face
of the sunbonnet girl in stasis, face
of my wife's mother daily, hourly changing.

In life we are, as my friend the poet says,
in death. We live arrayed
in the beauty and the muck derived
from the mind's elaborate spinning. Give me
therefore Solomon, therefore
my wife's sweet mother. Oh give me the mind
with its vast and unthinkable considerations!

Consider also the calm,
how it eases downward through the trunk
of its massive height,

how it quenches the thirst of the lily
opening itself as if voodoo
behind the coffin.

Consider darkness as a form of light.

||||||||||||||||||||||||||||||||||||||||||||||||||||||||||||||||||||||||||||||||||||

Watching My Granddaughter, 7,
Test for Her Purple Belt

FOR ALYSSA

Only a few seconds into the routine
and I'm convinced that, yes,
there is indeed enough mystery
to go around,

how the limbs on her
trim inexhaustible body
move so quickly and so precisely,
hands now open for the chop, now a fist,

her brother beside me looking on,
himself at 5 a karate kid,
his entire body, he tells me, magic,
and who am I to disagree,

my entire body a rabbit
pulled from the void of an improbable hat,
yesterday no less an enchantment
than today.

When she spars she holds her own
against whatever opposition,
you name it,
flood and famine, pestilence, fire

and ice—until having received at last
the purple belt
she bows, turns, walks quickly and precisely
back to the X that marks her spot—and

all things that go *bump* in the night.

||||||||||||||||||||||||||||||||||||||||||||||||||||||||||||||||||||||||||||||||||||

Not Dreaming

FOR NATE

Because my grandson is troubled
by bad dreams
I give him a dreamcatcher,
tell him to hang it in his bedroom window,
that I have instructed it to permit
only good dreams to enter.

My neighbor meanwhile
sits slumped in a wheelchair,
eyes heavy at half-mast,
face puffed and more than one click
off-center,
mouth as if carved
to make scary the Halloween pumpkin.
I was not always like this, he
manages to say, as if
standing before him I thought he was,
neither of us, I believe, dreaming.

That boy is the same grandchild who,
having been told to be patient,
asked, Why does patience
take so long?

At the stoplight I wait impatiently
for the light to change, as did my father,
who knew the value of patience.
When the light went green
he eased his old brown Dodge into the intersection,
there to be broadsided by impatience
augmented by booze. Broad daylight. Bright
blood. Early afternoon. My father, dead
on impact, not dreaming.

My grandson phones the next morning to say
he slept all night without calling out, without
screaming. That his dreams were good,
though he can't remember them. That the sun
is shining. That he is pretty sure
he'll never again have a bad one.

Two weeks ago, unable to sleep,
I went outside to observe the brisk fidelity
of a hunter's moon. Earlier
I had sat in a small church
in a small town
reminding God, in song, how great He is,
followed by dust to dust, followed by soup
and sandwiches in the basement. That night, not
dreaming, I toasted the moon
until the last of the toast was gone. Moon. No
water. No soil. No atmosphere. Nobody, then,
to tuck one's body in, to say goodnight,
to kiss one's cheek, to say, Sleep well. No
bed. No bug. No bite.

Discoveries

FOR KYLIE AND JAMIE

Believe this much: The strange new pool you are about to dive into
makes the return to the pool you are moving away from
possible. And this: That the sister who knows you
better perhaps than she believes she knows you
is about to begin to discover you
further.

In Colorado I find two rocks—sisters, perhaps—waiting patiently
to be discovered. Each in sunlight wears its flecks of mica
as if anxious for the party to begin. I take them home,
bathe them, set them in sunlight in the backyard.
When they are dry let the party
begin.

And this: That in the mountains I happened upon a length of aspen
that needed someone to walk with. With a new pocket knife
I trimmed and shaped it until the blade somehow slipped
and I sliced my left arm until blood red as my brother's
flowed like a mountain stream down
and into the cup of my hand.

Which I raise just now to offer this toast: Here's both to the one
who is leaving and to those who are left behind. And this:
To the strange new pool you are about to dive into,
pool that will sweeten your return
to the pool you are moving
away from.

Shooting the Rabbit

Now the dilemma is whether to dig out the old
Red Ryder air rifle, load it with shot
and tiptoe into the backyard,
or let the cottontail
finish its breakfast of hosta and dianthus.

> Grandfather's 12-gauge, after
> an explosion too violent
> ever to be prepared for,
> released an aroma not even
> the Fourth of July could
> measure up to. It hung
> suspended in the cold December air
> as if wanting to be taken in. And
> I took it in, acrid and sweet.
> And the cottontail lay
> splayed and amazed
> in the fresh white snow.

I resolve the dilemma by waiting, as always,
for my wife to resolve it. With her voice
and a yellow teatowel she spooks the rabbit,
calling it names not at all generic.

> We named our first son John,
> after my brother, who carries
> our other grandfather's name,
> grandfather blown away
> by indeterminate winds four years
> before my brother was born.

Had I shot the rabbit my wife, having many times
entreated me to shoot the rabbit,
would have denounced me for shooting the rabbit.
Isn't there something here worth taking in?

We sit meanwhile on the patio in metal
high-backed chairs that rock. Another burst
of early-morning news
hangs suspended in the mild April air, air
more acrid than sweet. We rock and rock,
amazed and grateful to be counted yet
among the living.

Nouns

A noun the size of Rhode Island
sits immobile on a dead limb
near the top of a legacy
sugar maple.

On this clear, bright, brisk morning
I had hoped to spot an adjective or two
with these new binoculars
I spent the last of this week's
allowance on.

Lovely, maybe, or maybe *serene*.
But it's a noun I'm looking at, noun
being the name of a person,
place, or thing.

Thing. When the noun, the thing,
spreads its wings, that couplet of things,
and lifts itself into another noun, the sky,
I lower the binoculars
to see more clearly more of this little universe
we nouns, collectively or alone,
presume to live in.

November 22, 1963

We leave Chaucer's Prioress
in Old Main's Room 321
to descend the stairs
to walk the campus to the Campus Center
to stand with a disillusionment of others
to watch the screen
to learn that the President is dead.

At Pershing Elementary a circle of children
stands looking up,
at its center a flagpole with the flag at half-mast.
In sharp sunlight the children are listening
to whatever it is a teacher is saying.
In an ancient Pontiac Catalina
with its transmission on its last legs
I drive by slowly, trying to spot
those children of my own.

I had excused myself from class
to take the call from my wife,
to learn from her what had happened.
When I returned to the class
to relay the information
I was not certain that
I had not been dreaming.

Now, back in the classroom, I gather my notes
and my copy of the *Canterbury Tales*,
inside of which rests the Prioress, that woman
with her finger on a medieval trigger
she, in her ecclesiastic madness,
cannot stop squeezing.

||||||||||||||||||||||||||||||||||||||||||||||||||||||||||||||||||||||||||||||||||||||||||||||

Theater

It's Oedipus, sure enough, I'd recognize that
blood-stained toga anywhere.

He's standing near the back entrance
to the theater,
under an overhang of leafy branches,
sneaking a smoke.

He nods, smiles, apologizes
for cutting so many of my classes, explains
that rehearsals have tied him down—hell,
man, not even a theater major
can be in two places at the same time.

I understand, or try to. He finishes the cigarette,
flips away the stub, smiles, nods,
turns and disappears, toga and all,
into the near end of the building.

In a couple of hours he will be blinded
by his own hand,
will have played the roles of perpetrator,
gumshoe, jury, judge.

It's mid-October. I leave the campus
to follow a narrow sidewalk
home. O what have I ever done
to deserve this? Whose father have I
ever slain or neglected—I mean,
other than my own?

||||||||||||||||||||||||||||||||||||||||||||||||||||||||||||||||||||||||||||||||||||

Moving On

FOR STEVE AND JANE

Why, on such a flawless, late-October morning,
do I think of loss?

Of my students' daughter's death,
of that poem I first read
as an unwashed college freshman, how
it moved me in ways I had never been moved before,
poet I had never heard of committing
both grief and confusion to paper,
writing—as the bells chimed, and after his remembering
antics made possible by the child's *restless heart*—

" . . . we are vexed at her brown study,
Lying so primly propped."

And now here am I, vexed also, walking the campus,
thinking of loss as the bird stays meanwhile
on the wing, as the gaillardia, that
hardy blanket flower, bends its yellow, russet head
as if to greet me, as those I know and do not know
wear the nearby street to sweet distraction
driving to and away from classes, others
late for work, someone somewhere
calling to someone, perhaps a daughter, pin oaks
rustling, speaking of those good old days
when they were acorns, and a full sun
against a cluster of euonymus
inducing a reenactment of the advent
of the burning bush.

Astonishing, isn't it, that what we designate as time
does not pause to stand with us
at those moments
of highest bereavement—how moving on
it reaches back the hand we take
to make the following
possible: Sunrise. Dayglow. Sunset. Moon. How
the bulbs we plant, despite the heaviest frost,
must surely one day rally into bloom.

||||||||||||||||||||||||||||||||||||||||||||||||||||||||||||||||||||||||||||||||||||||

August 12, 1992

For having lived long enough
to know what's indeed enough, this
reward: a young bur oak,
rising now just west of Old Main,
those responsible standing in a circle
around it, I standing in the circle with them.

When the storm with its ice and snow blows in
this tree will bend but
not quite break, in time will right itself
to keep on growing.

And I think of the son in Sophocles' *Antigone*
as he tries to convince his father to relent,
to withdraw the edict that, if kept in force,
will destroy not only the son's beloved Antigone,
but likewise the son himself. Sometimes to bend,
he says, is to show mercy. Not to bend, sometimes,
he says, is to show an absence
of mercy, with misery an everlasting consequence.

We stand in a circle with the bur oak,
freshly planted, at its center. Today
I am old enough to know what's indeed
enough. This tree. This circle. This moment.

This family.

||||||||||||||||||||||||||||||||||||||||||||||||||||||||||||||||||||||||||||||||||||||||||

After the Ice Storm

After the ice storm
I walk the campus to witness
the remarkably beautiful devastation,
ice into snow into heaviness
not even the limbs on the largest oak
could bear.

After the ice storm
I select a fallen limb from that
largest oak.
I would have it as something more
than a remnant, a token
reminder.

After the ice storm
I walk the campus with a walking-stick
smooth and as stout
as a farm boy's forearm. And I am not
surprised: it takes me back
to where it came from.

After the ice storm
I sense that time, having passed, goes right on
passing. So many survivors so
green now, so eager
to fill those many gaps
left by those who are gone.

||||||||||||||||||||||||||||||||||||||||||||||||||||||||||||||||||||||||||||||||||||||||

Connections: A Toast

Here's to the bur oak, *Quercus macrocarpa*, rising
just beyond my office window, here's to window,
to oxide and silicon, to their joining, here's to joining,
to fusion, pro and con, to transparency
that brings to the eye Renoir:
two young students, woman and man,
transecting the campus, here's to transecting, here's to
campus, over their shoulders bookbags no doubt containing
books, here's to books, Gray's *Anatomy*, perhaps,
let's hear it for Gray, let's hear it for anatomy, and

maybe something by Aeschylus or Plato, here's to Plato,
and while we're at it here's to Socrates,
to the goblet he raised to toast those immortal
kissing cousins, inquiry and innovation, here's to kissing,
to cousins, to inquiry and innovation, and perhaps
at the bottoms of the bags some thoughts
from Augustine or Jung, saint and otherwise,
here's to saint, here's to otherwise, Jung who said
It is not Goethe who creates Faust, it is Faust
that creates Goethe, here's to Goethe and Faust,

to a myriad of bone-and-brain creations,
to the act that marks each beginning,
to the moment whose enemy is stasis,
to the runner on first with stealing on his mind,
here's to the stolen base, the purloined kiss,
here's to motion perpetual, here's to mind, to flesh,
to the hitter at the plate, Jackie Robinson,
to the man on deck, Pee Wee Reese, to the hotdogs
in the box seats, to the peanuts in the gallery,
to Ebbets Field and to Fenway Park and to Rosa Parks
who refusing to ride sidesaddle

becomes a blue-chip conscientious ob-jec-tor—*There
is some shit I will not eat*—so here's to Rosa Parks,
to side, to saddle, here's to the horse
beneath the saddle, to sound horse and to Crazy Horse
whose hemlock was the feel of a cold bayonet,
whose words were prayer because they were not meant

as prayer—*It does not matter where this body
lies, for it is grass; but where this spirit is, there
it will be good for all of us to be*—and to the bird
with its coat of many colors, bird just now perched
on the topmost branch of the bur oak, *Quercus macrocarpa*,
trilling now Bach, now Beethoven, now Louis Armstrong,
trilling, with its unsplit tongue, one
steady and diverse and universal song.

Braids

> After all,
> we are partners in this land,
> co-signers of a covenant.
> At my touch the wild
> braid of creation
> trembles.
>
> *Stanley Kunitz, "The Snakes of September"*

Is this too much
to bargain for, the hope
that all things woven and braided

can somehow provide the covenant
to make us partners in a land
of multiple divisions?

One answer lies in the bright routine
of doing such braiding and such weaving
as we have the skills to do,

to dance then with our sacred arts
intact, art done with hands
that we extend by dancing, wearing,

as we do, history and good intentions
in our hair and on our shoulders,
our movements those of many channels

flowing among the many islands that serve
to make the river what it is, joinings
made possible by differences,

union through the handiwork of hands.

Proud

> Be dutiful, respectful, gentle and modest,
> my daughter. And proud walking.
>
> *advice to a young Sioux girl upon her becoming*
> *a woman, in* These Were the Sioux, *by Mari Sandoz*

And this also: *No people goes down*
until their women are weak and
dishonored, or dead
upon the ground. And I remember

watching my sister—dutiful,
respectful, gentle and
modest and proud walking—as she
cleared the counter in my

parents' café, cups
in one hand, plates stacked halfway
to heaven in the other, watched
her balance these

towers of porcelain all the way to the
kitchen, her body certain
and upright and
so newly woman it made me remarkably

proud to watch it, my own body
too young to know, beyond
feeling, what bodies might do when the
time comes for doing, death

and dishonor not
possible in my parents' café, where my
sister cleared the counter and
where, returning

from the kitchen, and wiping her hands
on a sky-blue apron, she winked
as a mother might wink
at a child at her unleavened brother.

Flight

> For I dance
> And drink and sing,
> Till some blind hand
> Shall brush my wing.
>
> *William Blake,* Songs of Experience

Almost aflight she spreads her wings of shawl,
anonymous in her countenance, yet colorful

in the reds and blues that constitute her wings.
Is she derived from circling birds? (All things

aspire to roundness, Black Elk said.)
With a lightness lighter than the silent dead

she very nearly leaves the whitened earth,
that tireless mother once more giving birth

to joy. If we indeed live at the mercy
of some immutable force that cannot see,

or care to see, the object that it sweeps
aside, or drowns, or devastates, or keeps

intact, then let us celebrate its wry
omniscience. O let us dance! And, dancing, fly!

Quest

> . . . a vision quest, typically a ritual trek into a natural remoteness
> where isolation and deprivation lead the sojourner into a new
> and keen awareness of existence, even of the cosmos itself,
> which brings about harmony and gives purpose to one's life.
>
> *William Least Heat-Moon,* "Vision Quest"

To be alone is the deepest deprivation,
I am told,
so doesn't it follow that from this

should come the deepest awareness?
I am told:
To be in isolation is the keenest pain—

one rung on the long ascent to harmony.
I am told
that purpose is what the eye detects

when clarity by way of deprivation,
I am told,
becomes the guide to lead the lonely

back to where the people, lonely also,
I am told,
await the return of the one whose quest

might make the cosmos understandable.
I am told:
To be in isolation is the keenest pain,

to be alone the deepest deprivation.
I am told:
To see most clearly is to survive, again.

||||||||||||||||||||||||||||||||||||||||||||||||||||||||||||||||||||||||||||||||||||||||||

Spheres

> For there is music wherever there is a harmony,
> order, or proportion; and thus far we may maintain
> the music of the spheres.
>
> *Sir Thomas Browne,* Religio Medici

And the dancer with a flourish
of parallels and spheres
says, Let there be not only day

and night, earth and sky and
all things warm and
breathing, but let there be also

symmetry and balance beyond
our meager compre-
hensions, parallels and spheres

too numerous to fathom or to
count, unfoldings
lovely in their infinite juxta-

positions, fleeting because so
briefly we discern
them—all this, and more, the

dancer says without so much
as one word spoken,
says it with the swaying and

the motions of an inveterate per-
formance, body
heavenly in its orbit going the certain

way of flesh and bone—going and
always going, inscrut-
able as what is lost, but never gone.

||||||||||||||||||||||||||||||||||||||||||||||||||||||||||||||||||||||||||||||||||||

Water

> Having the need to pray
> I come to the water's edge
> where dawn spreads out
> over the riverbank
> like a blessing of hands.
>
> *Geary Hobson, "Going to the Water"*

Going down to no great sea
to do no great business

I walk instead the bank
of this small Idaho stream,

its cold clear water wriggling
as if an ongoing serpent

over rocks and pebbles that
I enter the water to reach down

to pick up, to examine, to dry
against the denim of my jeans, to

return to the water that receives
them one by one,

water over them
returning them to brilliances

akin to what it must be like to be
so touched by hands

that never betray or leave you,
prayer without words so

divinely interminable,
water over stone with the shadow

of someone who needs to be here
just passing through.

<hr>

Sleep

> Oh sleep! it is a gentle thing,
> Beloved from pole to pole.
>
> *Samuel Taylor Coleridge, "The Rime of the Ancient Mariner"*

In sleep let there be no winter
with its crow

perched on the rib of the fallen,
no gulch sated

with its ghosts of prayers
not answered,

no hoops broken. In sleep
let there be creek

and calf, pipe and willow and
birdsong, breast

and bloom and cup, nation and
grass, and breath

that honors again and again,
by its leaving

and so surely returning, its
immutable source.

‖‖

Grass Woman

> Great green and yellow grasshoppers are everywhere
> in the tall grass . . . , and tortoises crawl about on the
> red earth, going nowhere in the plenty of time.
>
> *N. Scott Momaday,* The Way to Rainy Mountain

This material I am working with, she says,
is the blood of ancestors that
having soaked into the earth

found its way to this place, to this quarry
at the edge of Pipestone,
Minnesota, where hardened and layered

it waited patiently these many seasons
to be returned at last to the
realm of the living. Her voice is alto

delivering a chant as with her fingers she
rubs a miniature turtle
to a high reddish sheen. When she seems

satisfied, she looks at her handiwork and
says, as if speaking
to me through it, Treat this always with

reverence and respect, for it is sacred.
Then, raising her eyes
to meet mine, she says, This is my story,

this is my song. Then she asks, Are you a
storyteller? Do you sing?
I answer with a nod. Her eyes were green.

||||||||||||||||||||||||||||||||||||||||||||||||||||||||||||||||||||||||||||||||||||||||||||||||||||

Still Life Moving

> Who in the world is not waiting to be touched and filled?
> Love something your own size. Love the world.
>
> *Erica Funkhouser, "Still Life with Pewter Pitcher"*

Here, in pastel, you are no more in motion
than is the pear
beside the pitcher on the table, pitcher and

table no more in motion than the pear.
Yet seeing you
here immobile, we see likewise the form

beyond the still life moving, still life
breathing beyond the
stillness, and we remember how it was

to be told to stand perfectly still for only
a moment, told
not to move until the image by way

of something magic was recorded, how
good it felt when
after that interminable moment we were

told that the moment was over, how then
with one of our
hands we reached for the pear on the table,

reached for the pitcher, too, how then we
hurried to join
our friends who with pitchers and pears

were moving and breathing as if nothing,
not even the names
on the scroll of the dead, could deplete them.

Early July

As the Rialto burned
I stood across the street
in front of the dry goods store

less awake than asleep, the siren
having persisted until
everyone in Harper County, I swear,

stood filling a block-long stretch
on Main Street,
some in pajamas, it being early

July, only one day removed
from the jubilant cacophony
of cracker and rocket and buzz bomb,

and when someone said it was
probably leftover fireworks that did it
I believed him,

and someone else in a whisper
loud enough to be heard
blamed an arsonist, no doubt a Baptist

doing what God justifiably moved
him to do, movies
being the handiwork of Satan,

I believed that more so, because the flames
looked like hell
described by my Sunday school teacher,

and the lights and shadows cast
by the inferno made the faces
around me more demonic than eerie,

our local firemen meanwhile
swapping shouts and admonitions
as they directed long ropes of water

into the crackling maw of the conflagration
until nothing but anyone's guess
remained, nothing tomorrow to do

but rummage, maybe find something
of value only as a reminder
of how beautiful heaven must be.

||||||||||||||||||||||||||||||||||||||||||||||||||||||||||||||||||||||||||||||||||||||||||||||||||

After the First Good Early-Spring Shower

We'd drive to the overflow north of town,
my father and I,
to park the family jalopy in the overflow's channel,

then with our shoes and socks off and the legs
of our overalls rolled up
we'd stand shin-deep in moving water,

my father's mouth almost grinning. Maybe a bird,
an oriole, say, its orange
and black too striking not to be noticed,

would be losing then finding itself among the branches
of a cottonwood, and
maybe a mid-afternoon sun at our faces would be

making the cool water cooler. My father would dis-
engage the latches that
held down one side of the hood, and with that half

tucked up and out of the way he'd perform
the ritual, though he'd never
have called it a ritual, would remove the caps

from the battery and with a tin cup fill each cell
with water he'd have
dipped the tin cup into. I am telling you this because

we did things together so rarely, my father and I,
he with his unending work
and equally immortal silences, I with my fear

of disrupting, if not outright spoiling, either. Maybe,
but probably not, a yellow
Piper Cub from a cow-pasture airfield would cast

a slow eerie shadow over us, a blessing, maybe, or
maybe a premonition, and
I'd look up from the fleeing shadow to watch the

yellow bird with its baritone voice lose itself
to distance. Straining to see it
all, to see and to taste and smell and inhale it

all, I'd stand shin-deep in the current, Father
no less than the cells
becoming full, and with thin freckled fingers he'd

replace the caps, secure the hood, fill the tin cup
one more time. Maybe the oriole
would reappear, or a cloud from God knows where

would obscure the sun. And we'd drink from the
cup, soft water my father said
being good for both us and the battery, though I swear

as I raised the cup I saw many small things swimming.
When we'd settled back
onto the seats there'd be this long sad pause before

my father started the car—before the battery started
the car, before the water
in the battery started the car, before whatever it is

that made the water started the car—oriole, maybe,
if you go into it deeply
enough—or Piper Cub or sun that because some-

thing had moved the cloud away was shining.

Avon Calling

Once you have spent a lifetime
waiting in the front seat of a Chevy
for your mother to return

from having made her pitch or
from having derived the fruits
of an earlier successful pitch

you don't need to bother to learn
again the meaning
of relentless. Scribble

something in the dust
on the dashboard, then
watch as motes defined by sunlight

begin their relentless settling, their
relentless quest to return your
silly calligraphy to dust.

Inside the farmhouse your mother
disappeared into
odd syllables are moving from one

mouth to another—you have heard
them on those few occasions
when you bawled until your mother

relented and took you in: lipstick
and rouge, powder and blush, lotion
and body cream. Hush,

your mother said, and you did, and
the women talked and laughed
and closed their eyes and aahed,

smelling each other's wrists. It's an
old Chevrolet that might become
newer should these new products

prove to be all they are said to be,
Mother said. You study the dashboard
relentlessly, trying to decipher

those hieroglyphics abandoned no doubt
by a civilization that now must
surely be extinct. Inside the farmhouse

meanwhile the women testify, however
obliquely, to the relentlessness
of time that in the front seat of the Chevy

seems almost not to be passing. To
hurry it along you sit low
behind the wheel,

steering the old Chevrolet at breakneck
speeds into a high blue sky
maddeningly aromatic,

that smile on its sun younger by far
than the face that so re-
lentlessly wears it.

||||||||||||||||||||||||||||||||||||||||||||||||||||||||||||||||||||||||||||||||||||||||||

Titles

Because I have a memory for titles
I request "Beulah Land."

Grandfather smiles, nods, lifts
the red and black accordion to his chest,
works the leaky bellows and the keys
until the miracle of familiar sound occurs.

I am an unwashed boy
sitting on the pine-board floor
of a living room in a small farmhouse
too deep into disrepair to matter.

When Grandfather taps his foot
I wiggle mine.

Beyond a south window
walnuts drop their weary weight
from the limbs of the walnut tree.

Grandfather moves his lips
as if his lips are reaching
for something.

It's out there: *I'm living on the mountain
underneath a cloudless sky. . . .*

It is that moment between not dark and
dark. In the kitchen Grandmother
is at the sink, rattling dishes.

I move closer. If I am to live forever
what I must remember is the
title of another one before
this one ends.

‖‖

Looking for Scrap Iron at the Village Dump

We find more than we are
looking for—not iron to be sold
to Darnes, the half-blind man
who would sell it to the man
from Wichita in the black dump-
truck to be taken somewhere to be
melted down to make a bayonet,
say, to kill a Jap or a German
with—but items of incredible
interest because we cannot
identify them, one a rounded
length of weathered wood our
father identifies as a singletree,

and when we ask him to explain
he does, and we are impressed
with his knowledge and awed
by the greenness in his eyes as
he speaks, a greenness I believe
neither of us had ever seen before
as likewise we had not yet seen
the greenness in a field of ripening
lespedeza, Grandfather standing
at its edge with his hands in the
back pockets of his overalls, Father
beside him listening maybe as
intently as we listened, my brother
and I, to what it means to be a
singletree, to follow the rump
of a wide horse up one row and
down another, my brother and I
not only listening but nodding from
time to time, as if we understood,
as if somehow our nodding might
cause the words from the mouth
of our father, who so rarely spoke
with such renewal, to keep on going.

|||||||||||||||||||||||||||||||||||||||||||||||||||||||||||||||||||||||||||||||||||||||

Digging

Not to bury a dog or cat or
to discover China,

but to inhale whatever it is
the earth takes in

to make it earth. After
an easy rain

I lie alone on my back
with my eyes

closed, earth displaced
as a pillow. Many

years from now I'll read
in a poem, "The

Apprentice Gravedigger,"
how the poet

perceived himself as a
builder of holes,

how the most difficult
challenge of all

was the forming of one
for a child. But

at the moment I am bliss-
fully stuck

with the moment, earth
and two crawlers

having scented the hands
I have crossed

on the chest not far from
the lungs that in

spite of our history of loss
can't stop breathing.

‖‖‖

Distances

My Jack Armstrong pedometer
will tell me how far it is
around the paper route,
with its image of the all-American
boy on its face will measure distance

from the Champlin station
to Fanny Young's front porch
to Fenton's backyard filled
with weathervanes and birdhouses
and feeders and chimes all devised
and assembled by the hands of Fenton
to the final porch where old man
Werner will be standing
to receive the newsprint I wonder
if his old German eyes are up
to reading.

What it will not tell me is
how long I must wait
to receive it, how many
countless hours awake or almost
asleep I'll dream of it,
how many words will pass
from one mouth to another
as I hang out in the drugstore
or the pool hall or the barber shop
or the post office or the depot
or the cafe or the hatchery
or near the bins that hold
the hammers and the pliers and
the wedges and the hacksaws
in the business whose owner is what
Virgil at the feed store calls a shitbird

or in the dining room where
both the hour hand on the wall clock
and my father, off to work this morning
somewhere in another sphere,
are missing.

August

I am not old but old enough to believe
I know what Jimmy Stevens wants
when he invites my sister
into his Model-A. And because

I believe I know where he is going
I follow the car afoot, breathing
dust and exhaust until both
have left me

so far behind I must rely on what
I believe I know to get me
to where I believe they
are going. But I am

wrong. They aren't here,
meaning that wherever they are
I cannot find them, meaning
that whatever they might be doing

I cannot know, cannot put my small,
helpless body between them.
For a long time I sit in the weeds
at the side of the road that failed

me, inhaling dryness, looking up
and into the brilliance
of uncountable stars. August,
the month of my birth. I am alone and

not alone, long beans in moonlight
hanging from the limbs
of catalpas, coyotes with their howling
saying something I believe just now

I understand. For a long time I sit
in weeds somewhere between
those most mysterious cousins,
knowing and belief,

my sister somewhere in a Model-A
saying what I cannot hear, touching
what I cannot reach. There are many
small rocks in the road, far

too many to count, reflecting the moon-
rays. My plan is this:
to choose one of them to kick
all the way back to the farmhouse,

to save it then to remember how plentiful
this night was (to wash it and wash it
to give as a gift to my sister), how
remarkably empty.

||||||||||||||||||||||||||||||||||||||||||||||||||||||||||||||||||||||||||||||||||||

Darkroom

In the darkroom that smelled
not only of fixer and developer
but also of red earth and must,

darkroom that was the cave
we stored our abundance
of canned goods in—jars

and more jars of peaches, beans,
potatoes, row on row
of jams and jellies—I

worked a roll of film up and
down in a magic liquid
until in the reddish glow

of the magic safelight I saw
the negatives evolve, old man
posing serenely in a casket,

and the next day the images
from the printer so sharp
in their eventual glossiness

they brought tears to the eyes
of his wife, Edna, whose
hand-made pies in my

parents' cafe brought praise
from the mouths
of the customers, so many

lost now in sepia in the
grottos
of the no longer living.

━━

Saved

> For I have opened up toward heaven
> all the windows of my soul
> and I'm living on the hallelujah side.
> *old hymn*

It didn't last forever, that peace that passeth
understanding,
but while it lasted I was walking in cotton

so high it touched its kinfolk, those
cumulus mysteries
I once saw the face of Jesus in. I had been

called by the Holy Spirit to do whatever the
Holy Spirit
might dictate, had been saved and sanctified

and set aside for the greater glory of the Lord
God Almighty.
What happened precisely to account for my

fall from grace I don't know, can't remember,
but it happened,
all the windows of my soul gone foggy, all

the doors gone wobbly on their hinges, and
we moved again,
my mother and father and sister and brother

and I, moved to a place so far removed from
gloryland that
most of the time neither sun nor rain could

reach it. Four narrow rooms adjoining a long
narrow cafe filled
with country from a jukebox and aromas of

fried chicken and hot beef sandwiches from the
kitchen. The place
smelled good, and sounded good, too, when

it was filled with the words and laughter of
hungry customers, but
its long, long hours drove its owners, as one

of them testified later, beyond distraction.
When the music
ended and the last sweet scent from the kitchen

drifted into nihility I found myself unwashed
and alone
on the road to college, to what someone called

higher learning, and I was excited once again,
by Christ I was
down-in-my-heart excited, all around and above me

windows as certain as sin about to open.

Bits & Pieces

Those bits & pieces our lives are made of
have a patience (I swear it)
beyond the ken of Job. They are waiting

to be assembled by impatient folks like me
to be made sense of. I see
clearly the hoofprints in the cowlot into which

I coaxed the cows, then milked them, sitting
on a stool of weathered two-bys
hammered together by a father who when

he hammered his thumb held God account-
able. His brown teeth as he
did the hammering. The white milk as it

made its singular music against the tin walls
of the bucket. These bits
against the pieces of a later life, their reluctance

to fit together. But might they eventually, when
other bits & pieces so patiently
insinuate themselves? And does it matter?

In one of our kitchens I covered a bowl of ripe
mulberries with sugar, then
soaked them with milk drawn from the cisterns

of other cows. The girl I'd marry had a mother
whose birthmark is the orange afghan
I reach for when a north wind blows the safflower

from the feeder. This white porcelain cup survived
the rigors of our small cafe. My lips,
red from the berries, was why Evan Bullard

called me a pussy. I hold the cup in the hand whose
back with its brown liver spots
is my grandfather's. Should I praise or blame him?

When the hand struck Bullard's face it made a sound
relevant only to the ear.
I drink the black coffee as if indulging nectar, which

it is. Toast. Egg with a double yolk. How unlikely.
How lovingly it all goes down
together.

||||||||||||||||||||||||||||||||||||||||||||||||||||||||||||||||||||||||||||||||||||||||

We Take My Wife's Father Fishing One More Time

At the pond—an early afternoon
late in April—he sits
in the back seat of his Chevy
holding an open tackle box
as if tending an infant.

With that hand less tremored
he selects the jitterbug he can't
miss with. His mind, that rod
that bends to the slightest touch,
sends it far onto the pondwater,

singing. But there is nothing
but snag and snarl beneath the water,
old man with his mudcat teeth
goddamning whatever it is he's
hooked into, old man not fishing

yet fishing, eyes tangled, Chevy
rocking, one hand at the rod,
the other reeling, infant
with his rattling of sinkers and lures
about to fall down and go boom.

Flying over Chicago

When suddenly
we hit a bank of clouds
poof the lights of Chicago

go out, an entire city
gone in the twinkling of an eye
from something to nothing,

and it was an early American
poet, I believe,
who said that when we slip or

slam into nihility
we will still be happy, for
we will not be. Until the clouds

give way to starlight, both
above and maybe below,
I try to remember those eons

preceding my birth,
but what comes to mind is
always the gee and haw

of hearsay and history.
I cannot imagine the hole
without seeing the walls that

shape it, cannot stay awake
much longer, must not go
entirely to sleep.

At the Mayo Clinic

Almost embarrassed to be healthy
I sit waiting for my younger son, no longer
young, to return with the good news
all of us deserve: benign, treatable, nothing
to lose any additional sleep over.

Earlier, we awakened to a wet mid-March
snowfall, Minnesota doing its level best not
to disappoint, flakes so large
I walked all the way from our room
to the shuttle with my tongue out.

Our bodies do whatever they can, don't they,
to outlive themselves—medication
for the moment, humility before sleep
for the hereafter.

Your son disappears into that room
you were advised by way of a large sign
not to enter. You find a cushioned chair not
far from a long-leafed plant

to await his return. You know that
when you entered this place snow was falling,
covering alike the just and the unjust,
the upright as well as the fallen. Without

thinking too much about it
you nonetheless believe that when
you leave this place you will be grateful
to have been, to be being yet, one of them.

Daughters

FOR TERRY LYNN AND TRACY ANN

When you have daughters
bright and beautiful and so

filled with laughter that at certain
splendid moments it cannot be contained

it is difficult, isn't it, not to smile
for the most unlikely reason,

difficult not to subscribe to or
devise a system whereby what we

perceive as human might be sustained
indefinitely beyond the boundaries

of those finest moments, and difficult
not to fashion into words, or try to,

these lines that having begun go
right on going,

this hymn, let's call it that,
of gratefulness.

Walking and Looking Down

For one thing, it somewhat reduces the possibility
of that fatal misstep. For another,
it gives that small wad of large bills
the chance to be discovered.

But chiefly it enhances one's perception
of the biped, how one brace of feet
does the duck-walk, another the pigeon,
another a goofy compromise, another a tilting
this way or that, defying the elemental laws
of equilibrium. You become, as it were,
a somewhat authority, a Ph.D.
with a specialty in all things
kneecap downward: the fat calf, the lean calf,
the fallen arch, the foot flat as the iron

Grandmother hovered over, her bare feet
not unlike the acreage her German husband
tended, gumbo and rock, bunion
and hammertoe,

Grandfather guiding a one-bottom plow
behind a team of horses, plowing and looking down,
his specialties furrow and rein, gee and haw
and the switching of horsetail, his wife
in the farmhouse ironing—another
dress, another shirt, another (in a succession
she hopes to live to see the end of)
Tuesday morning.

Crossing Heaven

> If hell lay to the west,
> Americans would cross heaven
> to get there.
>
> *common saying around 1850*

No harps here, no cherubs with haloes
or choirs of angels singing. No gold. No
frankincense. No myrrh.

Only a small braided river dividing a valley
lush with vegetation
random as those who can hardly wait

to leave it, hell in the form of promises
somewhere ahead. To pass the time,
having spanked the pillows and

buried the children, you intone the words
you were taught to believe: *O there's
honey in the rock, my brother,*

honey in the rock for me. Underfoot,
a thick, patient layering of soil
awaits the seeds that one day

will sustain the offspring of those who
reluctantly or otherwise
change their minds. But at the moment

you are hellbent for that other paradise,
wealth and rumors of wealth
jingling like coins of the realm

in the pockets of your threadbare lives.